"The Catholic Commentary on Sacred Scripture is a landmark achievement in theological interpretation of Scripture in and for the Church. Everything about it is inviting and edifying. It is a wonderful gift to the Catholic Church and a model for the rest of us. Highly recommended for all!"

—**Michael J. Gorman**, St. Mary's Seminary and University, Baltimore

"When the Scripture is read in the liturgy, it is heard as a living voice. But when expounded in a commentary, it is too often read as a document from the past. This fine series unites the ancient and the contemporary by offering insight into the biblical text—verse by verse—as well as spiritual application to the lives of Christians today."

—**Robert Louis Wilken**, University of Virginia

"There is a great hunger among Catholic laity for a deeper understanding of the Bible. The Catholic Commentary on Sacred Scripture fills the need for a more in-depth interpretation of Scripture. I am very excited to be able to recommend this series to our Bible Study groups around the world."

—**Gail Buckley**, founder and director, Catholic Scripture Study International (www.cssprogram.net)

"This series represents a much-needed approach, based on good scholarship but not overloaded with it. The frequent references to the *Catechism of the Catholic Church* help us to read Holy Scripture with a vivid sense of the living tradition of the Church."

—**Christoph Cardinal Schönborn**, Archbishop of Vienna

"The Catholic Commentary on Sacred Scripture will prove itself to be a reliable, Catholic—but ecumenically open and respectful—commentary."

—**Scot McKnight**, *Jesus Creed* blog

✝ Catholic Commentary on Sacred Scripture

SERIES EDITORS
Peter S. Williamson
Mary Healy

ASSOCIATE EDITOR
Kevin Perrotta

CONSULTING EDITORS
Scott Hahn, Franciscan University of Steubenville
✝Daniel J. Harrington, SJ, Weston Jesuit School of Theology
William S. Kurz, SJ, Marquette University
✝Francis Martin, Dominican House of Studies
Frank J. Matera, Catholic University of America
George Montague, SM, St. Mary's University
Terrence Prendergast, SJ, Archbishop of Ottawa

Galatians

Cardinal Albert Vanhoye
and Peter S. Williamson

B
Baker Academic
a division of Baker Publishing Group
Grand Rapids, Michigan

Published by Baker Academic
a division of Baker Publishing Group
PO Box 6287, Grand Rapids, MI 49516-6287
www.bakeracademic.com

Printed in the United States of America

Originally published as *Lettera ai Galati* by Cardinal Albert Vanhoye, © Figlie di San Paolo, via Francesco Albani, 21, 20149 Milan, Italy. Translated and adapted courtesy of Paoline Editoriale Libri.

Library of Congress Cataloging-in-Publication Data
Names: Vanhoye, Albert, author.
Title: Galatians / Cardinal Albert Vanhoye and Peter S. Williamson.
Description: Grand Rapids : Baker Publishing Group, 2019. | Series: Catholic commentary on sacred scripture | Includes bibliographical references and index.
Identifiers: LCCN 2018037235 | ISBN 9780801049729 (pbk. : alk. paper)
Subjects: LCSH: Bible. Galatians—Commentaries. | Catholic Church—Doctrines.
Classification: LCC BS2685.53 .V36 2019 | DDC 227/.407—dc23
LC record available at https://lccn.loc.gov/2018037235

Nihil obstat:
Monsignor Robert Lunsford
Censor Librorum
August 8, 2018

Imprimatur:
Printed with Ecclesiastical Permission
Most Reverend Earl Boyea
June 28, 2018

The *nihil obstat* and *imprimatur* are official declarations that a book is free of doctrinal or moral error. No implication is contained therein that those who have granted the *nihil obstat* or *imprimatur* agree with the contents, opinions, or statements expressed.

In keeping with biblical principles of creation stewardship, Baker Publishing Group advocates the responsible use of our natural resources. As a member of the Green Press Initiative, our company uses recycled paper when possible. The text paper of this book is composed in part of post-consumer waste.

19   20   21   22   23   24   25   7   6   5   4   3   2   1

Contents

Illustrations   7

Editors' Preface   9

Note on Authorship   12

Abbreviations   13

Introduction   15

Outline of the Letter to the Galatians   27

An Unusual Beginning (1:1–5)   29

Strong Words: Paul Takes a Stand (1:6–10)   34

Part 1   **Paul Defends His Gospel by Telling His Story (1:11–2:21)**   41

Paul's Call to Preach Came by Divine Revelation (1:11–24)   43

Official Recognition of Paul's Gospel (2:1–10)   59

Confrontation at Antioch (2:11–14)   72

Paul's Gospel (2:15–21)   81

Part 2   **Arguments from Christian Experience and from Scripture (3:1–5:12)**   95

Three Quick Arguments for Faith over Works of the Law (3:1–18)   97

The Temporary Role of the Law, the Extraordinary Benefits of Faith (3:19–29)   119

Adoption as Sons and Daughters of God (4:1–11)   135

A Personal Appeal (4:12–20)   152

Another Argument from Scripture (4:21–31)   159

Concluding Summons to Live as Free People (5:1–12)   171

Part 3   Exhortation about How to Live as a Christian (5:13–6:10)   185

Freedom, Love, and Life in the Spirit (5:13–25)   189

Advice for Christian Community Life (5:26–6:10)   202

Paul's Final Words and Signature (6:11–18)   208

Suggested Resources   215

Glossary   217

Index of Pastoral Topics   221

Index of Sidebars   223

Map   224

Illustrations

Figure 1. Map: Possible locations of St. Paul's Galatian churches 21

Figure 2. Remains of Roman baths at Ancyra 22

Figure 3. Rural landscape from the southern region called Galatia 22

Figure 4. The overlap of the ages 32

Figure 5. *St. Paul Preaching at Athens* (Raphael, 1515) 45

Figure 6. Medallion of St. Paul in an icon frame 54

Figure 7. Medallion of St. Peter in an icon frame 54

Figure 8. St. James, the brother of the Lord 55

Figure 9. St. Peter's Church in Antioch 73

Figure 10. Etching of St. Peter and St. Paul in a fourth-century catacomb 75

Figure 11. St. Peter and St. Paul (de Ribera, 1612) 77

Figure 12. Moses (Lawrence the Monk, ca. 1408–10) 116

Figure 13. Pedagogue and child (Greek terracotta) 126

Figure 14. Jebel Musa, the traditional location of Mount Sinai 163

Figure 15. Ancient surgical instruments used for circumcision 173

Figure 16. Torah manuscript on parchment, ca. 1270 191

Figure 17. Map: The journeys of St. Paul 224

Editors' Preface

The Church has always venerated the divine Scriptures just as she venerates the body of the Lord. . . . All the preaching of the Church should be nourished and governed by Sacred Scripture. For in the sacred books, the Father who is in heaven meets His children with great love and speaks with them; and the power and goodness in the word of God is so great that it stands as the support and energy of the Church, the strength of faith for her sons and daughters, the food of the soul, a pure and perennial fountain of spiritual life.

Second Vatican Council, *Dei Verbum* 21

Were not our hearts burning [within us] while he spoke to us on the way and opened the scriptures to us?

Luke 24:32

The Catholic Commentary on Sacred Scripture aims to serve the ministry of the Word of God in the life and mission of the Church. Since Vatican Council II, there has been an increasing hunger among Catholics to study Scripture in depth and in a way that reveals its relationship to liturgy, evangelization, catechesis, theology, and personal and communal life. This series responds to that desire by providing accessible yet substantive commentary on each book of the New Testament, drawn from the best of contemporary biblical scholarship as well as the rich treasury of the Church's tradition. These volumes seek to offer scholarship illumined by faith, in the conviction that the ultimate aim of biblical interpretation is to discover what God has revealed and is still speaking through the sacred text. Central to our approach are the principles taught by Vatican II: first, the use of historical and literary methods to discern what the biblical authors intended to express; second, prayerful theological reflection to understand the sacred text "in accord with the same Spirit by whom it was written"—that is, in light of the content and unity of the whole Scripture, the living tradition of the Church, and the analogy of faith (*Dei Verbum* 12).

The Catholic Commentary on Sacred Scripture is written for those engaged in or training for pastoral ministry and others interested in studying Scripture to understand their faith more deeply, to nourish their spiritual life, or to share the good news with others. With this in mind, the authors focus on the meaning of the text for faith and life rather than on the technical questions that occupy scholars, and they explain the Bible in ordinary language that does not require translation for preaching and catechesis. Although this series is written from the perspective of Catholic faith, its authors draw on the interpretation of Protestant and Orthodox scholars and hope these volumes will serve Christians of other traditions as well.

A variety of features are designed to make the commentary as useful as possible. Each volume includes the biblical text of the New American Bible, Revised Edition (NABRE), the translation approved for liturgical use in the United States. In order to serve readers who use other translations, the commentary notes and explains the most important differences between the NABRE and other widely used translations (e.g., RSV, NRSV, JB, NJB, and NIV). Each unit of the biblical text is followed by a list of references to relevant Scripture passages, Catechism sections, and uses in the Roman Lectionary. The exegesis that follows aims to explain in a clear and engaging way the meaning of the text in its original historical context as well as its perennial meaning for Christians. Reflection and Application sections help readers apply Scripture to Christian life today by responding to questions that the text raises, offering spiritual interpretations drawn from Christian tradition, or providing suggestions for the use of the biblical text in catechesis, preaching, or other forms of pastoral ministry.

Interspersed throughout the commentary are Biblical Background sidebars that present historical, literary, or theological information, and Living Tradition sidebars that offer pertinent material from the postbiblical Christian tradition, including quotations from Church documents and from the writings of saints and Church Fathers. The Biblical Background sidebars are indicated by a photo of urns that were excavated in Jerusalem, signifying the importance of historical study in understanding the sacred text. The Living Tradition sidebars are indicated by an image of Eadwine, a twelfth-century monk and scribe, signifying the growth in the Church's understanding that comes by the grace of the

Holy Spirit as believers study and ponder the Word of God in their hearts (see *Dei Verbum* 8).

Maps and a glossary are included in each volume for easy reference. The glossary explains key terms from the biblical text as well as theological or exegetical terms, which are marked in the commentary with a cross (†). A list of suggested resources, an index of pastoral topics, and an index of sidebars are included to enhance the usefulness of these volumes. Further resources, including questions for reflection or discussion, can be found at the series website, www.CatholicScriptureCommentary.com.

It is our desire and prayer that these volumes be of service so that more and more "the word of the Lord may speed forward and be glorified" (2 Thess 3:1) in the Church and throughout the world.

Peter S. Williamson
Mary Healy
Kevin Perrotta

Note to Readers

The New American Bible, Revised Edition differs slightly from most English translations in its verse numbering of Psalms and certain other parts of the Old Testament. For instance, Ps 51:4 in the NABRE is Ps 51:2 in other translations; Mal 3:19 in the NABRE is Mal 4:1 in other translations. Readers who use different translations are advised to keep this in mind when looking up Old Testament cross-references given in the commentary.

Note on Authorship

This volume is unique in the Catholic Commentary on Sacred Scripture series (CCSS) in that it is based on a previously published work, Cardinal Albert Vanhoye's *Lettera ai Galati*, published in 2000 and revised in 2011. Peter S. Williamson, this volume's coauthor, adapted Vanhoye's Italian commentary for this series, using a translation by his wife, Marsha Daigle-Williamson. This commentary presents Cardinal Vanhoye's work, originally written for his students, along with some additional material to better serve ministers of the word and other readers. Williamson has adapted Vanhoye's commentary in three ways. First, he has added sidebars, pastoral application sections, a glossary, illustrations, suggested resources, and indexes—features that are characteristic of the CCSS. For some of these features Williamson was able to draw upon material from *Lettera ai Galati* or other writings by Cardinal Vanhoye, although the preponderance is Williamson's own work. Second, because it was necessary to condense the Italian commentary to meet the requirements of this series, Williamson has omitted some information and arguments that would be of interest to graduate students and scholars but are less pertinent to a pastoral commentary. Finally, in a few places Williamson has included in the text or footnotes other interpretations suggested by recent commentators.

Abbreviations

†	indicates that the definition of a term appears in the glossary
ACCS	Ancient Christian Commentary on Scripture: New Testament VIII, *Galatians, Ephesians, Philippians*, edited by Mark J. Edwards (Downers Grove, IL: InterVarsity, 1999)
BECNT	Baker Exegetical Commentary on the New Testament
Catechism	*Catechism of the Catholic Church*, 2nd ed. (New York: Doubleday, 2003)
CCSS	Catholic Commentary on Sacred Scripture
Denzinger	H. Denzinger, *Compendium of Creeds, Definitions, and Declarations on Matters of Faith and Morals*, 43rd ed. Edited by Peter Hünermann. Latin-English (San Francisco: Ignatius, 2012)
ESV	English Standard Version
Lectionary	*The Lectionary for Mass* (1988/2000 USA Edition)
LXX	†Septuagint
NABRE	New American Bible (Revised Edition, 2011)
NIV	New International Version
NJB	New Jerusalem Bible
NRSV	New Revised Standard Version
NT	New Testament
OT	Old Testament
RSV	Revised Standard Version

Books of the Old Testament

Gen	Genesis	1 Sam	1 Samuel	Tob	Tobit
Exod	Exodus	2 Sam	2 Samuel	Jdt	Judith
Lev	Leviticus	1 Kings	1 Kings	Esther	Esther
Num	Numbers	2 Kings	2 Kings	1 Macc	1 Maccabees
Deut	Deuteronomy	1 Chron	1 Chronicles	2 Macc	2 Maccabees
Josh	Joshua	2 Chron	2 Chronicles	Job	Job
Judg	Judges	Ezra	Ezra	Ps(s)	Psalm(s)
Ruth	Ruth	Neh	Nehemiah	Prov	Proverbs

Eccles	Ecclesiastes	Ezek	Ezekiel	Nah	Nahum
Song	Song of Songs	Dan	Daniel	Hab	Habakkuk
Wis	Wisdom	Hosea	Hosea	Zeph	Zephaniah
Sir	Sirach	Joel	Joel	Hag	Haggai
Isa	Isaiah	Amos	Amos	Zech	Zechariah
Jer	Jeremiah	Obad	Obadiah	Mal	Malachi
Lam	Lamentations	Jon	Jonah		
Bar	Baruch	Mic	Micah		

Books of the New Testament

Matt	Matthew	Eph	Ephesians	Heb	Hebrews
Mark	Mark	Phil	Philippians	James	James
Luke	Luke	Col	Colossians	1 Pet	1 Peter
John	John	1 Thess	1 Thessalonians	2 Pet	2 Peter
Acts	Acts	2 Thess	2 Thessalonians	1 John	1 John
Rom	Romans	1 Tim	1 Timothy	2 John	2 John
1 Cor	1 Corinthians	2 Tim	2 Timothy	3 John	3 John
2 Cor	2 Corinthians	Titus	Titus	Jude	Jude
Gal	Galatians	Philem	Philemon	Rev	Revelation

Introduction

Paul's Letter to the Galatians has long aroused the interest of readers because of the light it sheds on the early history of the Church, on Christian doctrine, and on the striking personality of its author. It keeps readers interested because its passionately expressed teaching is always relevant to Christian †faith and life.

As regards *history*, Galatians begins with an autobiographical section in which Paul relays firsthand information about his life prior to his conversion and the years after it, as well as his relationship with Peter and the church of Jerusalem. There is nothing quite like it in any of his other letters, which offer only occasional and fragmentary autobiographical information. Adding to the historical interest of Galatians is the challenge of relating its narrative to that of the Acts of the Apostles.

As regards *doctrine*, the Letter to the Galatians treats a central and essential element of Paul's theology—†justification by faith in Christ. Although this teaching merits regular review because it is foundational, there is a natural human tendency to forget it. Some scholars have argued that the main point of Galatians is no longer relevant to Christians. It deals with the choice between faith in Christ and the Mosaic †law, but most Christians today are not tempted to seek salvation through the law of Moses. However, while it is true that most Christians are no longer concerned about the need for circumcision and Jewish food laws (i.e., keeping kosher), the deeper question about the basis of our relationship with God remains. Are we relying on our own works or on Christ for salvation? For Paul the only foundation is faith in Christ: no human works can ever claim that role. The Catholic Church is faithful to this doctrine, teaching it at the Council of Trent and reaffirming it in the Catechism of the Catholic

Church (see 1987–2029). Catholic theologians have also expounded justification in their treatises on †grace. Nevertheless, because we human beings easily succumb to placing hope for our salvation in good deeds and good intentions, thus substituting human works for faith in Christ, it is always necessary to recall Paul's forceful insistence on justification by faith.

Of course, Galatians is not the only letter in which Paul expounds this doctrine. The Letter to the Romans offers a fuller exposition of the same themes. But Galatians holds its own unique points of interest. Compared to Romans, Galatians seems a bit like a first draft, with the disadvantages but also the advantages that entails. As for disadvantages, some passages in Galatians are hard to understand, some steps in Paul's arguments are missing, and some of his affirmations can seem a bit one-sided. As for advantages, Paul's writing in Galatians is more spontaneous, more animated, and more emphatic. This points to another difference. Paul's exposition in Romans is carefully constructed and has the tone of an academic lecture, as much as that is possible for someone with Paul's passionate temperament. Romans provides us with a theological treatise. Galatians, on the other hand, offers a deeply felt argument about a burning question. In Romans, Paul addresses a community that does not personally know him, so he expresses himself moderately and politely in order to win their acceptance. In Galatians, Paul is speaking to *his* Christians, people he evangelized. The tone is more personal, more direct, and even fierce because his letter is provoked by their unfaithfulness to his preaching. All of this makes his letter more colorful and lively.

We can add that in Galatians Paul presents himself as the defender of Christian freedom. The theme of freedom is not absent in Romans, but it comes across more forcefully in the fiery arguments and exhortations of Galatians. Freedom remains an important topic, even though attention today tends to focus on political rather than religious freedom. Just as there is a tendency among Christians to drift away from justification by faith, so also Paul's teaching about freedom is often neglected. It is natural for pastors to emphasize compliance rather than freedom, and easier to focus on the limits of freedom rather than on its essence. However, to communicate the Pauline perspective on Christian freedom is necessary to help people grow to maturity in Christ, provided that other aspects of the truth are not forgotten.

In addition to the historical information and doctrinal teaching it provides, Galatians holds a special psychological interest because of how clearly it reveals the *personality* of its author. A renowned French theologian, Auguste Sabatier, put it this way:

All the powers of Paul's soul shine forth in these pages. . . . There is nothing in ancient or modern literature to be compared with it. . . . Broad and luminous views, keen logic, biting irony—everything that is most forcible in argument, vehement in indignation, ardent and tender in affection, is found here combined and poured forth in a single stream, forming a work of irresistible power.[1]

Paul's tumultuous, explosive spontaneity elicits our interest, but it also presents difficulties for interpretation because it leads to many irregularities in his expression: interrupted sentences, ungrammatical constructions, enigmatic and paradoxical formulas, obscure allusions. To understand it fully we would need to understand the concrete circumstances he is addressing. Unfortunately, we have no other sources of knowledge about the situation of the Christians in Galatia on which to draw. The best we can do is to deduce the historical context from the letter itself. It is no wonder that commentators hold diverse opinions about various points in the letter.

Overview of Galatians

The circumstances that led Paul to send this letter are indicated in vivid terms immediately after his greeting (1:1–5). Paul expresses amazement that the Galatians are turning to "a different gospel" (1:6). The Apostle immediately denounces that so-called †gospel, saying that it arises from a desire "to pervert the gospel of Christ" (1:7). Then he strongly affirms the unchangeable nature of the gospel he has preached (1:8–9). The goals of the letter can be described as twofold: a passionate defense of the gospel Paul preached to the Galatians and a fierce attack on the Galatians' adherence to another gospel.

Most commentators agree that the letter has three basic sections, although they differ about where precisely these sections begin and end.[2]

The first section (1:11–2:21) defends the gospel that Paul proclaims on the basis of a series of events in his life. Its theme is clearly stated at the outset: "The gospel preached by me is not of human origin. For I did not receive it from a human being, nor was I taught it, but it came through a revelation of Jesus Christ" (1:11–12).

1. Auguste Sabatier, with George Gillanders Findlay, *The Apostle Paul: A Sketch of His Doctrine* (London: Hodder and Stoughton, 1899), 153–54.

2. Some prefer a division into two parts, the first doctrinal (1:6–5:12), the second exhortative (5:13–6:10). This division, however, does not distinguish between the autobiographical argument (1:11–2:21) and the doctrinal one (3:1–5:12). Other interpreters propose four divisions, distinguishing two successive proofs (3:1–47 and 4:8–5:12) in the doctrinal argument.

The second section (3:1–5:12) defends Paul's gospel more directly and at the same time combats the Galatians' adherence to another gospel with various arguments. The basic themes of this second part are forcefully introduced at the end of the autobiographical section. Paul declares that "a person is not justified by works of the law but through faith in Jesus Christ" (2:16). This thesis statement indicates that the "different gospel" that Paul opposes teaches that justification requires not only faith but also keeping the law of Moses. The Apostle Paul absolutely rejects that position. Some of the arguments he presents against it are based on the Galatians' experience of the faith (3:1–5; 4:12–20), while others are doctrinal and based on Scripture (3:6–4:11; 4:21–31). Concluding the second part is an exhortation to the Galatians to conduct themselves in accord with the truths Paul has just set forth (5:1–10).

The third section of Galatians (5:13–6:10) defends Paul's gospel against erroneous practical conclusions that readers might be tempted to draw. It rejects a false understanding of Christian freedom. The fact that Christians are free in regard to the law of Moses does not permit them to lead a dissolute life but rather summons them to a life of generous love under the inspiration of the Holy Spirit. This theme is introduced in the first sentence: "You were called for freedom, brothers. But do not use this freedom as an opportunity for the flesh; rather, serve one another through love" (5:13).

Up to the last sentence in this third section (6:10), Paul has dictated this letter to a secretary. He concludes with a few lines in his own hand, repeating a few points that are still on his heart, and ends, as he usually does, by wishing his recipients "grace" (6:18).

Genre

To interpret a text correctly, we need to be aware of its literary type or genre—that is, what kind of writing it is. We do not interpret a poem the way we read a business letter. To what genre does Galatians belong? Its traditional title, the Letter to the Galatians, reflects the fact that it belongs to the epistolary genre, and the way it is written corresponds to Greco-Roman letter-writing conventions. The beginning states the name of the sender, "Paul," and the name of the addressees, "the churches of Galatia," followed by the greeting, "grace to you and peace" (1:1–3). Another salutation ends the letter: "The grace of our Lord Jesus Christ be with your spirit, brothers. Amen" (6:18).

What kind of letter is Galatians? It is certainly not merely a letter of friendship, since Paul does not send personal news about where he is, what he is doing, or what he plans to do. Rather, Galatians is a pastoral letter, an apostolic intervention in response to a crisis that hangs over the Christian communities Paul established in a particular region. The letter contains a message that Paul wanted to address to these Christians that he was unable to present in person because he was elsewhere.

In recent decades, biblical scholars have sought to understand Galatians in light of studies of ancient †rhetoric.[3] However, although it is possible to find parallels in Galatians to various kinds of rhetoric, it seems better to recognize the distinctiveness of the letter's original setting. Galatians belongs to a persuasive genre that is not catalogued in ancient rhetorical treatises—namely, Christian preaching grounded in Scripture and the mystery of Christ, which summons its readers to faith and to life in the Spirit.

Where and When Was Galatians Written?

Today it is customary to indicate at the beginning of a letter the date and sometimes the place from which a letter is written. This custom, however, did not exist in antiquity. Paul therefore does not say where he was when he dictated his letter to the Galatians or when he did so. We can deduce that the letter was written more than fourteen years after the Apostle's conversion since Paul mentions visiting Jerusalem "after fourteen years" (2:1). But how much time passed between that visit and the composition of Galatians?

The answer depends on the relationship between the meeting in Jerusalem Paul refers to in Gal 2:1–10 and the Council of Jerusalem (approximately AD 48) recounted by Luke in Acts 15:4–29. Some commentators believe these are two different events[4] and that the Letter to the Galatians preceded the Jerusalem Council and was therefore written before Paul's second missionary journey (Acts 16:1–18:17), making Galatians the oldest of Paul's letters. However, the majority of commentators believe that Paul's mention of his visit to Jerusalem in Gal 1:18 and Luke's account of the Council of Jerusalem (Acts 15) refer to the same event, and therefore they date Galatians after the Council of Jerusalem.

---

3. Greco-Roman rhetoric distinguished three kinds of discourse corresponding to diverse situations that required persuasion: *forensic rhetoric*, intended to accuse or defend a person in court; *deliberative rhetoric*, addressed to a political assembly to argue for or against a proposed action; and *demonstrative rhetoric*, used on special occasions—a city festival, for instance—in order to praise and celebrate notable achievements. For a concise but helpful overview, see Michael Gorman, *Apostle of the Crucified Lord* (Grand Rapids: Eerdmans, 2004), 83–85.

4. Some commentators think that Acts 15 synthesizes the debates and conclusions of more than one meeting.

Internal evidence from Paul's letters makes this second view more probable. Comparing Paul's various letters shows a development in the Apostle's thought on certain points, suggesting the likelihood that 1 Thessalonians is the oldest letter and that Galatians was written closer in time to the Letter to the Romans. Romans is generally considered to have been written in early 58, when Paul was about to return from Greece to Jerusalem (see Rom 15:25). It is therefore likely that Galatians was written around the year 56 when Paul was in Ephesus. In support of this, an ancient prologue to Galatians says it was written from there.

Who Were the Galatians?

Paul addresses his letter to "the churches of Galatia" (1:2). Whom exactly that refers to is far from clear. Nowhere else does Paul direct a letter to "the churches" (plural) of an entire region; he always names a particular city (Thessalonica, Philippi, Corinth, Rome, Colossae), even when he intends to address the Christians in a whole province (see 2 Cor 1:1). Why doesn't Paul mention any city here? Perhaps Paul's communities in Galatia were located not in big cities but in small towns or villages, but this is only a guess.

Where is the region of Galatia? From comparing the accounts in Acts with what we know of historical geography, two possibilities for its location emerge, one northern and ethnic, the other southern and administrative. The "churches of Galatia" could be located in the region of Ancyra (present-day Ankara) in the north-central part of Anatolia (modern Turkey); this region was inhabited by a Celtic people who were called Galatians because they resided in Gaul before invading Asia Minor in the third century BC. The other possibility is the south-central part of Anatolia that constituted the Roman province of Galatia, which was inhabited by a variety of nationalities.

Both hypotheses find support in Acts. The southern hypothesis identifies Galatia with a region Paul evangelized on his first missionary journey (Acts 13:13–14:26). In his account of this journey, Luke does not mention Galatia, but he names the principal cities that Paul and Barnabas evangelized and refers to the regions of "Pamphylia" (13:13; 14:24), "Pisidia" (13:14; 14:24), and "Lycaonia" (14:6), parts of which belonged to Roman Galatia. After Paul and Barnabas's return to Antioch (14:26), Luke reports the controversy over circumcision for converted †Gentiles and the Council of Jerusalem, where the issue was discussed and resolved (Acts 15). After the council, on his second missionary journey, Paul passes through this same region again (16:1) before continuing toward the northwest and Macedonia (16:10–12).

© Baker Publishing Group

Figure 1. Possible locations of St. Paul's Galatian churches according to the northern and southern hypotheses.

Two passages in Acts, however, point to the northern hypothesis. They mention Paul's journey in "Galatian territory" (Acts 16:6; see 18:23). These two texts, the only ones in Acts that mention Galatia by name, show that Luke distinguishes between the "Galatian territory" (16:6) and the more southerly regions of Pamphylia, Pisidia, and Lycaonia that Paul evangelized earlier. We do not know, however, if Paul made the same distinction, since the names of the southern regions do not appear in his letters.

In the end, whether Paul was writing to north or south Galatia does not significantly impact the meaning of Galatians for Christian life. In either case, Paul teaches about justification by faith in Christ and about Christian freedom from the law of Moses. What shifts is our understanding of the historical context. According to the southern hypothesis, the letter could have been written before Paul's second missionary journey, and perhaps before the Council of Jerusalem. In the northern theory, on the other hand, the letter would come later, after the

Figure 2. Remains of Roman baths at Ancyra, located in the northern region called Galatia.

Council of Jerusalem, after he passed through the north "Galatian territory" for the first time on his second missionary journey (Acts 16:6). In this case, the letter might have been written during that journey, but more likely in the course of his third journey, after his second visit to that region (Acts 18:23). If the northern Galatia hypothesis is correct, Gal 2:1–10 could refer to the Council of Jerusalem. In our view, the close parallels between the letters to the Galatians and to the Romans tip the balance in favor of a later date for Galatians, making the northern hypothesis more probable.

Figure 3. Rural landscape from the southern region called Galatia.

Historical Setting

From the very beginning of his letter (Gal 1:6) Paul attacks the "different gospel" that his readers are on the verge of accepting. What was its content, and who was spreading it? Since the Galatians knew, Paul did not feel the need to explain, which makes it difficult for us to answer these questions. However, we can infer some things from the way the Apostle argues his case.

The first passage that is instructive in this regard is Gal 2:3–5, where the Apostle declares that during his visit to Jerusalem he had fought "so that the truth of the gospel might remain intact" for the Galatians (2:5). The context shows that the question revolved around circumcision: Titus, a Gentile convert, was not "compelled to be circumcised" (2:3). To be circumcised entailed an obligation to practice the law of Moses and adopt the Jewish way of life, especially Sabbath observance, regulations for †ritual purity, and food laws (5:3). Paul maintained that requiring Gentile Christians to keep the Mosaic law would reduce them to slavery, so he forcefully resisted the attempt (2:4–5).

From the chapter that follows (3:7–29), one can surmise that the rival gospel held that faith in Christ was not enough for a person to be justified before God. It was also necessary to enter into Abraham's family through circumcision (see Gen 17:9–14); indeed, without this sign of the †covenant it was not possible to have any part in Abraham's †inheritance, the blessings that God had promised to his descendants. It was likewise necessary to adhere to all the precepts of the law given on Mount Sinai (see Exod 24:3–8). While contemporary Christians do not often think about sharing in the blessings promised to Abraham, New Testament authors clearly understand life in Christ to be a fulfillment of these and other Old Testament promises.

The missionaries of the rival gospel did not lack ready arguments from the Old Testament. To these arguments, it seems, they added a critique of Paul and his way of evangelizing Gentiles. They insinuated that he was not a genuine apostle, since he was not one of the Twelve, and therefore ought to conform himself to the teaching and the practice of the apostles among the Jewish Christians in Jerusalem. They claimed that Paul was preaching a gospel that was merely human teaching, waiving necessary requirements in order "to please people" (Gal 1:10). In addition, he was not consistent, since in some circumstances he himself preached circumcision (5:11).[5] The goal of these insinuations from his opponents was, evidently, to undermine Paul's

---

5. Acts 16:3 reports that Paul had Timothy circumcised, although the situation was quite different from requiring circumcision of Gentile believers, since Timothy was born of a Jewish mother.

apostolic authority so that they could more effectively deny the validity of the gospel he preached.

Who were these opponents? Paul never identifies them clearly. He depicts them at the beginning of the letter as certain people "who are disturbing" the Christians in Galatia "and wish to pervert the gospel of Christ" (1:7). He is undoubtedly thinking about them when he talks about his opponents at the time of the meeting in Jerusalem: "false brothers secretly brought in, who slipped in to spy on our freedom that we have in Christ Jesus, that they might enslave us" (2:4). The troublemakers in Galatia certainly are of the same mentality as the †Judaizers of Acts 15:1, 5, who wanted to impose on Gentile converts the obligation of living like Jews. In the confrontation at Antioch (Gal 2:11–14), Paul reproved Peter for acting as though he agreed with the Judaizers. By refusing to eat with Gentile Christians, Peter was pressuring them to "live like Jews" (2:14).

We have to wait until Gal 4 to find another direct mention of Paul's adversaries, and there what is at stake is the personal loyalty of the Galatians. Paul does not name his opponents but says with feeling, "They show interest in you, but not in a good way; they want to isolate you, so that you may show interest in them" (4:17). This attempt to seduce his readers away from him pains the Apostle, since he cares deeply about his relationship with his Galatian Christians.

Although they may only be rhetorical flourishes, three sentences in Gal 5 suggest the possibility that the Apostle did not have specific information about these troublemakers. In the first sentence he asks, "Who hindered you from following [the] truth?" (5:7). In the second, he maintains that there is one person chiefly responsible, but he is unable to say who he is: "The one who is troubling you will bear the condemnation, whoever he may be" (5:10). In a third strong statement, he refers to a group: "Would that those who are upsetting you might also castrate themselves!" (5:12).

Paul's final remarks in his own hand at the end of the letter are more concrete. Here Paul states explicitly what was possible to surmise from chapter 2—namely, that the troublemakers are "trying to compel" the Galatians "to have yourselves circumcised" (6:12–13), the same language of compulsion used earlier in reference to Titus (2:3). To counter the strategies of these Judaizers Paul denounces their motives: they "want to make a good appearance in the flesh," meaning that they are trying to please people and avoid persecution for "the cross of Christ" (6:12), the true basis of justification. Before his own conversion, Paul persecuted the Church (1:13, 23). Now he is persecuted because he does not preach circumcision (5:11). Finally, Paul accuses these rival teachers of inconsistency: "Not even those having themselves circumcised observe the law themselves" (6:13).

These statements do not reveal the precise identity of the Judaizers; all we can tell is that they are Jewish Christians. It is important to see that Paul does not take aim at Jews in general but rather engages in an intramural polemic against certain Jewish Christian missionaries who observed the Mosaic law and wanted to impose laws specific to the Jewish people on Gentile converts. For us, the precise identification of Paul's adversaries and a detailed determination of their position are secondary. What primarily interests us is the content of the Apostle's teaching. In a certain sense we are indebted to the Judaizers since their error elicited such a vigorous reaction from Paul, forcing him to give expression to profound and essential aspects of our faith in a letter full of apostolic teaching and vitality.

The Letter to the Galatians and Christian Life Today

Besides the perennially important themes of justification by faith and Christian freedom, several other topics in Galatians stand out for their relevance to the Church of the twenty-first century.

- In an age that wants to trim the Christian message to conform to contemporary culture, it is necessary to recall Paul's uncompromising commitment to the unchanging gospel of Jesus Christ. Today it is not Jewish tradition that seeks to refashion the gospel but secular ideologies that would erase what is distinctive in its moral requirements, as well as theological currents that deny that salvation is available only in and through Jesus Christ. Paul's words echo through the centuries as a sharp warning: "Even if we or an angel from heaven should preach [to you] a gospel other than the one that we preached to you, let that one be accursed!" (1:8).

- The most-quoted verse in Galatians is probably 2:20: "I have been crucified with Christ; it is no longer I who live, but Christ who lives in me; and the life I now live in the flesh I live by faith in the Son of God, who loved me and gave himself for me" (RSV). While many things can be said about this verse, contemporary readers especially cherish the poignant declaration that grounds every Christian's identity in Christ's personal love and gift of himself "for me."

- Less noticed, but equally important for the sake of the new evangelization, is Paul's confidence that Christian life is marked by a palpable experience of divine power, so much so that the Apostle can cite it in argument: "Does, then, the one who supplies the Spirit to you and works mighty deeds among you do so from works of the law or from faith in what you heard?" (3:5). The Church must seek to recover Paul's confidence and the experience of the early Church.

- Although Galatians has sometimes been interpreted erroneously to teach the replacement of Israel by the Church, the letter is better understood as showing the close relation between Jews and Christians, since Abraham is our common father in faith (3:7–14).

- Through Gal 4:4–7 many Christians have grasped—and many still need to grasp—the life-changing truth that God has adopted us as his sons and daughters and has demonstrated that extraordinary fact by sending the Spirit of his Son into our hearts, raising us to a dignity that is scarcely imaginable.

- Finally, Paul's teaching in Gal 5:16–25 about the role of the Holy Spirit in empowering and guiding Christian conduct is nothing less than revolutionary. He begins with an extraordinary claim: "Live by the Spirit and you will certainly not gratify the desire of the flesh" (5:16). Then Paul interprets Christian experience by explaining the interior conflict between fallen human nature, "the †flesh," and the indwelling Spirit of God (5:17). To avoid confusion between these opposing principles of conduct, Paul contrasts the "works of the flesh" (5:19–21) with the good fruit that the Spirit produces: "love, joy, peace, patience, kindness, generosity, faithfulness, gentleness, self-control" (5:22–23). In doing so he demonstrates that being guided by the Holy Spirit leads to conduct that surpasses the law's demands (5:18, 23).

When Paul heard that the Christians in Galatia were beginning to accept the teaching of the Judaizers, it must have seemed to him an unmitigated disaster. He responded passionately, bringing to bear all his zeal, his love, and his powers of persuasion to return the Galatians to the right path. Nearly two thousand years later, we cannot help but be grateful for that trial, since it elicited from Paul such a wonderful clarification of the gospel and such rich teaching about how to †live as a Christian. Paul's gospel is that we are justified by faith in Jesus Christ, the one who loved us and gave himself for us on the cross (2:16, 20; 3:1). Christ freed us from the law so that we might live by the Holy Spirit and not gratify the desire of the flesh, so that through love we might serve one another (5:13, 16).

Outline of the Letter to the Galatians

Opening Greeting (1:1–5)
Reproof and Declaration of Loyalty to the Gospel of Christ
(1:6–10)

I. Paul's Defense of His Gospel with Autobiographical Arguments
(1:11–2:21)
   A. The Divine Origin of Paul's Gospel (1:11–24)
      1. Introduction to Part 1 (1:11–12)
      2. From Persecutor to Apostle (1:13–24)
   B. Official Recognition of Paul's Gospel (2:1–10)
      1. Second Visit to Jerusalem and a Controversy (2:1–5)
      2. Agreement among the Apostles (2:6–10)
   C. The Incident at Antioch and the Gospel of Paul (2:11–21)
      1. Paul Opposes Peter's Inconsistent Conduct (2:11–14)
      2. The Doctrine of Justification (2:15–21)
II. Arguments from Christian Experience and from Scripture
(3:1–5:12)
   A. Variety of Arguments (3:1–18)
      1. An Argument from Experience: The Gift of the Spirit (3:1–5)
      2. An Argument from Scripture: The Faith and Blessing of
         Abraham (3:6–14)
      3. A Legal Argument: The Priority of the Promise over the Law
         (3:15–18)
   B. The Temporary Role of the Law; the Superiority of Faith
      (3:19–4:11)

        1. The Provisional Nature of the Law (3:19–22)

        2. The Two Periods of Salvation History (3:23–4:7)

        3. Direct Address (4:8–11)

    C. An Appeal to Remember Their Love in the Past (4:12–20)

    D. Another Argument from Scripture and a Conclusion (4:21–5:12)

        1. The Two Sons of Abraham and Two Covenants (4:21–31)

        2. Concluding Exhortations and Admonitions (5:1–12)

III. Application to Christian Life (5:13–6:10)

    A. Freedom: Not License but Service in Love (5:13–15)

    B. The Power of the Spirit over the Flesh (5:16–25)

    C. Not Conceit but Solidarity (5:26–6:6)

    D. Do What Is Good (6:7–10)

Paul's Handwritten Postscript (6:11–18)

An Unusual Beginning

Galatians 1:1–5

All of Paul's letters to churches differ from other letters of his day in the way they begin, but Galatians is unique among them all. A typical greeting at the beginning of a letter is found in Acts 23:26: "Claudius Lysias to his excellency the governor Felix, greetings." ("Greetings" is literally "rejoice.") In contrast, Paul usually introduces himself as an apostle of Christ, mentions one or more of his coworkers as sending the letter with him, and names the church to which he is writing with a complimentary description of their relationship to God. He expresses a prayer-wish that his readers may enjoy †grace and peace. Paul normally follows his initial greeting by expressing thanks to God for the recipients of the letter and for God's work in their lives. However, the crisis that Paul discerns in Galatia that has motivated him to write this letter (see "Historical Setting" in the introduction, pp. 23–25) leads him to depart from his customary pattern.

Initial Greeting (1:1–5)

[1]Paul, an apostle not from human beings nor through a human being but through Jesus Christ and God the Father who raised him from the dead, [2]and all the brothers who are with me, to the churches of Galatia: [3]grace to you and peace from God our Father and the Lord Jesus Christ, [4]who gave himself for our sins that he might rescue us from the present evil age in accord with the will of our God and Father, [5]to whom be glory forever and ever. Amen.

NT: Acts 2:24; 9:15; 16:6; Rom 1:7; Gal 2:20
Catechism: Christ's gift his Father's will, 2824

1:1–4 As in his other letters, Paul begins Galatians with a prayer-wish for its recipients (v. 3). Instead of opening with "rejoice" (Greek *chaire*), as secular letters of that period normally did, Paul prays that his readers enjoy **grace** (*charis*), the gratuitous favor of God, and **peace**, an echo of the Jewish customary greeting (2 Macc 1:1). †Grace and peace come from a relationship with God that recognizes him as **our Father** and a relationship with his Son Jesus the †Messiah. By saying "our," Paul refers to the standing that he shares with the Galatians as a fellow Christian. His invocation of grace and peace from God and Jesus Christ suggests that his letter will be read at a liturgical gathering of the Christian community and expresses his participation in their assembly.

In other respects, however, this letter to the Galatians begins differently. Immediately after Paul's name and title of **apostle** is a jarring negative, **not**, which is then countered by **but**. This tone of controversy is very unusual at the beginning of a letter. Paul feels a need to immediately repudiate certain opinions about the nature of his apostleship and to vigorously affirm the divine origin of his apostolic calling. We can infer that opponents of his apostolate have discredited him with the Galatians, perhaps spreading the idea that he was not an apostle of Christ in the full sense of the term but only an emissary sent by the community in Antioch, the church from which Paul began his missionary work.[1] Paul firmly denies having received his commission **from human beings** or through the mediation of a human being such as Peter or one of the other apostles. Paul received his apostleship **through Jesus Christ and God the Father**.

It is important to note the contrast between "from human beings" and "through Jesus Christ" because it shows that for Paul, Jesus Christ is not merely a man but a divine person. Paul's use of prepositions here is also significant. The first part of the sentence uses two prepositions—"*from* human beings" and "*through* a human being"—which might lead a reader to expect a parallel expression, "*through* Jesus Christ *from* the Father." Instead Paul uses a single preposition, "through," for Christ and the Father, indicating the union of Christ with the Father. Likewise in verse 3, Paul employs a single preposition, "from," to indicate **God our Father and the Lord Jesus Christ** as the one source of grace and peace.

Paul's denial in this first sentence that his apostleship comes from human beings prepares for the first, autobiographical part of the letter (1:11–2:21), in which he will defend the divine origin of the †gospel he preaches (1:11–12). Other elements in his opening section prepare for the second, more doctrinal

---

1. Acts 13:1–3. See 2 Cor 8:23 for an instance when Paul uses the term "apostles" to refer to emissaries of the churches.

section (3:1–5:12). Paul immediately recalls fundamental points of †faith that the Galatians seem not to have fully grasped: Christ's resurrection (1:1) and the passion and death by which he gave himself for our freedom (1:4). The Galatians are in the process of turning back to slavery (4:9; 5:1)!

Like the earliest apostolic preaching, Paul presents the resurrection as the work of **God the Father who raised** Jesus.[2] To refer to the passion, Paul combines two other early formulations from the gospel traditions. The first is Jesus' statement that the Son of Man has come to "give" his life as a ransom for many (Matt 20:28; Mark 10:45); the second is that Christ died "for our sins" (1 Cor 15:3). Paul's wording, **Christ, who gave himself for our sins**, emphasizes the total personal commitment of Christ in saving us. Galatians 2:20 will emphasize this even more, speaking of Christ's love.

Christ's purpose in offering himself was to **rescue us** from the present evil age, a liberation analogous to that of the exodus, when God saw the affliction of his people and came down "to rescue them from the power of the Egyptians" (Exod 3:8; see 18:9–10; Acts 7:34). Such a goal is therefore perfectly **in accord with the will of our God and Father** (Gal 1:4), who wills salvation. On Christ's part, redemption is a work of obedience to the Father (see Rom 5:19; Phil 2:8) and of generous love for human beings (see Gal 2:20; Eph 5:2, 25–26). Instead of freeing people from Egypt, Christ frees people from **the present evil age**. This phrase refers to the distinction that Jews and Christians of Paul's day made between "this age" and "the age to come."[3] This present age is the world that was created "very good" (Gen 1:31) but now contains evil because it has become subject to Satan, "the ruler of this world" (John 12:31), on account of sin. The age to come will occur when God intervenes to establish his kingdom.

The Jewish people expected the transition from the present to the future age to take place in the days of the Messiah. They anticipated a clear-cut chronological separation between the ages:

The present age / The age to come

The early Christians, however, came to recognize that the future age was inaugurated at the resurrection of Christ (see vertical line 1 in fig. 4), although the present evil age remains temporarily until the return of Christ (vertical

2. Acts 2:24, 32; 3:15; 4:10; 1 Thess 1:10. Other texts emphasize the active role of Christ or the Spirit in the resurrection (Mark 16:6—see RSV; John 10:17–18; Rom 8:11; 1 Thess 4:14; 2 Tim 2:8—see RSV).

3. See Matt 12:32; 24:3; Luke 18:30; Eph 1:21; Heb 6:5. Sometimes the Greek word for "age" is translated "world" (e.g., Rom 12:2 RSV).

line 2). They were aware of living in the overlap between the present age and the age to come.

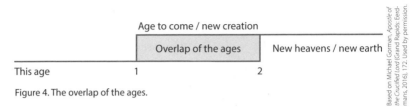

Figure 4. The overlap of the ages.

Christians no longer belong to the present age; instead, they belong to the "new creation" (Gal 6:15; see 2 Cor 5:17). They still find themselves in the world, but, having a new life in Christ, they must no longer conform themselves to this age (Rom 12:2).

In verse 4 Paul prepares for his doctrinal discussion, in which he will contrast the time of slavery to the †elemental powers of the "world" with the time of freedom obtained by Christ (see Gal 3:23–25; 4:3–5) and will vigorously urge the Galatians to stand firm in that freedom (5:1).[4]

By referring to the present age, Paul also sets the stage for the last part of the epistle, which is an exhortation to Christian living (5:13–6:10). Rescued and freed from the power of this evil age, Christians are responsible to †live in a manner that conforms to their new life in Christ. They have received the †eschatological gift of the Spirit, who opposes worldly and †carnal ways of living. The opposition between the present evil age and the age to come is reflected in the conflict between the †flesh and the Spirit in the life of the believer (5:16–25).

The thrust of the entire letter is thus already indicated in the first few verses. Paul has thought ahead of time about what he will say. This does not mean that his letter will be a carefully arranged discourse. Polished orators and methodical teachers are concerned not only to offer convincing arguments but also to express them in the most organized way. They prepare a well-ordered presentation arranged as clearly as possible in divisions and subdivisions, and they take time to correct every sentence, eliminating any obscurity, irregularity, and defect. Paul is not that kind of writer; instead, his style is explosive.[5] He thinks long and hard about what he wants to say, but reflects on his topic

4. In that discussion Paul will no longer use the word "age" (Greek *aiōn*) but will speak of the elemental powers of the "world" (Greek *kosmos*).

5. While some may question whether these remarks about Paul's writing style pertain to Romans, they clearly do not apply to Ephesians and Colossians, which some scholars believe were written by a disciple of Paul after his death. Other scholars, who consider these letters from Paul, attribute the difference in style to the aid of a secretary and perhaps to the additional time he had available to write these letters while a prisoner.

passionately without detailed attention to the form of his remarks. Although he has a clear goal in mind, when the time comes to begin dictating the letter, he does not step back to compose his thoughts in a meticulous manner (like the author of Hebrews, for instance) or to review his text and correct the style. Rather he advances full speed ahead, impelled by his passion and conviction.

This is especially true for the Letter to the Galatians, where Paul has scarcely identified himself before he begins presenting his argument. Other writers might devote more space to courteous pleasantries, but Paul considers the matter to be so urgent that he immediately gets down to business. Even the phrase **and all the brothers who are with me** (v. 2) may be intended to make a point. At the beginning of his other letters, Paul usually names one or more of his coworkers (Sylvanus, Sosthenes, and especially Timothy) as coauthors of the letter. Here no other individuals are named; there is only this general reference. The naming of only Paul himself as author forcefully asserts his personal authority. On the other hand, the fact that "all the brothers" are with him indicates that he is not isolated as he addresses the Christians in Galatia. His position is thus doubly reinforced.

Paul's terse manner of referring to his addressees as **the churches of Galatia**— there is no compliment or praise for them—is also a hint that tension exists. This tone contrasts with the wording in his other letters. For example, 1 Cor 1:2 contains no less than three expressions of appreciation and esteem: "to the church *of God* that is in Corinth, to you who have been *sanctified* in Christ Jesus, called to be *holy*." In Rom 1:7 Paul says, "to all the beloved of God in Rome, called to be holy." For the Galatians there is no mention of any churches "of God," no "beloved," no "called to be holy," since Paul wants to call their attention to an urgent problem.

Even the †doxological formula in verse 5—**to whom be glory forever**—can **1:5** be explained by Paul's perspective on the situation in Galatia. In his other letters, the Apostle never includes a doxology at the beginning. Why does he do so here? In his other letters the first words after the opening are usually, "I give thanks to God," or "I bless God." In those letters Paul goes on to thank God for the †grace abundantly poured out on the recipients of his letter. Here, however, the first words after his opening sentence will be very different. He does not say, "I give thanks," but "I am amazed," and follows with a stinging rebuke. Paul did not feel it was appropriate under the circumstances to express thanksgiving to God about the Galatians (even though he will later express the depth of his love for them, 4:19–20). On the other hand, he did not want to forgo giving glory to God. It is thus reasonable to infer that Paul's doxology compensates for the absence of an opening prayer of thanksgiving and signals in advance that Paul will not be praising the Galatians.

Strong Words: Paul Takes a Stand

Galatians 1:6–10

Paul's initial greeting hinted at a controversy. In the words that follow, he directly confronts the situation that has prompted the letter and expresses his vigorous response.

A Stern Reproof (1:6–10)

---

[6]I am amazed that you are so quickly forsaking the one who called you by [the] grace [of Christ] for a different gospel [7](not that there is another). But there are some who are disturbing you and wish to pervert the gospel of Christ. [8]But even if we or an angel from heaven should preach [to you] a gospel other than the one that we preached to you, let that one be accursed! [9]As we have said before, and now I say again, if anyone preaches to you a gospel other than the one that you received, let that one be accursed!

[10]Am I now currying favor with human beings or God? Or am I seeking to please people? If I were still trying to please people, I would not be a slave of Christ.

NT: Acts 15:24; 2 Cor 11:4, 14; 1 Thess 2:4; Jude 1:3
Catechism: the gospel, 75–76

These verses introduce the theme of the letter: the defense of Paul's †gospel and his fight against the Galatians' adherence to a distortion of the gospel. The content is presented not in an academic manner but with great intensity. Paul does

34

not begin by simply stating his topic, but rather immediately enters into battle brandishing his most potent weapon, a repeated anathema. Paul's language is not that of detached exposition, but of spirited confrontation.

Why is Paul so impassioned? As the rest of the letter makes clear, the Galatians have been listening to Jewish Christian teachers who say that it is not enough to believe in Christ and be baptized. They say it is also necessary for †Gentile Christians to be circumcised and to keep the †law of Moses (see "Historical Setting" in the introduction, pp. 23–25). Paul discerns that this teaching not only is mistaken but also fundamentally contradicts the gospel he was sent to proclaim. He will explain his reasons in 2:15–21.

His first words, **I am amazed**, express Paul's reaction to the situation: as-   **1:6**
tonishment and disappointment. He is saying in effect, "I did not expect this from you!" He sharpens his rebuke with sarcasm—he is amazed they are doing this **so quickly**. Paul charges the Galatians with desertion, made all the worse because of the person they **are so quickly forsaking**. It was God who **called** the Galatians, but they are turning their backs on him. He established them in a wonderful plan of generous love, the **grace [of Christ]**,[1] but they are leaving to go elsewhere. How foolish! How shocking and disgraceful! Paul does not explain the circumstances or say how he learned of this situation. He simply states what he sees.

Paul says they "are forsaking," present tense, because their shocking behavior is current: the Galatians are forsaking God's call now. Paul is watching the drama unfold and is dumbfounded. However, the use of present tense means that their desertion is not yet complete. At times commentators overlook this present tense and speak as though the Galatians have already completely abandoned their †faith. But Paul is not saying that they have already gone over to **a different gospel**, only that they are in the process of doing so. His letter is not a pronouncement of final judgment on a situation beyond repair but is an intervention to stop a development that is under way.

Paul wants to shock the Galatians with his first words. In all probability, they did not think they were turning their backs on God when they were discussing the need for circumcision. On the contrary, it is likely that their concern was to be even more faithful to God's will as it is expressed in the Scriptures they had, what we now call the Old Testament. Paul, however, sees things very differently: the Galatians are on a path to perdition. He wants to set a radical choice before them. The situation is extremely serious, so Paul uses strong words.

---

1. The NABRE uses brackets in the text to indicate words that are absent from some important ancient manuscripts.

The Meaning of "Gospel" in the New Testament

BIBLICAL BACKGROUND

Paradoxically, the noun "†gospel" (Greek *euangelion*, "good news") rarely appears in the Gospels (twelve times, never in Luke and John) but is used very often by St. Paul (sixty times!). In every instance the word refers to the preaching of the Christian faith. The books that we call Gospels were almost certainly not written when Paul wrote Galatians. Only in the second century did the word "gospel" come to refer also to the four canonical Gospels.

Both Paul and the authors of the Gospels use a verb that means "to announce good news, to preach the gospel" (Greek *euangelizomai*, from which we get "evangelize"). According to Matthew, Mark, and Luke, the gospel preached by Jesus centered on the good news that God was initiating his long-awaited kingdom and summoned those who heard to repent and believe. In the course of his ministry Jesus also revealed his own identity as the †Messiah (God's anointed king) and Son of God, although his disciples were not able to fully grasp what he was saying until after the resurrection.

The gospel preached by the apostles in Acts continued to announce the coming of God's kingdom but centered above all on Jesus as the Messiah and Son of God and on his death and resurrection, which fulfilled the Scriptures and confirmed his identity and message. The apostles summoned all to repent, believe, be baptized, and receive the gift of the Holy Spirit in order to attain salvation.[a] Although initially the apostles preached primarily to Jews, as Jesus had, after the incident with Cornelius (Acts 10–11) the apostles eventually preached the message to all †nations, starting from Jerusalem in fulfillment of Jesus' command and ancient prophecy (Matt 28:18–20; Acts 1:8; Isa 2:1–5). The form of the message the apostles preached to Jews, who already believed in the true God and knew the Old Testament, necessarily differed in some respects from what they preached to †Gentiles, who needed to turn from polytheism and idols to serve the true God. Acts includes sermons by Peter and Paul that illustrate the apostolic preaching to Jews (Acts 2:14–40; 13:16–41) and Gentiles (14:15–17; 17:22–31).

The first great controversy the early Church faced concerned whether Gentiles who believed in Jesus needed to become Jews by being circumcised and keeping the law of Moses in order to be †justified (Acts 15). In Galatians, Paul addresses this issue and shows that underlying this question is a crucial truth about the basis of our justification.

a. Acts 2:38–40; 4:12; 13:26, 48; 16:31; 28:28.

At first glance it seems that Paul contradicts himself, since he says the Ga- 1:7
latians are turning to "a different gospel," and then, **not that there is another**.
Although in 2:7 Paul will allude to two expressions of the †gospel, one proclaimed
to Jews and another directed to †Gentiles, here he is saying that the gospel of
his opponents is not authentic. It is a *different* gospel that subverts the true
gospel. What is this false gospel? Paul does not need to explain, because the
Galatians know what he is talking about: the requirement of circumcision and
observance of Jewish law that they have begun to add to †faith in Christ. They
do not understand what is wrong with this new teaching. What could be the
problem with adding these practices that Jews have followed for centuries? But
there is no room for doubt about Paul's diagnosis of the situation: the entire
gospel is at stake.

Paul describes himself as an apostle "set apart for the gospel of God" (Rom 1:8–9
1:1). When something concerns the †gospel, he immediately catches fire. To
Paul the idea of distorting the gospel is intolerable. He therefore responds with
tremendous vigor, pronouncing anathemas against whoever would proclaim
to the Galatians a different gospel than he preached. Twice Paul says, **let that
one be accursed** (Greek *anathema*). When it comes to the content of the faith,
Paul is not irenic; it is a matter of spiritual life or death. His conviction is so
great here that he feels the need to repeat and insist. In speaking about the
evangelizing of the Galatians that occurred earlier, he uses the first-person
plural (**we preached** . . . , **As we have said** . . .) because he had companions;
Timothy and Silvanus accompanied Paul on his second missionary journey
(Acts 15:40–16:4; 1 Thess 1:1). He then expresses himself in the singular (**and
now I say again**) because it is he alone who is dictating the letter.

A significant detail in verse 8 reveals both Paul's resoluteness and his pri-
orities. The Apostle begins with the unlikely hypothetical circumstance that
he and his companions in the apostolate would preach a different gospel.
Even in such an extreme case, Paul has no hesitation: the anathema would be
launched at them. This makes it very clear that Paul is defending not himself
but the gospel he has proclaimed. The issue is not his personal authority but
the truth of the faith. In the section that follows (Gal 1:11–2:21), the perspective will be different, and Paul will defend his own personal position. His goal,
however, will still be to defend the gospel as he proclaims it, proving that it
comes directly from Christ.

Paul even goes so far as to say that if **an angel from heaven** were to reveal a
different message, it must be rejected: the gospel of Jesus Christ is the standard
against which every revelation must be tested. These words of Paul remain

The Origin of *Anathema* in the Christian Tradition

In ordinary Greek usage the meaning of *anathema* was "votive offering" (e.g., Luke 21:5), but in the †Septuagint this word translates the Hebrew word *herem*, which means "set apart for destruction" for a religious reason (translated "ban" in Deut 13:16; Josh 6:17). In Galatians the meaning is analogous: the word *anathema* expresses a curse and therefore proclaims a separation from the people of God. Paul refers here not only to the judgment of God but also to the Church's most severe penalty for wrongdoing: excommunication (see 1 Cor 5:1–5; 1 Tim 1:20; Titus 3:10–11).

With these anathemas (and a third one in 1 Cor 16:22) Paul's letters are the means by which this term enters the Christian tradition. Later it was used in the solemn pronouncements of Church councils. Here are two examples from the canons of the Council of Trent:

> If anyone says that, without divine grace through Jesus Christ, man can be justified before God by his own works, whether they be done by his own natural powers or through the teaching of the law, let him be anathema.

> If anyone says that it is lawful for Christians to have several wives at the same time and that this is not forbidden by any divine law [Matt 19:9], let him be anathema.[a]

While doctrinal statements sometimes hold in tension different aspects of the truth or entail changes in the way that †faith is expressed or understood, no compromise is acceptable with statements that are contrary to the faith.

a. Denzinger, 1551 (Canons on Justification) and 1802 (Canons on the Sacrament of Marriage).

relevant, since both Islam and Mormonism proclaim different messages on the supposed authority of angels.

Why does Paul get so worked up about a "different gospel"? Is it only because of his fiery personality? According to Paul, the gospel is "the power of God for . . . salvation" (Rom 1:16). There is nothing more valuable to a human being and to the human race than eternal salvation. The gospel of Jesus Christ makes salvation available to all. An analogy may help to make Paul's perspective more intelligible. What is the value of a million dollars of counterfeit currency? Precisely nothing. Paul is concerned that his beloved Galatian Gentile Christians are about to exchange their good currency for counterfeit and lose everything. That is why his tone is so fierce.

Another analogy: when someone is about to drink poison unawares, the best way to help the person is not to smile and make small talk but to grab the glass out of their hand. It is a violent action, but it is the most loving thing to do. Paul's strong words to the Galatians also manifest charity. The Galatians are in the process of abandoning the gospel for a teaching that would lead them to forfeit their salvation by seeking it in religious observances rather than through faith in Christ. Paul has got to do something!

Following the two anathemas, Paul abruptly asks two questions in a challenging tone: **Am I now currying favor with human beings . . . ? Or am I seeking to please people?** According to this translation, Paul speaks negatively of "currying favor" and pleasing people. However, his first question could be translated more positively, "Am I now trying to persuade people?" In 2 Cor 5:11 Paul uses the same verb positively to describe his apostolate: "We try to persuade others." To spread the †faith, one must be persuasive. To persuade can be a very praiseworthy undertaking. But Paul has another meaning in mind: persuading people dishonestly by altering the †gospel message to make it more palatable (see 2 Cor 2:17). 1:10

It is the same with his second question: "Or am I seeking to please people?" In 1 Cor 10:33 Paul presents himself as an example to imitate since he aims "to please everyone in every way" for the purpose of bringing people to faith. He becomes like a Jew to win over Jews, and like those outside the †law of Moses to win them over as well (1 Cor 9:20–22). However, in 1 Thess 2:4 Paul firmly rejects the idea of wanting to please everyone—"We speak, not as trying to please human beings"—and in that context he links attempting to please people with deception, impure motives, greed for gain, flattery, and seeking human praise. It is the second kind of people-pleasing to which Paul refers in this Galatians passage, since in his final sentence he answers his own questions by declaring the incompatibility of seeking to please people and being a servant of Christ: **If I were still trying to please people, I would not be a slave of Christ.**

Reading between the lines, we can perceive that Paul's questions allude to accusations against him that he is indignantly rejecting. Paul has been accused of not telling the whole truth in his preaching and of concealing some of God's requirements. The implication is that he adapted his message to the ideas and tastes of his audience in order to obtain for himself a greater missionary success. Apparently, after Paul's departure, other preachers came among the Galatians and said something like this: "The gospel Paul proclaimed to you is incomplete. He kept back from you some important requirements, such as circumcision, in an attempt to be diplomatic. We, however, are bringing you the whole gospel truth, the full message of salvation. You should not rely on Paul so much."

To counter such fraudulent accusations, Paul launches the two crushing anathemas and then asks, in effect, "Have you heard these anathemas? In light of these, who can still say I am too diplomatic? Am I trying to please people by such anathemas? Obviously, I am not."

Reflection and Application (1:10)

The offense that Paul's opponents falsely accuse him of—changing, diluting, or downplaying the requirements of the gospel to make it more palatable—can be a very real temptation for preachers, teachers, and all Christians. The pressure to alter our message is greatest precisely at the points where the teaching of Christ and his Church diverges most sharply from the beliefs and practices of the surrounding culture. The topics about which Christians today are tempted to change the message or remain silent vary, but include the uniqueness of Christ, the reality of hell, Scripture's teaching about sexual morality, Christ's teaching about marriage, and the sacredness of human life. Among the devout it is tempting not to speak about gossip, judging others, God's mercy toward sinners, leadership as service, Jesus' teaching about money, and Christ's call to move beyond our circle to seek the lost.

It is easy for us in church leadership roles, whether lay or ordained, to become overly concerned with pleasing others to the neglect of pleasing Christ. For people in ministry, the visible approval of other people can subtly replace the invisible approval of God as the goal of our labors. Some people will esteem us because we hold a high position, attract a large following, or manage to avoid conflict, and we may be tempted to evaluate ourselves the same way. But serving Christ often requires taking a stand that will not please others, that makes us unpopular, or that will cost us promotions. Paul's words remind us whose approval we must seek: "If I were still trying to please people, I would not be a slave of Christ."

Part 1

Paul Defends His Gospel by Telling His Story

Galatians 1:11–2:21

Paul's Call to Preach Came by Divine Revelation

Galatians 1:11–24

After a very energetic introduction (1:6–10), Paul begins the first part of the letter, which presents evidence from his own life story to show that the †gospel he proclaims is authentic. His presentation divides into three sections. In the first section (1:11–24), Paul shows that the gospel he preaches comes from a divine revelation of Christ and not from human teaching. In the second (2:1–10), Paul reports on his meeting with the apostles in Jerusalem and records its conclusion: the authenticity of his gospel was officially recognized.[1] In the third (2:11–21), he recounts a confrontation with Cephas (Peter) in defense of the gospel as he taught it. Paul uses that occasion to establish the fundamental point of the letter: †justification comes through †faith in Christ and not through works of the †law (2:16–21).

The Divine Origin of Paul's Gospel (1:11–12)

---

[11]Now I want you to know, brothers, that the gospel preached by me is not of human origin. [12]For I did not receive it from a human being, nor was I taught it, but it came through a revelation of Jesus Christ.

NT: Matt 11:25–27; 1 Cor 15:1–9
Catechism: divine origin of the gospel, 74–75
Lectionary: 1:11–20: Vigil of Sts. Peter and Paul

1. For an explanation of what was distinctive in Paul's proclamation of the gospel, see the commentary on 2:2 and the sidebar, "Paul's Gospel," p. 62.

1:11–12   After the explosion of anathemas in verses 8–9, Paul adopts a calmer tone to make his case. He addresses the Galatians as **brothers** (to be understood inclusively as "sisters and brothers"), a term used among Jews and taken up by Christians. Among Christians, however, it refers no longer to a kinship due to race, but rather to a brotherly relationship based on our relationship to Christ and our adoption as children of God (1:4; 3:26–28; 4:5–7).

Paul's principal affirmation concerns the nature of **the gospel preached by me**: it is **not of human origin**. It is not a message devised by a human being or conformed to the tastes of human beings. In support of this, the second sentence explains the divine origin of this †gospel. Paul specifically denies that in his own case the gospel was received through the teaching of a human being. According to Acts 2:42, the first Christians "devoted themselves to the teaching of the apostles." All subsequent generations of Christians have heard the gospel of Christ through the apostles' teaching, transmitted through Scripture and Tradition. But the Apostle Paul did not learn the gospel this way; rather, he received it directly **through a revelation of Jesus Christ**.

The word "revelation" here translates the Greek word *apokalypsis* and indicates God's disclosing something previously unknown.[2] Here Paul is speaking not about the literary genre of apocalypse but rather about a divine initiative to reveal something by vision or prophecy.

Paul calls it a "revelation of Jesus Christ." The phrase could mean that Jesus is the person who does the revealing or that he is the person who is revealed. Here it means both, because Jesus revealed himself to Paul (Acts 9:3–5), and a few verses later Paul says it was God who "was pleased to reveal his Son to me" (Gal 1:15–16). There is no contradiction, since at the same time that Christ revealed the gospel about himself, God was revealing his Son to Paul.[3]

So in verses 11–12, Paul gives an initial defense of his gospel: he denies it has a human origin and declares its divine origin. In itself this second point is the more important, and we would therefore expect it to be the main topic of the

---

2. Using the verb form of this word, Dan 2:47 †LXX states that "God is a *revealer* of mysteries." "Apocalypse" eventually came to refer to the literary genre to which a portion of the book of Daniel belongs (Dan 7–12). This literary genre developed during the two centuries before Christ as a way to present revelation from God. The best example of this genre is John's Revelation, described as *apokalypsis* in Rev 1:1. In the New Testament this word is also used for prophecies and visions (1 Cor 14:6, 26; 2 Cor 12:1, 7) and for the glorious revelation of Jesus at his return (1 Cor 1:7; 1 Thess 2:7; 1 Pet 1:7, 13).

3. In a Gospel text closely related to this passage (Matt 11:25–27), the act of revealing is attributed first to the Father and then to the Son. In fact, the Father confers on the Son the work of revelation. This pattern is analogous to what Paul teaches about redemption itself. It is the Father who "handed [his Son] over for us all" (Rom 8:32), but at the same time it is the Son who has "given himself up" for us (Gal 2:20; see 1:4).

Figure 5. *St. Paul Preaching at Athens* (Raphael, 1515).

first part of the letter (1:11–2:21). However, in the verses that follow, Paul says very little about the revelation he received, but rather expands on the negative part of his statement, in which he denies any dependence on human beings for the content of his gospel.

From Persecutor to Apostle (1:13–17)

¹³For you heard of my former way of life in Judaism, how I persecuted the church of God beyond measure and tried to destroy it, ¹⁴and progressed in Judaism beyond many of my contemporaries among my race, since I was even more a zealot for my ancestral traditions. ¹⁵But when [God], who from my mother's womb had set me apart and called me through his grace, was pleased ¹⁶to reveal his Son to me, so that I might proclaim him to the Gentiles, I did not immediately consult flesh and blood, ¹⁷nor did I go up to Jerusalem to those who were apostles before me; rather, I went into Arabia and then returned to Damascus.

OT: Isa 49:6; Jer 1:5
NT: Mark 7:3–13; Acts 7:58–8:3; 9:1–31; 13:47; 22:3; Rom 1:13; Phil 3:4–6
Catechism: Christ's divine sonship and faith, 442; uniqueness of Paul's apostleship, 659
Lectionary: 1:11–20: Vigil of Sts. Peter and Paul

The autobiographical part of the letter begins here. Paul is about to tell his readers the story of his conversion. Scholars and ordinary readers alike are interested in comparing what Paul himself writes about this period of his life with the account that Luke gives (Acts 7:58–8:3; 9:1–31). But Paul writes about himself and what he did in the past, not for the sake of autobiography, but rather to make a point. Consequently, he does not attempt to report everything thoroughly, but selects the facts that are useful for his purpose, the defense of his †gospel.

1:13–14   The first fact is his **former way of life** in Judaism, which did not in any way dispose him to become an apostle of Christ. Elsewhere Paul tells us that he belonged to the party of the Pharisees (Phil 3:5), a group that the Gospels depict as fiercely opposed to Jesus. The Pharisees strictly separated themselves from †Gentiles in order to maintain their particular understanding of †ritual purity. The fact that Paul became an apostle of Jesus Christ, and especially to Gentiles, was due to an extraordinary act of God's †grace and power. Although Paul does not say so explicitly, his amazing transformation confirms the divine origin of the gospel he proclaims and undermines the allegations of his opponents who are contesting his apostolic standing.

Verses 13 and 14 reveal Paul's passionate temperament. Fierce language like **persecuted, beyond measure**, and **destroy** describes his former behavior. These terms show that Paul is not trying to soft-pedal or excuse his actions as a persecutor. On the contrary, by saying that he persecuted **the church of God**, he underscores the gravity of his conduct. When he refers to zeal for his **ancestral traditions**, he displays a flash of pride, an attitude that other passages in his letters confirm (1 Cor 15:10; Phil 3:6).

When he begins by saying, **You heard of my former way of life,** he implies that the Galatians heard his story when they were first evangelized. Either Paul or one of his apostolic companions had told it, and he does not need to repeat it. He limits himself to recounting the facts that are relevant for his argument. The first part of Paul's life was **in Judaism**, an expression not found elsewhere in the New Testament. The word "Judaism" (in its Greek form) made its appearance at the time of the Maccabees (see 2 Macc 2:21; 8:1; 14:38 RSV). When Antiochus IV wanted to impose a Greek way of life ("Hellenism" in 2 Macc 4:13) on the Jews, many Jews heroically resisted in order to maintain a lifestyle in conformity to the laws of Moses and their traditions. At that time, faithful

Jews faced persecution at the hands of Gentiles. In Paul's case, however, a Jew became a persecutor of his own people who formed—although he did not yet know it—the Church of God.

Initially, Paul perceived Christianity to be a grave threat to Judaism and reacted with extreme intensity. He persecuted the followers of Jesus "beyond measure."[4] In Acts where details of this persecution are given, Luke writes,

> Saul . . . was trying to destroy the church; entering house after house and drag-ging out men and women, he handed them over for imprisonment. (Acts 8:3)

> Now Saul, still breathing murderous threats against the disciples of the Lord, . . . asked . . . for letters to the synagogues in Damascus, that, if he should find any men or women who belonged to the Way, he might bring them back to Jerusalem in chains. (Acts 9:1–2)

To describe Paul's actions, Luke uses the same Greek word as Paul does here and in 1:23 for "destroy"—a word meaning "to ravage or annihilate." It is used in the New Testament exclusively of Paul, "who in Jerusalem ravaged those who call upon this name" (Acts 9:21).

To explain the motive for this fierce persecution, Paul adds that he surpassed **many of** his **contemporaries** in Judaism. We would like to know how old Paul was at that time, but we are not given that information. When describing his fervent Jewish practice, Paul says he was **even more a zealot** than others his age for his "ancestral traditions." To practice Judaism includes not only keeping the †law but also observing a whole way of life entailing many traditions. The first Christians, although they were Jews, did not follow all these traditions. Jesus' teaching gave them a certain freedom with respect to "the tradition of the elders" (Mark 7:1–13; see Matt 15:2–6), and they were therefore accused of speaking against the law (Acts 6:13–14). Paul's zeal for the ancestral traditions—he calls them "*my* ancestral traditions"—drove him to persecute Christians relentlessly.

All of this clearly shows that Paul was in no way disposed to receive the gospel from the Church, much less to preach it. Paul's proclamation of the gospel—especially a gospel freed from the traditions of the elders to which Jews felt bound—cannot be explained by human influence.

After a vigorous description of his previous negative condition, one might **1:15** expect a sharp contrast through a detailed account of the positive side, the "reve-lation of Jesus Christ" that Paul received (v. 12). That expectation, however, is

---

4. This expression is characteristic of Paul, who is the only one to use it in the New Testament (Rom 7:13; 2 Cor 1:8; 4:7, 17).

unfulfilled. Paul does not even minimally describe the content of the revelation he received. Elsewhere he says that Christ "appeared to me" (1 Cor 15:8), and thus he has "seen Jesus our Lord" (1 Cor 9:1), but of this he here says only a little (Gal 1:16).

Nevertheless, there is something very solemn about the words Paul uses to refer to the divine revelation he received that shows the exceptional importance of the event. Paul uses two verbs to describe God's initiative in his life. God, **who from my mother's womb had set me apart and called me**, is the one who determined Paul's vocation. Both verbs solemnly affirm the divine character of Paul's vocation and thus implicitly the divine origin of his gospel.

The way Paul refers to his vocation connects it to both that of the prophet Jeremiah and that of the "servant of the Lord" in Isaiah. God said to Jeremiah,

> Before I formed you in the womb I knew you,
> > before you were born I dedicated you,
> > *a prophet to the nations* I appointed you. (Jer 1:5, italics added)

Paul's awareness of being "the apostle to the Gentiles" (Rom 11:13) and of being called to "proclaim [Christ] to the Gentiles" (Gal 1:16) would have naturally led him to meditate on Jeremiah's vocation to be "a prophet to the nations," since in both Greek and Hebrew the word for "†nations" is the same as the word for "†Gentiles." Paul realized that his own calling was not an afterthought but was, like Jeremiah's, the result of a divine choice before he was born. Instead of using the verb "dedicate" or "appoint," as in Jer 1:5, Paul uses "set apart" as he does in Rom 1:1. The same verb is also used in Acts 13:2 for the missionary vocation of Barnabas and Paul, where it refers to God's choice of someone for a special mission.

While Jeremiah does not speak of God "calling" him, Isaiah's second Song of the Servant of the Lord does speak of being called:

> Before birth the LORD *called me*,
> > from my mother's womb he gave me my name. (Isa 49:1, italics added)

This prophecy would have caught Paul's attention because it declares God's plan for the Gentiles:

> It is too little, he says, for you to be my servant,
> > to raise up the tribes of Jacob,
> > and restore the survivors of Israel;

I will make you a light to the nations,
>   that my salvation may reach to the ends of the earth. (Isa 49:6)

Acts records that Paul applied this text to his own apostolate to the Gentiles (Acts 13:47).

Paul indicates the completely gratuitous nature of God's choosing him: it was **through his grace**. He is very aware that his vocation is not due to his merits. How could a persecutor deserve to be called an apostle? Paul recognizes he is the beneficiary of the very generous love of God.

Although similar to the vocations of the greatest prophets, Paul's vocation **1:16** is greater since God did not reveal "his Son" to any of them. But Paul reports that God **was pleased to reveal his Son to me**. The word "pleased" emphasizes God's affectionate favor toward Paul.

The revelation is doubly divine because its author is God and its content is the Son of God. The divine sonship of Christ is the principal *doctrinal* element of the revelation the Apostle received, but here Paul receives a revelation of the *person* of God's Son. A personal relationship with Christ the Son of God is Paul's greatest treasure (2:20). In Phil 3:7–8 Paul affirms, "Whatever gains I had, these I have come to consider a loss because of Christ. More than that, I even consider everything as a loss because of the supreme good of knowing Christ Jesus my Lord."

The Bible uses the expression "son of God" in a variety of senses. The fact that here Paul refers to Jesus as the Son of God in the strongest sense of the term—that is, as fully divine—is clear for a few reasons. First, the fact that Jesus' sonship is divinely revealed implies it is a divine mystery. Second, the fact that in the Greek text Paul uses the definite article, literally saying, "*the* Son of him," lets us know that the sonship of Jesus Christ is unique (see the sidebar, "'Son of God' in the Bible," below). A third indication is the contrast observed in 1:1 and 1:12 between "human beings" and "Jesus Christ" that places Jesus on the divine side of the contrast. Finally, we have noted how Paul links Jesus Christ with God the Father in 1:1 and 1:3, unexpectedly using a single preposition to introduce both of their names.

Rather than speak of the revelation "to me," as the NABRE and most translations render this phrase, Paul literally says that God revealed his Son "*in* me," indicating the interior effect of this revelation. What happened to Paul was not only something external that had the objective result of changing his mind. Rather, as in every divine vocation, Paul experienced an inner attraction that captured him in the depths of his soul. The revelation Paul received had an apostolic purpose: **so that I might proclaim him to the Gentiles**.

"Son of God" in the Bible

BIBLICAL BACKGROUND

The original language of Scripture sometimes contains nuances of meaning that are not easily translated into English. For instance, "his Son" in Gal 1:16 translates a Greek phrase that literally says "the son of him." The presence or absence of the article ("the") makes a difference in what is meant by the phrase "son of God" in the Bible.

A few texts in the Old Testament speak of the "sons" of God to designate angels or his people (see Deut 32:8; Job 1:6; Wis 12:19, 21). Some texts refer to particular people as sons of God—for example, the Davidic king (2 Sam 7:14; Ps 2:7) or the righteous person (Wis 2:18 RSV). Israel in a collective sense is sometimes called "God's son" (Exod 4:22; Jer 31:20), although the Septuagint, the Greek translation of the Old Testament, never uses the article in these texts.

However, in Gal 1:16 and many other New Testament passages, Jesus Christ is called "*the* Son of God" or "his Son" using the article in Greek (although the definite article does not appear in English). These expressions appear in Paul's earliest letter (1 Thess 1:10) and in 1 Cor 1:9 and 2 Cor 1:19. The way in which the New Testament refers to Jesus as the Son of God is unique, distinct from all other references to "son of God" in the Bible.

It is to be noted that the revelation Paul received, profound as it was, is not the main point of the sentence in which it appears; he mentions it only as background ("But when [God] . . ." [v. 15]) to introduce what he wants to emphasize: **I did not immediately consult. . . .** This is the train of thought that Paul will complete in verse 17 and the narrative that follows.

Reflection and Application (1:16)

When Paul and his companions preached, those who heard them not only heard their arguments for the †gospel; they encountered Christ in and through them. Paul reminds the Thessalonian Christians of their experience of him and his companions:

Our gospel did not come to you in word alone, but also in power and in the holy Spirit and [with] much conviction. You know what sort of people we were [among] you for your sake. And you became imitators of us and of the Lord. . . .

With such affection for you, we were determined to share with you not only the gospel of God, but our very selves as well, so dearly beloved had you become

to us. . . . You are witnesses, and so is God, how devoutly and justly and blame-
lessly we behaved toward you believers. As you know, we treated each one of you
as a father treats his children. (1 Thess 1:5–6; 2:8, 10–11)

An important way in which the presence of the Holy Spirit becomes manifest
is through the demeanor and character of those who proclaim the gospel.

Later in Galatians, Paul speaks of Christ's presence in him: "I live, no longer
I, but Christ lives in me" (2:20). Because Paul was living in Christ and Christ
was living in Paul, people could not help but take notice and respond, whether
positively or negatively. For Paul to be a missionary, he needed a revelation of
Jesus in his inmost self—and so do we. Paul's example shows us how important
it is for anyone involved in evangelization or ministry to cultivate their personal
relationship with Jesus. The more Christ lives in us and we †live in him, the
more people will encounter him when they encounter us.

After reporting with such solemnity the revelation he received, Paul speaks of **1:17**
what he did "immediately" thereafter. Luke reports that the first effect of Christ's
appearance to Paul was apostolic: "He began at once to proclaim Jesus in the
synagogues, that he is the Son of God" (Acts 9:20). Luke's account is surprising
and significant, because normally a new convert does not become an apostle
"immediately" but needs to complete a lengthy catechesis and formation. Paul
could have said, "I immediately began to proclaim the faith," but rather unexpectedly he speaks of what he did *not* do: **I did not immediately consult flesh
and blood, nor did I go up to Jerusalem to those who were apostles before
me** (Gal 1:16–17). One can see that Paul's pressing concern when writing to
the Galatians is not to give an account of his missionary activities but to affirm
the independence of his apostolic testimony, denying any dependence on other
people, even those who were the most authoritative.

Before a person makes a very important personal decision, it is helpful to
consult relatives, friends, or other people with experience, but Paul did not do
that. Certain that he had received divine revelation, he did not want to subject
that revelation to "†flesh and blood," to human beings in all their limitedness. It
is even more significant that Paul did not feel the need to be in contact with the
apostles in Jerusalem. When referring to them, Paul uses a phrase that shows his
awareness of being an apostle in the full sense of the word, even though he was
not chosen by Jesus as part of the Twelve (see Matt 10:1–4; Mark 3:13–19; Luke
6:12–16). He describes the apostles in Jerusalem as "those who were apostles
before me," which clearly implies that he himself has become an apostle and
suggests that this occurred at the time of his revelation. The same perspective

is found in 1 Cor 9:1, where Paul asks, "Am I not an apostle? Have I not seen Jesus our Lord?" Knowing that he was appointed as an apostle by Christ himself, Paul did not need the approval of the other apostles.

Paul's manner of speaking could leave the impression that he had no contact with anyone and was not connected to any Christian community, but he does not say that. Paul wants to demonstrate the directly divine origin of the †gospel that he preaches. He does not deny being in relationship with the Christian community in Damascus; he denies only having "consulted" anyone to be sure of his gospel (see the sidebar, "Paul's Gospel," p. 62).

The sentence finishes by saying what he did do: **rather, I went into Arabia . . .** , probably referring to the region south of Damascus. The Greek verb used to describe his going to Arabia bears the nuance of going away.[5] Instead of going to Jerusalem, he distanced himself from it. He does not explain the reason or the goal of his trip to Arabia, nor does he say what activity he was involved in there. Solitary meditation? Preaching the gospel? The only point he wants to make is that by being in Arabia he was far from Jerusalem and could not be in contact with the apostles and the church in Jerusalem. The independence of his vocation and of his gospel is thus proved. Paul owes nothing to human beings, not even to the apostles who preceded him. Instead of being merely a disciple of the apostles, as his opponents may have asserted, Paul found himself suddenly elevated to the rank of apostle by virtue of the revelation he received.

Paul does not report the duration of his time in Arabia—months? years?—but he does explain that before going to Jerusalem he **then returned to Damascus**. This statement provides indirect confirmation of Acts that when Paul received the "revelation of Jesus Christ" (Gal 1:12), he was near Damascus (Acts 9:3).[6]

Reflection and Application (1:17)

For the Apostle Paul to demonstrate the authenticity of his message, it was necessary to insist that he received it independently of the mediation of any other human being—that his apostleship and his †gospel came directly from Jesus Christ. Paul needed to defend the message he proclaimed against people who may have tried to compare it unfavorably with the teaching of others who claimed to be apostles.

---

5. Greek *aperchomai*, "to depart from," in contrast to "go up [*anerchomai*] to Jerusalem."
6. Acts does not report Paul's time in Arabia but only recounts Paul's conversion and preaching in Damascus prior to his going to Jerusalem (Acts 9:19–26). Either Luke did not know that Paul went to Arabia in between stays in Damascus, or, more likely, he compresses his account, leaving out unnecessary details.

However, for later generations of Christians, including ourselves, the situation is nearly the opposite. The authenticity of the gospel we believe and proclaim is determined by its continuity with the gospel proclaimed by Paul, Peter, and all the apostles. Since the second century the Church has recognized certain writings of the apostles and some of their coworkers as inspired and authoritative Scripture and, along with Sacred Tradition, as constituting the deposit of †faith. By the end of the fourth century a consensus emerged regarding the contents of these Scriptures testifying to the revelation of Christ: the twenty-seven books of the New Testament. Because God has revealed himself fully in his Son Jesus Christ (John 1:18; 14:9; Heb 1:1–4), the Church awaits no further public revelation before his return in glory (Catechism 66).

When people today receive prophecies or visions, these divine communications are called "private" revelation since they do not add to the deposit of faith and are not binding on the faithful. They are to be tested for their conformity with Scripture and Tradition. We look to the bishops, as those appointed by Christ to guide the Church, to make authoritative judgments on private revelation when necessary (Catechism 67, 801).

Paul's Eventual Contact with Peter (1:18–20)

---

¹⁸Then after three years I went up to Jerusalem to confer with Cephas and remained with him for fifteen days. ¹⁹But I did not see any other of the apostles, only James the brother of the Lord. ²⁰(As to what I am writing to you, behold, before God, I am not lying.)

NT: Matt 5:33–37; 16:18; John 1:42; Jude 1:1
Catechism: brothers of the Lord, 500; oaths, 2154
Lectionary: 1:11–20: Vigil of Sts. Peter and Paul

Paul denied having had any contact with the apostles immediately after his   **1:18**
conversion (1:17). Here he acknowledges going to Jerusalem and finally having some contact later. He minimizes its significance, however, specifying that the contact occurred later (**after three years**), that it was brief (**fifteen days**), and that it was limited to **Cephas**—that is, Peter—and James. It is clear that for Paul, Cephas was the most important apostle, and it was he whom Paul went to Jerusalem to meet three years after encountering Christ on the road to Damascus.

The Greek verb Paul uses for **confer with** can mean either "to seek to know" or "to question" a person to obtain information. Paul's coming to Jerusalem to

Cephas Is Peter

BIBLICAL BACKGROUND

Cephas is a Greek form of an Aramaic word (*kēfā*) that means "rock"; Kephas would be a more accurate English spelling than Cephas, since the name begins with a *k* sound. The Fourth Gospel records that Jesus gave this new name to Simon, Andrew's brother: "'You are Simon the son of John; you will be called Cephas' (which is translated Peter)" (John 1:42). The other Gospel writers also record Jesus giving Simon the new name, but they use a Greek word for "rock" (*petros*, Peter) rather than the original Aramaic (Matt 16:18; Mark 3:16; Luke 6:14).

According to Matthew, Jesus explains this name in reference to the special role of leadership Peter is called to exercise: "You are Peter, and upon this rock I will build my church" (Matt 16:18). After Jesus, the person mentioned most often in all four Gospels is Peter. In every list of the Twelve, Peter's name comes first. Acts shows Peter exercising this role of leadership in a variety of ways (e.g., Acts 1:15; 2:14; 5:29; 15:7). The importance of the meaning of Simon's new name to the early Church is evident from the fact that Cephas is the only Aramaic name we know of that the New Testament authors chose to translate into Greek. Barnabas continued to be known by his Aramaic name, while Paul used a Roman name (*Paulos*) in place of his Hebrew name Saul.

Unlike other New Testament writers, Paul usually refers to Peter by his Aramaic name, Cephas, four times in 1 Corinthians and four times in Galatians (1:18; 2:9, 11, 14; but see 2:7–8). Paul's use of Cephas may be due to his initial acquaintance with Peter in an Aramaic-language environment (1:18) or perhaps because Galatians and 1 Corinthians were written before "Peter" replaced "Cephas" in common usage among the Greek-speaking churches.

Figures 6–7. Medallions of St. Paul and St. Peter in icon frames, made in Constantinople ca. 1100.

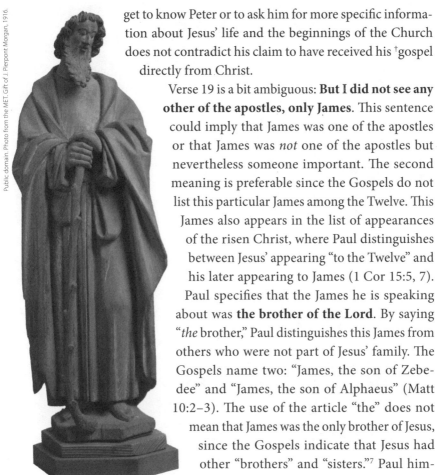

Public domain. Photo from the MET. Gift of J. Pierpont Morgan, 1916.

Figure 8. St. James, the brother of the Lord (oak sculpture, Netherlands, ca. 1500).

get to know Peter or to ask him for more specific information about Jesus' life and the beginnings of the Church does not contradict his claim to have received his †gospel directly from Christ.

Verse 19 is a bit ambiguous: **But I did not see any**   **1:19** **other of the apostles, only James.** This sentence could imply that James was one of the apostles or that James was *not* one of the apostles but nevertheless someone important. The second meaning is preferable since the Gospels do not list this particular James among the Twelve. This James also appears in the list of appearances of the risen Christ, where Paul distinguishes between Jesus' appearing "to the Twelve" and his later appearing to James (1 Cor 15:5, 7). Paul specifies that the James he is speaking about was **the brother of the Lord**. By saying "*the* brother," Paul distinguishes this James from others who were not part of Jesus' family. The Gospels name two: "James, the son of Zebedee" and "James, the son of Alphaeus" (Matt 10:2–3). The use of the article "the" does not mean that James was the only brother of Jesus, since the Gospels indicate that Jesus had other "brothers" and "sisters."[7] Paul himself speaks in the plural about "the brothers of the †Lord," distinguishing this category from that of "the apostles" (1 Cor 9:5). In Palestinian Judaism, "brother" could refer to many different kinds of relatives, including cousins.[8] Paul's word choice suggests that the expression had become a title of honor; he says not merely "the brother of Jesus" but "the brother of the Lord," pointing to the relationship of James with the glorified Christ. Acts speaks of this James as a leader of the Jerusalem church (see Acts 12:17; 15:13; 21:18).

By saying **before God, I am not lying**, Paul swears that he is telling the   **1:20** truth. Why did the Apostle feel the need to swear after reporting a detail that

---

7. See Matt 12:46–47; 13:55–56; Mark 3:31–32; Luke 8:19–20; John 2:12; 7:3–10; Acts 1:14.
8. See Catechism 500 on the "brothers" of the Lord.

does not seem very important? We do not know. Perhaps Paul's opponents were trying to diminish his apostolic authority by saying that Paul was not really an apostle but only a disciple of the apostles because he had spent time in Jerusalem being instructed by them. Or perhaps his opponents were saying that Paul's teaching differed from that of the other apostles, so he avoided communication with them. Either of these would be grounds for the †Judaizers to argue that the Galatians should accept their version of the †gospel rather than Paul's.

The presence of Paul's oath confirms the defensive nature of this part of the letter. Paul is defending himself in order to defend his gospel. Paul was accustomed to calling on God as his witness, a form of swearing (2 Cor 1:23; 11:31; 1 Thess 2:5). He did not observe the prohibition against swearing given by Jesus in the Sermon on the Mount (Matt 5:33–37) and repeated in James 5:12. Either Paul did not know of this prohibition or did not interpret it in an absolute manner but understood it as an exhortation to honesty in speech.[9] Paul did not hesitate to swear to what he was saying, because he was being completely sincere (2 Cor 1:17–20; 2:17–23; 4:2; 1 Thess 2:3–6).

Lack of Personal Acquaintance with the Churches of Judea (1:21–24)

---

[21]Then I went into the regions of Syria and Cilicia. [22]And I was unknown personally to the churches of Judea that are in Christ; [23]they only kept hearing that "the one who once was persecuting us is now preaching the faith he once tried to destroy." [24]So they glorified God because of me.

NT: Acts 9:26–30; 11:25–26; 22:3

1:21   After his brief visit with Peter, Paul again **went** far away from Jerusalem and the apostles. He mentions two **regions** but no cities. **Syria** suggests Damascus or Antioch (see Acts 11:26); **Cilicia** was the region of Paul's hometown of Tarsus (see Acts 9:30). Paul mentions Antioch in Gal 2:11, but he never speaks of Tarsus in any of his letters. In 1:21 he does not describe his activity in these places, but the report of the churches of Judea in verse 23 indicates that Paul was engaged in evangelization.

---

9. Catholic tradition has followed St. Paul in not interpreting this prohibition as excluding all oaths; see Catechism 2154.

Although Paul has acknowledged brief contact with Peter and James, he **1:22** highlights the absence of a relationship with **the churches of Judea**, stating they did not know him personally but only heard about his conversion. He specifies that he is speaking of churches **that are in Christ**, since the word translated "churches" could refer to non-Christian assemblies.[10]

As a consequence of his geographical distance, the Christian churches in **1:23** Judea did not know Paul except by hearsay. They heard about the extraordinary transformation he had undergone from being a persecutor of the Church to being a missionary of the Christian faith. Some biblical scholars dispute that anyone can speak of Paul's "conversion," since verses 15–16 speak only of the "revelation" he received. While it is true that Paul did not change from paganism to the worship of the true God as Gentile Christians did, nonetheless verse 23 depicts a radical conversion—a complete change of direction: **the one who once was persecuting . . . is now preaching the faith he once tried to destroy**. In Phil 3:7–11 Paul says of this conversion that he set aside everything he previously valued in order to put Christ first in every aspect of his life.

The conclusion of the churches of Judea demonstrates that they discerned **1:24** the hand of the †Lord in these events: **they glorified God**. Ending the first section of his defense this way shows Paul's †rhetorical skill (1:13–24). If he had declared the extraordinary character of his conversion himself, someone might have challenged the value of his testimony (John 5:31; 8:13). Paul therefore prefers to report the testimony of others and their response of praise to God. It is an admirable conclusion, expressing Christian faith and advancing Paul's argument that God had intervened dramatically in his life and—his main point—that his †gospel has its beginning from that revelation of Christ.

The theological message of this brief unit (Gal 1:11–24) is found in Paul's explicit assertion of the divine origin of his apostleship and doctrine. God acted to turn a persecutor into an apostle of Christ. God's intervention consisted in a revelation of Jesus Christ as the Son of God, a revelation that was to be communicated to the †Gentiles. Both the revelation of Jesus as God's Son and the mission to the Gentiles are of fundamental importance in Paul's discussion with the Galatians, and they do not cease being fundamental for the †faith of the whole Church up to the present time. The doctrine of the Apostle Paul is not mere theological speculation; it belongs to divine revelation.

---

10. The Greek word for church, *ekklēsia*, means "assembly" (see Acts 19:32, 39, 40) and in the †Septuagint refers to the congregation of Israel (Deut 23:3–4; 1 Chron 13:2, 4).

Reflection and Application (1:11–24)

Our joy as Christians is founded on the fact that God has entered into history to save us and that the †gospel is no mere human philosophy or ideology, but is God's own message to the human race about how we can be saved from the power of sin, Satan, and death forever. Paul fought for the purity of this message, refusing to accept any distortion or compromise. At the heart of this message is the saving death and resurrection of Jesus Christ, which establishes us in a right relationship with God. The human predicament caused by sin requires a divine remedy. No one could have imagined what that remedy would entail. It was necessary for God himself to reveal it in the gospel.

Official Recognition of Paul's Gospel

Galatians 2:1–10

Continuing his autobiographical account, Paul presents another argument in defense of the †gospel as he understands and proclaims it. To this point he has insisted on his independence as an apostle, based in part on his lack of contact with the other apostles. Now he will show that the content of his gospel was approved by the leadership of the church in Jerusalem. Paul thus responds to another likely insinuation of his opponents: that his message is incompatible with that of the twelve apostles appointed by Jesus.

The passage divides into three parts: (1) an introduction that explains the circumstances of Paul's second visit to Jerusalem (vv. 1–2); (2) a brief mention of a controversy with "false brothers" (vv. 3–5); and (3) an account of the official recognition of Paul's gospel (vv. 6–10). The introduction has a tranquil tone and simple style. But in the second part, when Paul discusses the controversy, his prose shows signs of agitation, which makes it a little hard to follow his thought. A calmer though insistent tone characterizes the third part.

Another Visit to Jerusalem, with Controversy (2:1–2)

¹Then after fourteen years I again went up to Jerusalem with Barnabas, taking Titus along also. ²I went up in accord with a revelation, and I presented to them the gospel that I preach to the Gentiles—but privately to those of repute—so that I might not be running, or have run, in vain.

NT: Acts 15:1–5, 12

2:1 Once again Paul offers a chronology that can be interpreted in different ways. What is the starting point of the **fourteen years** before his next trip to **Jerusalem**? Does this time include the three years in Arabia (1:18), or is he not counting them? Since Paul wants to emphasize the independence of his apostolic ministry, if it were seventeen years that he had been largely away from Jerusalem, he would probably make that clear. Thus it is probable that the three years are included, eleven years have passed since his meeting Cephas, and the events he is about to describe occurred fourteen years after his conversion.

This raises a historical question: What is the connection between this visit to Jerusalem that Paul describes in 2:1–10 and the events of Acts 15, commonly referred to as the Council of Jerusalem? According to Acts 15, Paul and Barnabas go up to Jerusalem and present a report of their mission to a meeting of the apostles and elders, who reach a decision about what will be required of †Gentile Christians. The question of the relationship between the meeting in Gal 2 and that in Acts 15 is complex, and there is far from perfect agreement among scholars, but the majority believe that both passages refer to the same events (see the sidebar, "Paul's Visit and the Jerusalem Council [Acts 15]"). If Paul's conversion occurred in AD 35 (as some scholars suggest), and the years are counted inclusively (as was the custom at the time), his first meeting with Cephas occurred in 37 and the Council of Jerusalem in 48.

Paul's mention of the presence of **Barnabas** matches the account in Acts, which reports that prior to the trip to Jerusalem Paul and Barnabas had gone on mission together and had proclaimed the gospel to Gentiles as well as Jews (see Acts 13:4–14:28). Thanks to Acts, we know that Barnabas was a "Levite, a Cypriot by birth," a generous Christian held in high esteem by the church in Jerusalem (4:36–37). Barnabas was sent to Antioch to pastor the growing church in that city; when he saw the large number of new converts, he went to Tarsus and recruited Paul to help him (11:22–26). In the first part of their joint mission, Barnabas is named first and has the lead role among the missionaries, but after their visit to Antioch in Pisidia (13:46), Paul is usually named first. However, in Paul's account in Galatians of the events in Jerusalem, he speaks in the first-person singular as the person with the primary responsibility (except for Gal 2:5), while the role of Barnabas is secondary (2:1, 9). This agrees with Luke's account of the Council of Jerusalem in Acts 15, where Paul's name is consistently mentioned first, except in the letter from the council to the church in Antioch (Acts 15:25).

Paul's Visit and the Jerusalem Council (Acts 15)

BIBLICAL BACKGROUND

A comparison of the accounts of Paul's second visit to Jerusalem, when his way of presenting the †gospel to †Gentiles is approved (Gal 2:1–10), and of the Council of Jerusalem (Acts 15) reveals some similarities but also some differences.

The similarities include the facts that Paul and Barnabas go up to Jerusalem to discuss whether Gentile Christians need to be circumcised, since there are some who want to impose this requirement. Both Peter and James participate in the discussions, and the outcome is favorable to the position held by Paul and Barnabas—namely, that Gentile Christians will not be required to be circumcised.

The differences include the reason that occasions the Jerusalem meeting: Paul cites a revelation from God as the reason for his trip to Jerusalem, while Acts reports a controversy that had arisen. Paul mentions that Titus accompanied him and Barnabas, and that John was a party to the final agreement, but Luke mentions neither Titus nor John. Paul says he laid out his gospel privately to those of repute (Gal 2:2), while Acts describes first a meeting of the apostles and elders to investigate the matter (Acts 15:6), then a larger session (15:12). Acts does not recount Barnabas and Paul presenting their gospel; rather, they report "the signs and wonders God had worked among the Gentiles through them" (15:12). At the end of the account in Acts there is a list of additional requirements asked of the Gentile Christians, but Paul makes no mention of them in his account.[a]

The issue is complicated, and the data do not easily yield a solution that satisfies every question. Nevertheless, none of the differences in detail are irreconcilable (e.g., Paul may well have received his revelation when praying about the controversy, Acts does not mention every person involved in an event, etc.). On the whole the points in common are more substantial than the differences, so the majority of exegetes hold that Paul and Luke refer to the same series of events but present them from different viewpoints.

a. Another difference is that, according to the account in Acts, Paul's coming to Jerusalem for the council was not his second journey to this city as a Christian, as Paul says here in Gal 2:1, but his third. His first is mentioned in Acts 9:26–30; his second is a charitable relief mission mentioned in Acts 11:30 and 12:25. The one in Acts 15:2 would therefore be the third. However, Luke seems uncertain about the chronology of the relief mission, introducing it somewhat vaguely (Acts 11:27).

Titus was a close coworker of Paul's (2 Cor 2:13; 8:23) and a Gentile, to whom one of Paul's pastoral letters was later written. Paul's bringing Titus with him to Jerusalem may have been intended to put a human face on the Gentile mission for the leaders in Jerusalem.

Paul's Gospel

BIBLICAL
BACKGROUND

Paul uses various terms to speak of the †gospel. Sometimes he calls it just "the gospel" (Gal 2:5, 14); other times he calls it "the gospel of Christ" (1:7), "the gospel preached by me" (1:11), or "the gospel that I preach to the Gentiles" (2:2). Reading the beginning of the letter (1:6–7), one has the impression that there is no difference between the gospel preached by Paul and "the gospel of Christ." The only difference seems to be a difference of place and audience. Instead of preaching in the land of Israel, Paul is preaching in pagan †Gentile territory. However, the fact that Paul came to Jerusalem to present his gospel to church leaders clearly implies the presence of certain differences. In 2:2 it is impossible to substitute "the gospel of Christ" for "the gospel that I preach to the Gentiles." Paul could not write "I presented the gospel of Christ to them," because the apostles in Jerusalem knew that gospel much earlier than Paul.

Paul's gospel is therefore not identical with the gospel of Christ but is a specific way of presenting it. Paul realized that preaching the gospel to pagan Gentiles required some differences in content. Paul needed to discern: What are the essential elements of the gospel of Christ? Which elements of Jewish tradition are necessarily tied to the gospel—and thus need to be presented to Gentiles—and which are not? This kind of discernment would not have been easy for a Jew raised to worship God according to Jewish traditions. However, Paul had received a revelation of the mystery of Christ that enlightened his understanding. He realized that preaching to the Gentiles, far from being a circumstance that led to distorting the gospel of Christ, led to a clearer and more profound recognition of what is specific to Christian faith, distinguishing it from nonessential elements of Jewish tradition.

However, the existence of two ways of presenting the gospel, and two ways of living it out in the Church—one for Jews and another for Gentiles (see commentary on 2:7)—could not fail to raise serious problems. A discussion and clarification by the apostles was indispensable.

2:2   Paul recounts that his trip to Jerusalem was undertaken **in accord with a revelation**. He does not give the least hint of the form this revelation took. It could have been an interior illumination or perhaps a prophetic word given through someone else, which the community recognized as the voice of the Holy Spirit (see Acts 13:1–2). In Jerusalem, Paul **presented** his gospel to the leaders of the Church to hear their judgment about it. Paul does not say "the gospel that I was preaching" but **the gospel that I preach**, indicating that he did not change his manner of preaching the gospel afterward.

Paul refers to the Jerusalem leaders to whom he presented his gospel by a word the NABRE translates in different verses as **those of repute**, those "*reputed* to be important," and those "*reputed* to be pillars" (Gal 2:2, 6, 9, italics added).[1] The same word appears in Mark 10:42, where it is translated as "those . . . recognized" as rulers, which captures the sense better. The meaning is not that the leaders appear to be something that does not correspond to reality. Texts from Euripides, Plato, and other Greek writers show that these expressions designate recognized leaders, people with titles who have a public charge that confers visibility and not merely appearance. Paul probably uses this general term because the group was composed not exclusively of apostles but also of presbyters (according to Acts 15:6) and because he wants to highlight the official character of the meeting and its conclusion.

Paul concludes Gal 2:2 by expressing his personal goal for the meeting: **so that I might not be running, or have run, in vain**. The Greek phrase translated here "so that I might not" is used only by Paul in the New Testament, and it always refers to a fear or danger to avoid.[2] Some interpreters want to deny any concern here on Paul's part since Paul has no doubts about his gospel. But Paul is not expressing anxiety that he has made a mistake about the gospel. Rather, the context indicates that Paul's concern for the fruitfulness of his ministry has to do with the importance of maintaining communion with the church in Jerusalem. It was not enough to preach the gospel accurately. It was also necessary to maintain unity with the mother church. True fruitfulness in ministry requires the preaching of the truth but at the same time the building and preserving of unity. Without unity, Paul would be running "in vain." This is why he felt it necessary to present his way of preaching the gospel to those responsible and to reach an explicit agreement with them.

The way Paul expresses himself reveals humility on his part and not the rigid and prideful attitude that some interpreters attribute to him. Paul did not write, "I presented my gospel to them to force them to recognize the correctness of my position"; instead he wrote, "I presented my gospel to them to avoid the danger of my running in vain." Through divine revelation, he understood the need to maintain unity with the mother church in Jerusalem (2:1).

---

1. This phrase in v. 2 is the same in the RSV as in the NABRE. The NRSV ("acknowledged leaders") and NJB ("recognised leaders") catch the nuance better.

2. Paul expresses a similar fear in 4:11, using the same Greek phrase, writing, "I am afraid on your account that perhaps I have labored for you in vain." In that context, Paul expresses concern regarding the results of his ministry if the Galatians do not persevere in the truth, in which case Paul would have labored in vain.

Paul's Resistance to "False Brothers" (2:3–5)

---

[3]Moreover, not even Titus, who was with me, although he was a Greek, was compelled to be circumcised, [4]but because of the false brothers secretly brought in, who slipped in to spy on our freedom that we have in Christ Jesus, that they might enslave us— [5]to them we did not submit even for a moment, so that the truth of the gospel might remain intact for you.

NT: Acts 15:1–2, 5, 24; 2 Cor 11:13

2:3   Paul notes at once the initial result of the meeting: **Titus** was not **compelled to be circumcised**. "Those of repute" in Jerusalem did not require circumcision for Titus as a necessary condition for full [†]ecclesial communion. Titus is referred to as a **Greek**, a word Paul often uses interchangeably with "[†]Gentile."[3] Paul had received Titus into the Church and had made him his companion and coworker without requiring him to be circumcised.[4]

This is the first time in the letter Paul provides us a specific indication of the controversial issue and the content of the "different gospel" he excoriates in 1:6–7. Paul was preaching the [†]gospel without requiring circumcision of the Gentiles who converted. His gospel did not include circumcision even though, according to Gen 17:14, it was a mandatory condition of belonging to God's [†]covenant people. Paul's opponents wanted to impose this requirement on Gentile converts (Gal 5:2, 3, 6, 11; 6:12–13), but Paul understood the teaching of Scripture differently, as he will explain. As far as Paul is concerned, resisting the imposition of circumcision on Gentile believers is essential!

2:4   Paul's mention of circumcision brings to his mind the extreme tension of the period immediately before his second visit to Jerusalem.[5] According to Acts, visitors arrived in Antioch from Judea who began telling the Gentile Christians there, "Unless you are circumcised according to the Mosaic practice, you cannot be saved" (Acts 15:1). That teaching aroused "no little dissension and debate by Paul and Barnabas" (15:2). Luke notes that the same disturbing discussions were taking place in Jerusalem: "But some from the party of the Pharisees who had become believers stood up and said, 'It is necessary to circumcise them and

---

3. See Gal 3:28; Rom 1:16; 2:9–10; 10:12.

4. The situation of Titus contrasts with that of Paul's other close coworker, Timothy, whom Paul circumcised because his mother was Jewish and he had been raised Jewish, although his father was a Gentile (Acts 16:1–3; 2 Tim 1:5; 3:15). Presumably, unlike the Gentile Christian Titus, Timothy lived as an observant Jewish Christian, as Paul did (see the sidebar, "Did Paul Keep the Law of Moses?," pp. 174–75).

5. Verse 3 has been commented upon in the previous section.

St. Augustine on the Purpose of the Letter to the Galatians

LIVING TRADITION

Augustine summarizes the circumstances and purpose of Galatians with admirable clarity in the opening words of his commentary:

> The reason why the Apostle writes to the Galatians is so that they might understand what it is that God's grace accomplishes for them: they are no longer under the law. For though the grace of the gospel had been preached to them, there were some from the circumcision who still did not grasp the real benefit of grace. Despite being called Christians, they were still wanting to be under the burdens of the law—burdens which the Lord God had not imposed on those serving righteousness, but on those serving sin [1 Tim 1:8–11]. That is, he had given a righteous law to unrighteous people to point out their sins [Rom 3:20], not take them away. He takes away sins only by the grace of *faith which works through love* [Gal 5:6].
>
> So then, these people were wanting to put the Galatians, who were already under this grace, under the burdens of this law, claiming that the gospel would be of no benefit to them unless they were circumcised and submitted to other carnal observances of Jewish custom.[a]

a. Translation by Eric Plumer in *Augustine's Commentary on Galatians: Introduction, Text, Translation, and Notes* (Oxford: Oxford University Press, 2003), 125.

---

direct them to observe the Mosaic law'" (Acts 15:5). Recalling this period as he writes years later, Paul shows his feelings in a tumultuous style and slightly confusing syntax. He categorizes his opponents as not true Christians but **false brothers**.[6] According to Paul, these †Judaizers **slipped in to spy on our freedom**, aiming to **enslave us**.

The immediate context indicates what freedom and what enslavement he is referring to, and the section on doctrine that follows will explain it more deeply. Because of the freedom from the †law Christ brings, Gentile believers like Titus are free to maintain their own cultural identity. In Paul's eyes, to oblige Gentile Christians to become Jews, to submit to the obligations that the law of Moses imposed on Israel, would be slavery, an unacceptable restriction (see Gal 4:9–10; 5:1). Paul makes clear that the freedom he is defending is not open to discussion but is part of life in Christ for Gentile believers. Later he

---

6. See 2 Cor 11:13, 26 for similar strong language by Paul. The letter from the apostles and elders to the Christians in Syria and Cilicia at the end of the crisis describes these teachers of circumcision only as unauthorized: "We have heard that some of our number [who went out] without any mandate from us have upset you with their teachings and disturbed your peace of mind" (Acts 15:24).

will explain that freedom from the law of Moses belongs to all who believe in Jesus, whether Gentile or Jew (2:19–20; 5:18; see the sidebar, "Paul's Nuanced View of the Law," pp. 146–47).

2:5   Paul records his and Barnabas's fierce resistance to the maneuver of the false brothers: **to them we did not submit even for a moment**. One possible approach would have been a temporary concession to circumcise Gentile converts in order to keep the peace, but Paul and Barnabas did not accept any kind of compromise. They remained immovable **so that the truth of the gospel might remain intact**. For Paul the question was not simply a matter of †ecclesial discipline but of doctrine, because what was at stake was nothing less than "the truth of the †gospel." This truth consists in the complete efficacy of the redemptive death of Christ and consequently the rejection of any kind of additional means of †justification (see 2:16–21).

Some translations say "so that the truth of the gospel might remain with you," implying that the Galatians had already been evangelized when Paul was defending his gospel in Jerusalem. However, the Greek is better rendered **for you**, indicating that Paul's stand in Jerusalem was for the sake of the Gentiles he would evangelize in the future, including the Galatians. This explicit reference to the Galatians as beneficiaries of Paul's struggle confirms what we can surmise—namely, that they were confronting the same issue that had arisen in Jerusalem some years earlier. The decision on this question taken in Jerusalem would thus be illuminating for the Galatians, so Paul is eager to report it.

The Outcome: Agreement among the Apostles (2:6–10)

---

⁶**But from those who were reputed to be important (what they once were makes no difference to me; God shows no partiality)—those of repute made me add nothing. ⁷On the contrary, when they saw that I had been entrusted with the gospel to the uncircumcised, just as Peter to the circumcised, ⁸for the one who worked in Peter for an apostolate to the circumcised worked also in me for the Gentiles, ⁹and when they recognized the grace bestowed upon me, James and Cephas and John, who were reputed to be pillars, gave me and Barnabas their right hands in partnership, that we should go to the Gentiles and they to the circumcised. ¹⁰Only, we were to be mindful of the poor, which is the very thing I was eager to do.**

NT: Acts 9:15; 15:6–29; 24:17; 1 Tim 1:11

Paul leaves aside the false brothers and returns to those **reputed to be**   **2:6**
important—that is, the recognized leaders (see commentary on 2:2)—to report the outcome of his meeting with them. However, as soon as he mentions
them, he unexpectedly adds a parenthetical remark expressing some reserve:
what they once were makes no difference to me. What does Paul mean? He
expresses indifference to something about the Jerusalem church's most prominent leaders—James, Peter, and John—and to justify his position, he invokes
a principle that is very dear to him: **God shows no partiality.**[7] This principle
affirms that God is not impressed with a person's external appearance, which
can so easily influence human judgment—wealth or poverty, physical strength
or weakness, beauty or ugliness, noble or common origin, even being part of
the chosen people or not. What characteristic of **those of repute** does Paul have
in mind? It cannot apply to their position of authority in the Church, since the
argument he is making in support of his †gospel rests on their authority. Quite
possibly Paul is expressing indifference toward a cult of personality surrounding those who "once were" the relatives and closest companions of Jesus during
his earthly ministry, something that Paul's opponents were using to make his
apostolate seem inferior.

In any case, the important point is that "those of repute" had not imposed
any addition to the gospel Paul laid out to them (see 2:2). Being fully united
with other members of the Church did not require converted †Gentiles to adopt
the Jewish way of life in any way.[8] Not only did this outcome give Paul and the
Gentile Christians breathing room, but the meeting in Jerusalem brought about
a formal recognition of Paul's apostolate and an agreement about a division of
labor in their future ministry (v. 9).

These very positive results occurred **when** the Jerusalem leaders **saw that**   **2:7**
Paul **had been entrusted with the gospel** to the Gentiles. How did they see
that? Acts explains that when Paul and Barnabas "arrived in Jerusalem, they
were welcomed by the church, as well as by the apostles and the presbyters,
and they reported what God had done with them" (Acts 15:4) and "the signs
and wonders God had worked" (15:12).[9] The divine assistance evidenced by

---

7. In the Bible, God's impartiality is an important aspect of his justice toward human beings (see
Deut 10:17–18; Sir 35:14–17; Acts 10:34–35; Rom 2:9–11; 1 Cor 1:26–29).
8. The letter summarizing the conclusions of the Council of Jerusalem mentions four expectations
of Gentile Christians—namely, that they "abstain from meat sacrificed to idols, from blood, from meats
of strangled animals, and from unlawful marriage" (Acts 15:29). Rather than requiring Gentile Christians to become Jews, these requirements appear to be based on Mosaic regulations for Gentiles living
among the people of Israel (see Lev 17:8–18:30).
9. Paul expresses himself in a similar way in Rom 15:18–19: "I will not dare to speak of anything
except what Christ has accomplished through me to lead the Gentiles to obedience by word and deed,

miracles given to Paul in his apostolate to the Gentiles and the tremendous fruitfulness of this apostolate clearly demonstrated that Paul was not mistaken when he affirmed he had received his mission from God.

The Jerusalem leaders' recognition of the importance of Paul's mission is expressed in terms that are more than flattering: **just as Peter** was entrusted with the gospel **to the circumcised**. Paul's mission is paralleled to Peter's! The four Gospels are unanimous in attributing to Peter the first rank among the Twelve, and Acts of the Apostles confirms his unique role.[10] Now Paul attains a similar position, and his gospel is set as a parallel to Peter's. There could not be a more positive response to Paul's mission.

Paul cared deeply about this parallel. He mentions it twice (Gal 2:7–8) and then repeats the parallel a third time when describing the agreement reached with "James and Cephas and John" (v. 9). Instead of referring to Peter by his Aramaic name, Cephas, as he does on every other occasion in his letters,[11] in verses 7–8 he uses the Greek name *Petros* twice. It is not clear why Paul does this. Perhaps the oral gospel traditions that were being taught in the churches of Galatia used the Greek form of Peter's name, and Paul wanted to reinforce his readers' understanding of what was being said about his apostleship in relation to Peter's.

Paul distinguishes two forms of the gospel, one entrusted to himself and one to Peter. For Paul it is **the gospel to the uncircumcised**. For Peter it was the gospel "to the circumcised." These expressions that seem odd to us evidently refer to non-Jews and Jews, respectively. The word "gospel" is used, even though the intended distinction is between the two apostles' diverse fields of mission. Paul's mission was to evangelize the Gentiles (the term can also mean "the †nations," vv. 8–9); Peter's was to evangelize the Jews. This clear distinction between the two missions is a simplification. Paul also evangelized his fellow Jews (see 1 Cor 9:20 and the accounts of Paul's preaching in synagogues in Acts), while Peter had an important role in initially evangelizing and receiving Gentiles into the Church (see Acts 10).

The phrases that the NABRE translates as "the gospel to the uncircumcised" and "to the circumcised" could also be rendered "the gospel of the uncircumcised" and "of the circumcised," suggesting not only two different audiences but also a certain difference in the content of the message. Paul does not specify the

---

by the power of signs and wonders, by the power of the Spirit [of God], so that from Jerusalem all the way around to Illyricum I have finished preaching the gospel of Christ."

10. See, e.g., Matt 10:2; 16:18–19; Mark 3:16; Luke 6:14; 22:31–32; John 1:42; 21:15–17; Acts 1:15; 2:14, 37–38; 3:4, 12; 4:8.

11. 1 Cor 1:12; 3:22; 9:5; 15:5; Gal 1:18; 2:9, 11, 14.

points of difference, but the context tells us that Paul did not require Gentile Christians to be circumcised, or to observe the dietary laws or other †ritual regulations found in the †law of Moses (see the sidebar, "Paul's Gospel," p. 62). His gospel was a gospel of the "freedom that we have in Christ Jesus" (Gal 2:4). Jewish Christians continued to observe the law of Moses (see Acts 21:20), although they did not regard their keeping the law as the foundation of a right relationship with God (Gal 2:15–16; Acts 15:8–11), and they set aside some traditional interpretations as Jesus did,[12] especially those that hindered relations with Gentiles (Acts 10:9–29; 1 Cor 9:1, 19–21; see the sidebar, "Did Paul Keep the Law of Moses?," pp. 174–75).

Paul adds a parenthetical clause in verse 8 to make clear that this entrustment **2:8** of each version of the gospel was not simply an administrative division of labor. Rather, the proof that God had entrusted their respective fields of ministry to Peter and to Paul was God's own operation in and through them to make their work effective. God had conferred on Paul an ability that corresponded to his mission, a capability that was not merely human. "Who is qualified for this?" Paul asks in 2 Cor 2:16. He answers, "Our qualification comes from God, who has indeed qualified us as ministers of a new covenant" (2 Cor 3:5–6). God **worked in Peter** to make him an apostle to the chosen people, and he **worked also** in Paul to make him an apostle to **the Gentiles**.

James, Cephas, and John **recognized** that the fruitfulness of Paul's mission **2:9** must be attributed to a **grace** given to him. Paul often uses the expression "the grace given to me,"[13] especially in regard to his apostolic vocation to the Gentiles (see Eph 3:8). At other times he presents his vocation as a "ministry" (*diakonia*) entrusted to him,[14] expressing another aspect of this very rich reality. Referring to his ministry as a †grace indicates Paul is aware that he did not deserve this marvelous gift from God and he feels deeply grateful.

After the confirmation of Paul's ministry and the recognition of the grace given to him comes an agreement. Paul emphasizes that the decision came from the men of greatest authority in the Church, **who were reputed to be pillars,** and that the agreement was not just expressed in speech but was demonstrated by a solemn gesture. Everyone could see that **James and Cephas and John** gave **their right hands** to Paul and Barnabas as a sign of **partnership** (Greek *koinōnia*). This word is significant because it goes beyond the meaning

---

12. See Matt 5:31–32, 38–41; 15:1–2; Mark 7:1–23; also Matt 12:1–8 and other occasions when Jesus departed from Pharisaic interpretations of the Sabbath.
13. Rom 12:3; 15:15; 1 Cor 3:10; Eph 3:2, 7–8.
14. See Rom 11:13; 2 Cor 3:6–9; 4:1; 5:18; 1 Tim 1:12.

of agreement and expresses personal bonds of cooperation and solidarity. It reveals that the distinction between the apostolic territories did not mean a separation between the people. Communion among apostles who are engaged in diverse missions guarantees the unity of the Church.

The order in which "James and Cephas and John" are mentioned has sometimes been used as an argument against the primacy of Peter, because Cephas is listed second rather than first. However, the order of three names does not necessarily signal a hierarchy of position. In 2 Cor 13:13 Christ is named first, then the Father, and then the Holy Spirit, but it does not follow that Christ has preeminence over the Father. Rather James is named first because, as the lead elder of the church of Jerusalem,[15] he was the most prominent leader in Jewish Christianity, and his support for Paul's apostolate made it likely that other leaders of the Jewish-Christian part of the Church would accept it as well. James seems to have had a special apostolate to the Jews. The way that Paul describes the respective missionary responsibilities is not geographical. Paul does not say, "We go to the nations, and they go to the land of Israel." Instead he says, "We go to the Gentiles, and they go to the circumcised." "The circumcised" designated all Jews, even those who lived among pagan nations. The Letter of James, in fact, is addressed "To the twelve tribes in the dispersion" (James 1:1), which is in line with this agreement.

While Peter's ministry is focused on fellow Jews, this does not mean that he restricts his activities to the land of Israel. He ministers to Jews in the diaspora—and apparently to Gentiles there also. Paul is about to recount that not long afterward Cephas came to Antioch and lived among the Gentile Christians (Gal 2:11–14). In 1 Corinthians, Paul mentions that among the factions in the Corinthian church was the party of Cephas (1 Cor 1:12; 3:22), and he also speaks of Cephas's journeys (1 Cor 9:5).

2:10   A stipulation is added to this declaration: **to be mindful of the poor**. The Christians in Jerusalem were not wealthy. Luke speaks, for example, of the case of the widows for whom "the daily distribution" of necessary items was organized (Acts 6:1). Paul immediately affirms that he shares the Jerusalem leadership's concern for the poor. He shows that concern years later in the collection he organized "for the poor among the holy ones in Jerusalem" (Rom 15:26; see 1 Cor 8). The collection also serves as a concrete expression of the communion between the Gentile and Jewish Christian churches, something that Paul considers very important (Gal 2:2).

---

15. See Acts 15:13–29. Hegesippus (AD 110–180) and Clement of Alexandria (150–215) both describe James as the first bishop of Jerusalem.

The theological message of this short passage concerns †ecclesial order and unity. Paul shows the priority he places on unity among various sectors of the Church. His apostolate does not consist solely in proclaiming the truth of the gospel but also in building unity. For that unity to be firm, it must be grounded in the Church's recognition of the work of the †Lord in all its diversity. Unity does not mean uniformity.

Reflection and Application (2:6–10)

Paul tells us that when the leaders of the Church in Jerusalem "saw that I had been entrusted with the gospel" and "recognized the grace bestowed upon me," they gave him their full support for his mission to the †Gentiles. In other words, James, Peter, and John discerned that God was at work through Paul because of the conversions and miracles, even though to all appearances Paul did not have the same pedigree for ministry that they did as belonging to the Twelve or as Jesus' "brother."

Are our eyes open to seeing God's grace in the fruitful ministry of our brothers and sisters who do not have the same qualifications we have—whether education, ordination, or some other official role? The New Testament is quite clear that Christ builds up his body through charisms, gifts of the Spirit, given to each of the baptized.[16] Sometimes the Lord works through those we least expect, and we, like Peter, John, and James, must humbly acknowledge his hand and give thanks, careful to avoid the sin of those who refused to believe in the ministry of John the Baptist and of Jesus (Matt 21:32).

This holds true for our brothers and sisters who belong to other churches. According to Vatican II's *Decree on Ecumenism*, "Very many of the significant elements and endowments which together go to build up and give life to the Church itself can exist outside the visible boundaries of the Catholic Church."[17] This reminds us to esteem our separated brothers and sisters and to pray more fervently for unity, so that the sharing of the gifts we have all received may be complete.

---

16. Rom 12:4–8; 1 Cor 12:4–11; Eph 4:7, 11–16; 1 Pet 4:10–11.
17. Second Vatican Council, *Unitatis Redintegratio* 3.

Confrontation at Antioch

Galatians 2:11–14

The final section of Paul's autobiographical argument reports a dramatic turn of events. After recounting how the Jerusalem leaders had recognized Paul's ministry, approved his †gospel, and formed a partnership with him for the preaching of the gospel, Paul now informs his readers about a public confrontation between Peter (Cephas) and himself that took place in the church of Antioch. It would be easy to imagine Paul choosing not to disclose a public disagreement with the most prominent leader in the early Church, lest it seem to undermine his side of the argument. But it is an indication of Paul's self-confidence that he not only tells the story but also insists that Peter was in the wrong and he was in the right. To defend his understanding of the necessary and practical implications of the gospel, Paul does not refrain from criticizing the conduct of the most authoritative apostle. Instead, he makes use of the occasion to introduce his doctrine of †justification.

The Confrontation with Peter (2:11–14)

---

¹¹And when Cephas came to Antioch, I opposed him to his face because he clearly was wrong. ¹²For, until some people came from James, he used to eat with the Gentiles; but when they came, he began to draw back and separated himself, because he was afraid of the circumcised. ¹³And the rest of the Jews [also] acted hypocritically along with him, with the result that even Barnabas was carried away by their hypocrisy. ¹⁴But when I saw that

Figure 9. St. Peter's Church in Antioch.

**they were not on the right road in line with the truth of the gospel, I said
to Cephas in front of all, "If you, though a Jew, are living like a Gentile
and not like a Jew, how can you compel the Gentiles to live like Jews?"**

NT: Acts 10:28–29; 11:2–18; 15:1; 1 Tim 1:5; James 3:17; 1 Pet 2:1
Catechism: Peter and the papacy, 880–82

Paul has been recounting a series of events linked by repetition of the word   **2:11**
"then" (1:18, 21; 2:1). The sequence, however, is interrupted in verse 11: **But
when Cephas came to Antioch . . .**[1] The rest of the sentence reveals Paul's
temperament: he is not the kind of leader who is afraid of conflict. Paul did not
criticize Peter's conduct behind his back but rather had the courage to confront
him **to his face**. Peter's importance in the Church is implicitly acknowledged
by the fact that his conduct matters so much. Paul is not shy in recounting his
own audacious response but gives a strong reason for it: Cephas **clearly was
wrong**. Other translations capture better a nuance of the Greek: "he stood

1. The NABRE begins the sentence with "and"; Paul, however, has switched to a Greek word that often
indicates a contrast. As to "when," Paul's wording is not completely clear about whether the incident in
Antioch took place before or after the meeting in Jerusalem. Some biblical scholars believe it was prior
to the resolution in Jerusalem, which might provide a more logical sequence of events.

The Church of Antioch

Antioch, located three hundred miles north of Jerusalem on the Orontes River near the Mediterranean coast (in present-day Turkey), was the leading city of the Roman province of Syria and third-largest city in the empire after Rome and Alexandria. This Antioch, which was distinct from other cities bearing the name, including Antioch in Pisidia where Paul and Barnabas evangelized on their first mission (Acts 13:14–52), was an important center of early Christianity.

Acts of the Apostles reports that Jewish Christians fled to Antioch during the persecution that followed the martyrdom of Stephen (Acts 11:19). There they proclaimed the †gospel to Jews and, for the first time on a wide scale, to †Gentiles, who warmly welcomed the message. To care for the large number of new converts in Antioch, the church in Jerusalem sent Barnabas, who in turn went to Tarsus to invite Paul (then called Saul) to come and assist him. It was in Antioch that disciples of Jesus were first called Christians (Acts 11:19–26). It was from Antioch that Paul set out on what would later be called his three missionary journeys (Acts 13:1–3; 15:35–41; 18:22–23).

condemned" (RSV) or "self-condemned" (NRSV). The sense is not quite that of a judicial condemnation, but it has an analogous meaning.

2:12–13   Paul now explains the situation. His criticism concerns a change of behavior on Peter's part that had negative consequences. The issue was whether Jewish Christians would share meals with †Gentile Christians. In order to maintain †ritual purity, Jews normally abstained from eating with non-Jews. Acts 10 alludes to this practice. Having entered the home of Cornelius, a non-Jew, Peter states, "You know that it is unlawful for a Jewish man to associate with, or visit, a Gentile." Then he adds, "But God has shown me that I should not call any person profane or unclean. And that is why I came without objection when sent for" (Acts 10:28–29). When Peter returned to Jerusalem, some of the Jewish believers confronted him, saying, "You entered the house of uncircumcised people and ate with them" (11:2–3). In fact, while the †law of Moses says that certain foods (such as pork) cannot be eaten, nothing in it explicitly forbids Jews from eating with Gentiles, but Jewish traditions did. A Jewish writing from around the second century BC depicts Abraham instructing Jacob,

> Separate yourself from the gentiles,
> and do not eat with them,

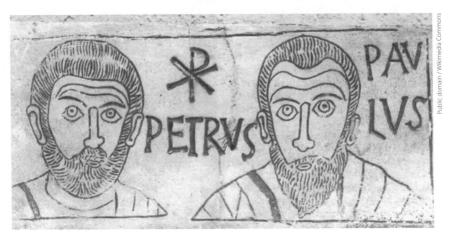

Figure 10. Etching of St. Peter and St. Paul in a fourth-century catacomb.

and do not perform deeds like theirs.
And do not become associates of theirs.
Because their deeds are defiled,
and all of their ways are contaminated, and despicable, and abominable.[2]

The problem of sharing meals was not identical with that of circumcision, which Paul talked about in the preceding paragraph (Gal 2:1–10), for this was a question of imposing a requirement on converted Gentiles. Here the question is how Jewish Christians should conduct their relationships with Gentile Christians.

When Peter first came to Antioch, **he used to eat with the Gentiles**. Apparently, that was not a problem for him (Acts 10:28–29). But then some Jewish Christians who were associated with **James** arrived from Jerusalem, although Paul does not say James sent them. From the context we understand that these new arrivals were committed to a strict observance of Jewish traditions, including not eating with Gentiles to avoid impurity, traditions that Peter himself had observed prior to his experience at the house of Cornelius (Acts 11:2–3). Now Peter found himself facing a difficult choice: **he was afraid of the circumcised**, probably meaning "the circumcision faction" (NRSV), those who continued to

2. *Jubilees* 22:16 (trans. O. S. Wintermute), in *The Old Testament Pseudepigrapha*, ed. James H. Charlesworth (New York: Doubleday, 1985), 2:98. Some scholars say that the underlying issue was whether Jewish Christians could eat nonkosher food at the homes of Gentile Christians. But Gal 2:12 makes no mention of dietary regulations, while Acts 10:28–29 explicitly focuses on the Jewish belief that Gentiles were unclean. Peter changes his view on this matter as a result of the visions he receives, the angelic summons to the house of Cornelius, and the fact that the Holy Spirit descends on the Gentiles, proving that God had cleansed their hearts by faith (Acts 10:1–11:18; 15:8–9).

think that Gentile Christians should be circumcised.[3] If he continued eating with Gentile Christians, he would lose the trust of this faction in Jerusalem and perhaps arouse their opposition to the Gentile mission. He chose to avoid these potential difficulties, at least for the time being: **he began to draw back and separated himself** from meals with Gentiles. Peter's choice was based not on doctrine but on pragmatic grounds. It had, however, significant repercussions, since the other Jewish Christians of the church in Antioch began to imitate his practice. Even **Barnabas**, Paul's mission partner in evangelizing Gentiles, was **carried away** in this bad direction. The result was a division of the church of Antioch into two groups, Jewish and Gentile. The Gentile Christians would soon get the impression that to avoid being regarded as unclean and to be able to share meals with Jewish Christians, their older brothers and sisters in the †faith, they needed to submit to Jewish observances. Alternatively, the church in Antioch would be divided into Jewish and Gentile communities, undermining the unity of the new humanity in Christ (Gal 3:28).

Paul refused to tolerate this situation. He recognized the behavior of Peter and his imitators as a pretense, as dishonest. Peter was concealing his convictions and acting as though he shared the ideas of the strict party of Jewish Christians who were aligned with James. Paul speaks of **hypocrisy**, using a Greek word that refers to pretending something that is not true. Sincerity is an important Christian virtue commended in the writings of Peter, James, and Paul (1 Tim 1:5; James 3:17; 1 Pet 2:1), and Jesus himself denounces hypocrisy in the Gospels (e.g., Matt 23).

2:14   Paul sees more than a mere human failing here. He recognizes that Peter's conduct is not consistent **with the truth of the gospel**. It leaves room for a practice to arise that is dangerous to the †faith, a division between Jewish and Gentile Christians on the false grounds that the latter remain unclean (Acts 10:28; 15:9). Therefore he intervenes forcefully, reproving **Cephas** in public in order to put an end to the pretense.

Paul's penchant for antithesis and paradox is reflected in his words to Peter. The contrast between Jew and Gentile is emphasized by the alternation of terms: **If you, though a Jew, are living like a Gentile and not like a Jew, how can you compel the Gentiles to live like Jews?** Paul thus highlights the contradiction in Peter's behavior. To express the contrast more sharply, Paul compresses the narrative. He says, "You . . . are living like a Gentile," when it would have been

---

3. Acts 21:20–24, although describing a situation some years later, attests to the presence of thousands of Jewish Christians in Jerusalem who were "all zealous observers of the law," some of whom may still have held that Gentile Christians should be circumcised.

more precise to say, "Until now you were living like a Gentile, but now you have gone back to living like a Jew." Paul also overstates the matter for effect. Cephas is not directly "compelling" Gentile Christians to become Jewish; rather, his conduct is exerting an unintended moral pressure on them.

It is worth noting that Paul's approach does not in any way call into question Peter's doctrine or his customary conduct. It only concerns his recent behavior that was not consistent with his basic position. To stop Peter's false actions that were causing public scandal, Paul reveals Peter's inconsistency, thus putting an end to the false impression that Peter considered Gentile Christians unclean.

Figure 11. St. Peter and St. Paul (oil painting by Jusepe de Ribera, 1612).

Paul does not report Peter's reaction to this confrontation but instead moves on to explain the doctrine of justification that underlies his refusal to require that Gentiles practice circumcision and other Jewish customs. Some authors speculate that Peter rejected Paul's correction, arguing that if Peter agreed with him, surely Paul would have reported it.[4] But the nature of Paul's correction was not an argument that left room for discussion, since it was a public disclosure of Peter's inconsistent practice. Besides, if it were generally known that Peter rejected Paul's correction, that fact would render this part of Paul's argument unpersuasive, since the testimony and practice of Peter would contradict it.

It is important to remember that the only perspective Galatians gives us on the matter is Paul's. To have a fuller picture of this event, we would need to hear from Peter. Since he did not leave a record, the best we can do is to imagine his position. According to the agreement in Jerusalem, Peter was to take concern

---

4. Some scholars have read this text as marking a division between Pauline and Petrine Christianity. However, evidence of such a division is lacking in the New Testament or in the earliest Christian writings, and later Christian tradition witnesses to the unity of Peter and Paul, liturgically commemorating them together (see also 1 Cor 3:22; 15:5; and 2 Pet 3:15).

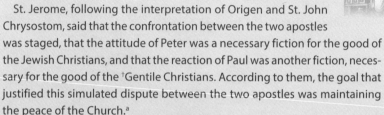

Paul's Confrontation with Peter in the History of Interpretation

LIVING TRADITION

Paul's account of his confrontation with Peter at Antioch has long made readers uneasy because of Christian veneration of Peter as the rock on whom Christ has built his Church (Matt 16:18). A variety of paths for avoiding this difficulty have been tried over the course of history.

St. Jerome, following the interpretation of Origen and St. John Chrysostom, said that the confrontation between the two apostles was staged, that the attitude of Peter was a necessary fiction for the good of the Jewish Christians, and that the reaction of Paul was another fiction, necessary for the good of the †Gentile Christians. According to them, the goal that justified this simulated dispute between the two apostles was maintaining the peace of the Church.[a]

This interpretation did not satisfy St. Augustine, who wrote to St. Jerome to explain the reasons for his disagreement. He did not accept that Sacred Scripture should be full of fictions not presented as such, and he maintained that a pretend controversy would be unworthy of the two apostles. The argument on this point in the correspondence between Augustine and Jerome was long (AD 395–405) and intense. In the Middle Ages, St. Thomas Aquinas summarized it in his exegesis of Gal 2:11–14 and sided with St. Augustine: Peter truly was in the wrong, failing to foresee the negative consequences of his actions.[b]

In the time of the Reformation, Luther referred to this incident repeatedly, interpreting his own situation in its light, placing himself on the side of Paul and the pope on the side of Peter. But this was a polemical misuse of the text, seeking to justify his rejection of papal authority. We have seen that in his questioning of Peter, Paul neither denies Peter's role of leadership nor accuses him of teaching false doctrine, but rather he accuses Peter of adopting a mode of conduct that was hypocritical and inconsistent.

a. See John Chrysostom, *Homily on Galatians 2:11–12*, in ACCS VIII:26, 28–29; Jerome, *Epistle to the Galatians* 1.2.11.
b. See Augustine, *Epistle to the Galatians* 15 (1B.2, 11–16); excerpts in ACCS VIII:27–29. See Thomas Aquinas, *Commentary on St. Paul's Letter to the Galatians*, trans. F. R. Larcher, OP (Albany, NY: Magi, 1966), chap. 2, lecture 3, http://dhspriory.org/thomas/SSGalatians.htm#23.

for proclaiming the †gospel to Jews (Gal 2:9), and the normal position of Jewish Christians was to remain faithful to Jewish observances (Acts 21:20). They had strong reasons to remain faithful to their heritage: respect for the †law that

God gave to his people, the duty to preserve solidarity with their countrymen, and a concern to proclaim the †Messiah to them. They did not see any reason to abandon their traditional way of life. No doubt it was difficult for some to accept that the law of Moses and Jewish traditions were not required of Gentile Christians who had recently come to share in the †inheritance of Israel through the Messiah. Peter did not wish to upset them.

In this context, Peter's conduct is at least understandable. Nevertheless, Galatians is not simply a historical document but is also a part of inspired Scripture. Consequently, it is important to recognize that Scripture has not privileged Peter's point of view, whatever that might have been, but that of Paul. That does not place everything about Paul's way of handling the situation or his perspective beyond question. Nevertheless, the doctrine of inspiration does guarantee the judgment on the issue firmly expressed by Paul in the text and explained more clearly in the verses that follow. Christians are not called to accept circumcision or other "works of the law" to be justified. Rather, they are free of impurity and full members of God's †covenant people on the basis of the only valid foundation for relationship with God—namely, †faith in Christ, "who gave himself for our sins . . . in accord with the will of our God and Father" (Gal 1:4).

We may also conclude that Paul's example should be followed in refusing to compromise the truth of the gospel. The Apostle Paul often exhorts his readers to follow his example (see 1 Cor 4:16; 11:1; Phil 3:17; etc.), and this is conveyed to all subsequent generations as inspired teaching.

Reflection and Application (2:11–14)

A characteristic of Catholic †faith is love and respect for Peter's successor, the bishop of Rome. As the vicar of Christ and pastor of the whole Church, the pope enjoys a special assistance of the Holy Spirit when he teaches about faith and morals in the course of his ordinary ministry (Catechism 882, 892). Furthermore, the Church holds that when the pope "proclaims by a definitive act a doctrine pertaining to faith or morals," the Holy Spirit preserves his teaching from error, so that the Church may never be deprived of the †gospel (Catechism 891, quoting *Lumen Gentium* 25).

However, the Church has defined papal infallibility in a very limited way, because as this text shows, Peter himself was capable of making mistakes in the way he fulfilled his ministry. Moreover, it is a fact of history that some popes, especially during the Middle Ages and Renaissance, were very worldly men who scandalized many and greatly harmed the Church through their evil conduct. Thanks be to God that in the last couple of centuries the Church has been blessed with a series of holy popes more like Peter than like his unworthy successors. Nevertheless, divine assistance does not guarantee that the words and actions of even holy popes will always be good or wise, as this passage from Galatians illustrates. This is all the more reason why we Catholics should pray that the Lord guide the pope and the bishops and that they may be docile to his Holy Spirit.

Paul's Gospel

Galatians 2:15–21

Finally, we arrive at Paul's explanation of the theological error of those who wanted to require circumcision of the †Gentile Christians: they have a false understanding of the basis of our relationship with God. This section of the letter (Gal 2:15–21) briefly states the fundamental doctrinal teaching of Galatians. Just as a student writing a composition states his or her main idea before presenting the evidence in support of the thesis, this section, and especially verse 16, is Paul's thesis statement, for which he will present arguments in the doctrinal part of the letter (3:1–5:12).

Paul's Thesis Statement (2:15–16)

---

¹⁵**We, who are Jews by nature and not sinners from among the Gentiles,**
¹⁶**[yet] who know that a person is not justified by works of the law but through faith in Jesus Christ, even we have believed in Christ Jesus that we may be justified by faith in Christ and not by works of the law, because by works of the law no one will be justified.**

OT: Ps 143:2; Ezek 36:22–32
NT: Rom 1:18–32; 3:20–26
Catechism: justification, 1987–96

Paul begins by describing the position of the Jewish Christians, including Peter **2:15** and himself, using the first-person plural: **We . . . are Jews by nature**, meaning,

What Does It Mean to Be Justified?

BIBLICAL BACKGROUND

Understanding †justification can be a bit challenging, in part because English uses words derived from two roots, *just-* and *right-* (just, justice, justify, justification, righteous, righteousness) to translate Greek words based on a single root, *dik-*. Besides that, English translations of the Bible differ in the terminology they employ.

In the Old Testament, to be *righteous* or *just* (*dikaios* in the †Septuagint) meant to be like Noah, whose conduct was good, in harmony with God's ways, and who therefore enjoyed a good relationship with him that included his acceptance and blessing (Gen 6:9). To be unrighteous or unjust meant to be someone whose conduct was evil and contrary to God's ways, a condition that led to judgment and condemnation (Gen 18:23–19:13). For Israel, God's †covenant people, righteousness primarily meant to live out faithfully their covenant relationship with God by keeping the †law they received through Moses (Deut 6:25). Righteous conduct was not a means of earning a good relationship with God, but of remaining in the covenant relationship God had graciously given them (Deut 7:6–14). To be *justified* (*dikaioō* in the Septuagint) originally meant to be judged as righteous by God because one's conduct was good, in harmony with God's ways. Faithful Jews hoped to be accepted as righteous, or justified, by God on the day of judgment as a result of keeping the law of Moses (Ps 37:28–29; Wis 3:1–9; Dan 12:2–3).

But in the light of his encounter with the risen †Lord, Paul understood righteousness and justification more deeply. He realized that the righteousness based on keeping the law was inadequate (Gal 3:10–11) and provisional (3:22–25; 4:1–5). He reflected on many Old Testament texts that spoke of the universality of sin (he quotes many of them in Rom 3:9–19) and concluded that no human being will be justified on the basis of their conduct, since no one is truly just or righteous in God's sight (Pss 14:1–3; 143:2; Rom 3:10, 20).[a] Through the prophets God had promised to bring to pass an infinitely better way of addressing the problem of sin (Jer 31:31–34; Ezek 36:22–27). What was

by birth. As Jews, he says, we do not belong to the category of **sinners from among the Gentiles**. Here Paul presupposes the Jewish evaluation of the †Gentile world as morally corrupt because it lacked knowledge of God and of his †law.[1] The judgment that Gentiles are sinners and unclean in contrast to Jews, who keep the law and are righteous (Ps 1:2–5), was one of the motives of the †Judaizers to avoid eating with Gentile Christians.

1. Other biblical texts use similar language (see 1 Macc 2:48; Matt 26:45; Eph 2:12); Paul explains the situation of the Gentiles at some length in Rom 1:18–32. Nevertheless, the traditional Jewish understanding was not a complete perspective, as Peter discovered (Acts 10:34–35) and as Paul teaches (Rom 2:14–16).

needed was for the person to be justified in a more radical sense—namely, to be *made righteous* by a divine act that not only grants forgiveness of sins but also transforms the person from within. The basis of this justification is Christ's loving gift of himself on the cross for our sins (Gal 2:20). This discovery leads Paul to regard his previous righteousness based on keeping the law as "so much rubbish." Instead Paul aims to "gain Christ and be found in him, not having any righteousness of my own based on the law but that which comes through faith in Christ, the righteousness from God" (Phil 3:8–9).

Paul found confirmation in Scripture, especially Gen 15:6 and Hab 2:4, that the way human beings are justified is through †faith. Through faith in Jesus and baptism, the believer is united with him in his death and resurrection and receives his Holy Spirit.[b] This is true justification, which places a person in a harmonious relationship with God (see comment on Gal 3:6, p. 102).

Does justification by faith mean that conduct does not matter? Not at all. Paul, along with other New Testament authors, teaches that every person will someday face judgment before Christ on the basis of their works (Rom 2:5–11; 2 Cor 5:10).[c] Those who have persevered in faithfulness to Christ, in whom faith is at work through love (Gal 5:6), who have sown to the Spirit rather than the †flesh (6:8), will be judged by Christ as righteous (Matt 25:21, 23; 2 Tim 4:8). The New Testament refers to this positive final judgment sometimes as justification (Matt 12:36–37 RSV; Rom 2:13), sometimes as salvation (Rom 5:9–10; Phil 1:28). Like initial justification, final justification is founded on faith in Christ and his faithfulness toward us.

a. The Catholic Church believes that because of the special role in salvation history for which Mary was chosen (Luke 1:28), God preserved her from original sin and from actual sin. Nevertheless, even Mary was not justified because of her conduct; rather, her righteous conduct was possible because she was justified by †grace from before her birth on the basis of her Son's future sacrifice (Catechism 491–93).

b. See Gal 2:19–20; 3:27–28; 4:4. First Corinthians 6:11 is particularly clear on the role of the Holy Spirit in justification: "You were justified in the name of the Lord Jesus Christ and in the Spirit of our God."

c. See also John 5:28–30; Gal 6:7–9; Rev 20:12–13.

Paul's response is to point out that Jewish Christians implicitly recognize that **2:16** their own previous standing before God was also compromised, since **even we have believed in Christ Jesus that we may be justified**—that is, put in a right relationship with God. From the beginning of their proclaiming the †gospel at Pentecost, the apostles summoned everyone to †faith in Jesus to receive the forgiveness of sins that went beyond what was available under the Mosaic †law.[2] Paul's point is that Jewish Christians also believed in Christ to obtain forgiveness

2. Acts 2:38; 5:31; 10:43; 13:38; see also Luke 24:47.

What Are "Works of the Law"?

Throughout the history of interpreting Galatians there have been a variety of interpretations of what Paul means by "works of the †law." St. Augustine, the Protestant Reformers, and many Christians have applied the term broadly to mean all good works, which they correctly insist cannot †justify a person. Some ancient and recent commentators have understood "works of the law" to refer exclusively or primarily to identity markers in the law of Moses that set apart the Jewish people from the †Gentiles, such as circumcision, a kosher diet, and observance of the Jewish liturgical calendar. In the opinion of these interpreters, the inclusion of Gentiles among God's people in Christ makes these identity markers obsolete, at least for Gentile Christians. The third view is that "works of the law" refers to observance of the law of Moses as a whole, including both moral precepts and rules for religious conduct. Study of the contexts of the six places where Paul uses this phrase indicates that the third view is preferable.[a] Whenever Paul speaks of "works of the law," he refers to keeping the whole law of Moses.

Nevertheless, Paul's focus in Galatians is indeed on Jewish identity markers such as circumcision and dietary rules that the †Judaizers wanted to require of Gentiles as well. It is likewise true that in other texts Paul speaks generically of "works," without reference to the law of Moses, as inadequate for justification (Rom 4:2, 6), election (Rom 9:11), and salvation (Eph 2:8–9), confirming that Paul is also concerned to emphasize the primacy of divine grace and the radical insufficiency of human effort (Rom 11:6).

a. See Rom 3:20, 28; Gal 2:16; 3:2, 5, 10; in a majority of these contexts Paul explicitly refers to Jews. See the sidebar, "Paul's Nuanced View of the Law," pp. 146–47.

and be †justified. This implies that they recognized themselves to be sinners, even though they did not belong to the category of "sinners from among the Gentiles" (2:15). In addition, they recognized that they could not be justified by the law of Moses.

Paul's analysis of the situation of the Jewish Christians was new because it showed the inadequacy of the common opinion that doing the **works of the law** ensured justification—that is, being judged righteous by God on the basis of one's conduct. The problem with the common opinion was that it did not take into account the fact that Jews as well as †Gentiles find themselves in a state of sin, from which the law is radically incapable of freeing them (3:21). Elsewhere Paul explains that, by its nature, law cannot justify a sinner; it can only show that he or she is guilty and liable to punishment (3:21–23; Rom 3:20; 7:7–13; see the sidebar, "Paul's Nuanced View of the Law," pp. 146–47).

Thanks to Paul's insight that following the law of Moses fails to resolve the problem of sin, he can combat the error at the root of the teaching of the †Judaizers. They placed observance of the law in a necessary role alongside faith in Christ for justification. In other words, they established their spiritual confidence on the dual foundation of faith in Christ and observance of the law. Paul, however, recognizes that these two foundations are incompatible. Whoever seeks justification through keeping the law aims at a righteousness of his or her own (Phil 3:9) and is thus engaged in a kind of self-justification. Whoever, on the other hand, puts his or her faith in Christ radically renounces self-justification and receives justification as a free gift from God, obtained through the passion of Christ, who suffered "for our sins" (Gal 1:4). This is the choice: to rely on works of the law or to believe in Christ. The Jewish Christians had chosen faith in Christ, but they needed to realize that they were thereby excluding works of the law as the basis of or a necessary means of maintaining a right relationship with God.

Paul strongly insists on this position here both because he is convinced it is true and because it is fundamental to the doctrinal discussion that follows. The structure of Paul's sentence in verse 16 is stylistically magnificent and makes his message unmistakable:

> [We] who know that a person is not justified by works of the law but
> through faith in Jesus Christ,
> even we have believed in Christ Jesus that we may be justified by faith in
> Christ and not by works of the law,
> because by works of the law no one will be justified.

In one sentence Paul states his point three times! He employs three key terms—"justified," "works of the law," and "faith [or "belief"] in Christ"—and repeats them each three times.

The end of the sentence declares in an absolute way that **by works of the law no one will be justified**. With these words Paul supports his assertion by alluding to a psalm where the psalmist says to God,

> Do not enter into judgment with your servant,
> for no one living will be justified before you. (Ps 143:2 †LXX)

If no one living can be justified—that is, judged to be righteous—when God is judge, it follows that "works of the law" do not change that fact.

"Faith in Christ" or "the Faithfulness of Christ"?

The phrases "†faith in Christ" (Gal 2:16; 3:22) and "faith in the Son of God" (2:20) have raised lengthy discussions among scholars because the Greek can be translated in a variety of ways.

The simplest and traditional interpretation followed by most English translations is to render the Greek phrase *pistis Christou* as "faith in Christ." The central affirmation of verse 16 clearly has this meaning, since it says, "we have believed in Christ Jesus." Consequently, the NABRE translates the two instances of *pistis Christou* in that verse as "faith in Christ."

However, there are other ways of understanding the phrase. It is possible that Paul is referring to "faith *from* Christ," with the nuance that Christ is the source of our faith. We have believed in Christ because Christ gave us the faith to do so.

Another possibility is to attribute *pistis* to Christ. If we translate *pistis* as "faith," we have "the faith of Christ," similar to "the faith of Abraham" (Rom 4:16). Galatians 3:6 says, "Abraham believed." So did Christ believe? The difficulty is that neither Paul nor any other New Testament writer attributes the act of believing to Christ, even though the verb *pisteuō*, "to believe," is used more than 240 times. This fact confirms that the New Testament does not regard Christ as a believer like everyone else: his relationship with God is of a completely different order.

However, there are two other meanings of *pistis*, either of which is appropriately attributed to Christ—namely, faithfulness or fidelity (see Rom 3:3–4) and trustworthiness. We can say that a person is †justified by Christ's faithfulness to God and to us, manifested in his gift of himself for our sins in obedience to God's will (see Gal 1:4). We can also say that a person is justified by the absolute trustworthiness of Christ, by Christ's being the solid support on whom our faith rests. Every act of faith or trust between persons is always the encounter of *pistis* on two sides, one who offers a sturdy support and one who accepts that support. If a text speaks explicitly of a faith that relies on someone, it is speaking implicitly of a support that is offered by another. To be justified by the trustworthiness of Christ, it is necessary for us to rely on his trustworthiness—that is, to trust in him.

Although in some instances the context of *pistis Christou* may point to one interpretation rather than another, usually we are not forced to choose. We can recognize ourselves as justified by our faith in Christ at the same time we realize that we are justified by his faithfulness, and that his trustworthiness is a firm foundation for our faith.

The good news is that this same verse (Gal 2:16) explains how a person is justified. Rather than present oneself to God to be judged as righteous on the basis of one's own observance of the law, one can believe in the †Messiah Jesus, which enables the person to receive God's free gift of †grace that restores lost innocence and imparts righteousness to the sinner.

The Apostle begins here his vigorous battle against the assertions of the Judaizers that Gentile Christians must observe the law of Moses, an argument that he pursues without letup until the end of the letter.

Application to Peter's Conduct (2:17–18)

---

¹⁷But if, in seeking to be justified in Christ, we ourselves are found to be sinners, is Christ then a minister of sin? Of course not! ¹⁸But if I am building up again those things that I tore down, then I show myself to be a transgressor.

After having clearly and vigorously set forth his thesis in verse 16, Paul confirms his point through a discussion of Peter's conduct that is notoriously difficult to untangle.[3] Verse 18, which is clearer, helps us understand verse 17. In verse 18 Paul has in mind the change in Peter's conduct. By eating with †Gentile Christians, Peter had torn down, so to speak, the wall of Jewish separatism. The †Judaizers regarded this act as a culpable transgression. However, in reality it was based on Peter's adherence to Christ. Seeking **to be justified in Christ** (v. 17), Peter had understood that he was free in regard to Jewish traditions. If Peter had been sinning by eating with Gentile Christians, one would have to conclude that Christ had led him to sin, making Christ **a minister of sin**, which is an absurd conclusion. Consequently, the premise must be utterly rejected. It cannot be said that Peter's earlier behavior was sinful.

But when Peter later caved to the demands of the Judaizers and separated himself from Gentile Christians, he was **building up again those things that he tore down**—that is, Jewish separatism. It was then that he truly showed

2:17–18

3. Paul's change from a first-person plural in v. 17 to a first-person singular in v. 18 makes the logic harder to follow. Paul is referring to Peter and himself in v. 17 when he speaks of seeking justification in Christ. Then he uses "I" in a generic sense in v. 18, illustrating his point by his example.

Some interpreters do not think that Paul is continuing to refer to Peter's behavior in these two verses. According to them, the first-person singular of v. 18 may indicate that in these two verses Paul has moved on from an account of the Antioch incident and is now speaking of Jewish Christians in general, including himself.

himself **to be a transgressor** (2:18). He was right when he tore down that wall, and "he clearly was wrong" (2:11) when he rebuilt it.[4]

Paul's Confession (2:19–21)

---

[19]**For through the law I died to the law, that I might live for God. I have been crucified with Christ;** [20]**yet I live, no longer I, but Christ lives in me; insofar as I now live in the flesh, I live by faith in the Son of God who has loved me and given himself up for me.** [21]**I do not nullify the grace of God; for if justification comes through the law, then Christ died for nothing.**

NT: Rom 6:6; 7:1–4; 2 Cor 5:14–15; Gal 5:24; 6:14
Catechism: justification, 1987–96
Lectionary: 2:19–20: St. Paul Miki and Companions; Common of Saints

Now Paul explains the basis of †justification by †faith and explains how his relationship with Christ changes his relationship to the †law of Moses.

Verses 19–21 are in the first-person singular. Paul describes his own situation as a Christian, not to depict an exclusive privilege afforded to him, but to illustrate the situation of every Christian. What Paul says in the preceding verses about justification would lack a foundation if Paul's case were unique. This description is essential to his argument, and the style of these verses is well suited to their sublime content. There is a strong antithesis between death and life. There are bold paradoxes: to die to the law through the law, to die to †live, to live crucified with Christ. Here Paul describes a profound union with Christ that every baptized believer is called to live out.

2:19   Paul's first highly paradoxical statement has left many commentators perplexed. What does **through the law I died to the law** mean? In Greek, Paul uses "†law" here without the definite article ("the"), which opens the way to various interpretations. Fortunately, the key to Paul's paradoxical statement is found in its immediate context: **I have been crucified with Christ**. Paul has died to the law of Moses through the law because he was crucified with Christ.

---

4. See Douglas J. Moo for a somewhat different view: "Jewish-Christians object that discarding the law means that they will be considered just like 'Gentile sinners' (see v. 15) and that Christ will therefore, in effect, be promoting sin. Paul strenuously rejects any such notion (v. 17b), arguing that it is only if the law is reestablished as a standard of right conduct (as Peter implicitly did at Antioch) that Jewish-Christians who no longer follow it could be truly considered sinners (v. 18). What Jewish-Christians need to do is imitate Paul, who, in order truly to live for God, has replaced his attachment to the law with an attachment to Christ (vv. 19–20)" (*Galatians*, BECNT [Grand Rapids: Baker Academic, 2013], Kindle loc. 4224).

Christ actually died, and he died "through the law," in the sense that his death came as a result of a legal condemnation (see John 19:7).[5] At the same time, he died "to the law," because the law has no more power over a dead person, especially if that person possesses a new life that is no longer earthly and is therefore completely removed from the jurisdiction of the law (Rom 7:1). This is precisely the case of the risen Christ, who "lives for God" (Rom 6:10). So Paul died to the law when he died and rose with Christ in baptism (Rom 6:3–8).[6]

Paul's death to the law of Moses is shared only by other Jewish believers who, like Paul, were previously subject to the law of Moses (Rom 7:1–4). However, every Christian, Jew and †Gentile alike, has been united to Christ's death on the cross through †faith and baptism (see Rom 6:3–5) in order to **live for God** in union with the risen Christ (see Rom 6:8–10). Later in the letter Paul will return to explain the role of the law of Moses in salvation history (Gal 3:15–4:7) and then to explain the Christian's rule of life in place of the law (5:13–25).

"I have been crucified with Christ." What a bold declaration! It demonstrates the strongest bond with Christ, a warm and personal identification with him (see also Phil 3:7–11). At the same time it expresses a dual conviction: (1) believers have in a real sense died and been raised with Christ in baptism (Rom 6:2–5, 11; Col 2:12), and (2) this event goes beyond the bounds of historical chronology and is an ever-present reality. Paul uses the verb in the perfect tense, which in Greek expresses the enduring result of a past action: I was crucified, and I still am. This corresponds to the concrete situation of believers. As we continue to †live on earth, Christ's passion is being actualized in our lives, which in turn affects our participation in the life of the risen Christ. Paul refers to this dynamism in 2 Cor 4:11: "We who live are constantly being given up to death for the sake of Jesus, so that the life of Jesus may be manifested in our mortal flesh."

The believer's participation in the life of the risen Jesus is already present: **I**   2:20 **live, no longer I, but Christ lives in me**. This statement completes the perspective. Paul, who says he has undergone death (v. 19), clarifies that now he lives, but he lives as risen from the dead. Having died to his own self, his own ego, he is made alive by Christ. The death to himself is simultaneous to his death to the †law and shows that his break with the law is not to be understood as opening the way to egoism and license. On the contrary, it is a matter of renouncing oneself to make room for the life of Christ, a life of generous love (Rom 7:4).

---

5. Some suggest instead that Christ's death was "through the law" in that it was a voluntary acceptance of the law's just penalty for the sins of the human race.

6. Paul addresses this subject in a more understandable way in Rom 7:1–4.

Paul's affirmation that "Christ lives in me" introduces a claim that is completely new. Paul is saying that one person, Christ, lives in another, the believer, in such a real way that the life of the believer should be attributed to Christ rather than to the believer.

The statement that follows allows us to enter more deeply into this mystery, as Paul tries to define the believer's situation more precisely. At first Paul says, "It is no longer I who live" (NRSV). Then he adjusts this statement, acknowledging that his (and our) mortal existence on earth is not ended: **Insofar as I now live in the flesh**. By "†flesh" Paul refers to the human condition with its limitations and weaknesses, a difficult existence that is exposed to temptation, suffering, and death. Paul has said, "Christ lives in me." Now he clarifies this affirmation too, saying, **I live by faith in the Son of God**. We can understand now in what manner Christ takes possession of Paul's life. It is not a question of a violent occupation and control of another person's personality, which is what occurs in demon-possessed people. It is also not a question of a state of inspiration described by various authors, be they pagans like Plato or Jews like Philo of Alexandria, in which a person temporarily comes under the influence of a divine spirit. Paul speaks elsewhere of the mystical ecstasies he has experienced (see 2 Cor 12:1–4). What he says here, however, is not confined to privileged moments but entails his whole earthly life. By means of †faith, the life of Christ permeates Paul. Christ does not impose himself on Paul but makes his divine life available to Paul, inviting a response of faith. The absolute trustworthiness of the Son of God opens up for Paul the possibility of a life of faith, which is the life of Christ in him and his life in Christ, a marvelous reciprocal interiority. Jesus' farewell discourse in the Gospel of John has much to say about this mutual indwelling.[7] Faith does not present itself as a mere assent of the mind to certain truths, but as the surrender of one's whole being to the person of Christ (see the sidebar, "What Does Paul Mean by 'Faith'?," p. 100).

The end of Paul's sentence provides the foundation for everything. His faith and ours is founded on the trustworthiness of the Son of God, **who has loved me and** has **given himself up for me** (literally, "handed himself over for me"). There are two reasons that Christ is a secure foundation for faith: on the one hand, his infinite greatness and power as the Son of God; on the other, the extreme love he has shown toward us. Christ's love for us was demonstrated in his passion; his divine sonship was fully manifested in his resurrection (see Rom 1:4).

7. John 14:15–21, 23; 15:1–11; 17:20–23, 26.

Paul's wording draws upon earlier teaching from the apostolic tradition. His affirmation is similar to the one in Gal 1:4, which combined two traditional ways of speaking about Jesus' death: Christ's death "for our sins" (1 Cor 15:3) and Jesus' words about the Son of Man coming to "give his life as a ransom for many" (Mark 10:45). Here, however, Paul introduces two important changes. Above all, Paul has personalized the affirmation. Instead of saying, "for our sins" or "for many," he says, "for me." This singular "me" was included in the plural "many," so the statement contains no new information. Its expressive value, however, is quite different. Instead of a general statement of fact about the significance of Jesus' death, we find a direct expression of a personal relationship that cannot be reduced to an abstraction. The result is a paradox: Who could have ever imagined that the Son of God could give himself up for me, a mere man and a sinner at that?

The paradox is reinforced by the second change in Paul's choice of words. In this sentence Paul does not use the verb "give" (Greek *didōmi*) as in Gal 1:4 and Mark 10:45, but he uses "give up" (*paradidōmi*), which means to "hand over" or "deliver" a person to his or her enemies. There are numerous Old Testament passages in which God "delivers" his people to their enemies in order to punish them for their unfaithfulness (Judg 2:14; 6:1, 13; 13:1). Paul's use of *paradidōmi* aptly characterizes the passion. Judas "handed over" Jesus to the Jews (Matt 26:15, 45); the Jews "handed him over to Pilate" (Matt 27:2); Pilate in the end "handed him over to be crucified" (Matt 27:26). The same verb is found in Isaiah's great prophecy about the servant of the Lord: he was "handed over because of their sins" (Isa 53:12 [†]LXX). Despite these precedents, Paul's wording is original since he makes the statement reflexive: rather than *being given over*, Christ *gave himself over* to his own enemies to be mocked, mistreated, and put to death. He did all this "for me," Paul says. What unfathomable depths of generosity! What a mystery!

The key to the mystery lies in another affirmation that appears for the first time here in the writings of the New Testament: Christ's breathtaking initiative is a manifestation of love. The synoptic Gospels do not make this motivation explicit as Paul does.[8] The past tense of "who has loved me" raises the question, Why does Paul not use the present tense and say "the Son of God who *loves* me" (see Rev 1:5)? The reason is in the connection between "has loved" and "has given himself up." Paul is referring to the concrete past event in which the Son of God fully manifested his love: his death on the cross.

---

8. Christ's motive for his death on the cross, his love, is explicitly spoken of later in the Johannine writings (see John 13:1; 15:13; 1 John 3:16; Rev 1:5).

There is one more element that is new in what Paul declares here. While
1 Cor 15:3 speaks of *Christ* dying for sins, and Matthew and Mark speak of *the
Son of Man* giving his life as a ransom (Matt 20:28; Mark 10:45), here Paul attributes this initiative of love to *the Son of God*, a title that expresses the identity
of Jesus in his profound and mysterious relationship with the Father.[9] This is
precisely the way Christ was revealed to Paul at his conversion on the road
to Damascus (see Gal 1:16). This act of love of which the Apostle now speaks
is even more impressive: "The Son of God . . . gave himself for me" (author's
translation). What disproportion there is in this exchange! What certainty we
can have about its efficacy! What the Son of God has done is decisive for Paul's
life and for everyone who will accept this gift.

2:21   After this stupendous sentence (vv. 19–20), Paul adds a quick, sharp conclusion that brings us back to the controversy. In it he combines a spontaneous personal declaration—**I do not nullify the grace of God**—and a new argument—**if
justification comes through the law, then Christ died for nothing**.

"The †grace of God" is the freely given favor of God offered to us in the mystery of Christ's passion, which Paul has just spoken of. Through the redemptive
love of his Son, God offers us the free gift of †justification. To seek justification
in any other way constitutes disdain for this free gift, and therefore nullifies it.
What unthinkable ingratitude! Paul rejects this idea absolutely.

Once again Paul speaks paradoxically: he denies that justification, the estab-
lishment of justice, comes through the †law. In the everyday world of human
affairs, justice is established through law, but when it comes to our standing
before God, law is of no help. We are sinners, and the law is incapable of making us just. The only solution is Christ's death for our sins. Whoever, on the
contrary, claims that the law is necessary for justifying us before God empties
Christ's death of its efficacy. The monstrous absurdity of this consequence demonstrates with glaring clarity how indefensible the position of the †Judaizers is.

Paul concludes here the first part of his letter. This section was primarily
intended as a defense of his †gospel by means of autobiographical arguments.
The Apostle, however, was not able to restrain himself from beginning his
theological argument in these final verses, anticipating the second part of the
letter, which is devoted to doctrine.

The principal affirmation of the first part of the letter (1:11–2:21) concerned
a fundamental truth: the divine origin of the gospel Paul preached. The Apostle's

---

9. Of course, the synoptic Gospels also acknowledge Jesus as the Son of God (e.g., Matt 27:54; Mark
1:1; Luke 1:35).

proclamation was transmitted to him not through human teaching but through a revelation he received of Jesus Christ the Son of God. To establish that point, Paul presented his vocation as a continuation of that of the prophets (1:15) and showed the independence of his apostolate from that of the Twelve (1:16–24). Then he told how his apostolate was officially recognized by the Church authorities in Jerusalem (2:1–10) and also how he boldly defended the practices of his gospel in the face of Cephas's accommodation to the Judaizers (2:11–14). Finally, Paul laid out for the first time the content of his gospel, using the language of justification (2:15–21). The works required by the law of Moses are not able to render sinners righteous. The only solution is to accept by †faith God's gift of justification founded on Christ's death for sinners.

Reflection and Application (2:19–21)

Ignorance of the gospel. The Christians of Galatia are not the only ones to get confused about the content of the gospel. Peter Kreeft, a professor of philosophy at Boston College, writes about the ignorance of many Catholics about how we are saved.

> The life of God comes into us by faith, through us by hope, and out of us by the works of love. . . . But many Catholics still have not learned this thoroughly Catholic and biblical doctrine. They think we're saved by good intentions, or being nice, or sincere, or trying a little harder, or doing a sufficient number of good deeds.[10]

Dr. Kreeft has asked hundreds of his students this pointed question: "If you should die tonight and God asks you why he should let you into heaven, what would you answer?" His findings? "The vast majority of them simply don't know the right answer to this, the most important of all questions, the very essence of Christianity. They usually don't even mention Jesus!"[11] Ralph Martin comments:

> In our efforts toward evangelization, we must be clear on the content and substance of the gospel message, or else the means chosen and the results obtained will be quite ambiguous. While programs, plans and processes of evangelization are important, clarity of content is indispensable. What has been *revealed* to us

10. Peter Kreeft, "Luther, Faith, and Good Works," *National Catholic Register*, November 10, 1991, 8.
11. Peter Kreeft, "Protestants Bring Personal Touch to the Life of Faith," *National Catholic Register*, April 24, 1994, 1, 7.

about what it means to be a Christian? What is the *truth* that God wants us to communicate to others? In short, what is the gospel message?[12]

The basis of our justification.[13] To justify sinners means not only to forgive their sins but also to make them truly righteous before God. The Apostle explains that the only way to obtain this justification is by faith in Jesus. Keeping the law is not enough to transform a sinner into a righteous person, because the law is unable to change a person's deeply wounded interior life.

The law can command only from outside. However, the grace of Christ works in the intimate interior of a human being, bringing him or her to righteousness and holiness before God. For this reason the Apostle can say, "It is no longer I who live, but Christ who lives in me; and the life I now live in the flesh I live by faith in the Son of God, who loved me and gave himself for me" (2:20 RSV).

The certainty of Christ's love for me. No matter how often people say, "Jesus loves you," or "Christ died for you," it is not uncommon for a person to wonder deep down whether that statement is really true. It is easier to imagine that Christ loves humanity and died for the sins of the world than to believe that he died for me. Or a person may accept this truth in theory but find it hard to grasp its personal significance. St. Paul's extraordinary testimony in 2:20 can help, if we invite the Holy Spirit to enlighten our hearts. Paul has come to realize that Jesus' death on the cross was not just for humanity as a whole but rather was a voluntary offering of Christ's life for him personally despite his grave sins (1 Cor 15:9; Gal 1:13; 1 Tim 1:15), and not only for him, but for every person who has ever lived. Because he is the infinite Son of God who knew us before we were born, he was able to offer himself for each one of us. When we are tempted to wonder whether Christ really loves us, the place to look is not inside ourselves to feelings that come and go, but rather beyond ourselves to the cross of Christ, the irrefutable proof of Jesus' love for you and me. Christ's words at the Last Supper, repeated in the Eucharist, are properly understood as addressed personally to each of us: "Take this, all of you, and eat of it, for this is my Body, which will be given up for you." Our response is equally personal: "Lord, I am not worthy that you should enter under my roof, but only say the word and my soul shall be healed."

---

12. This reflection is from "What Is Our Message?," in *John Paul II and the New Evangelization*, ed. Ralph Martin and Peter S. Williamson (Cincinnati: St. Anthony Messenger, 2006), 18.

13. This reflection is taken from Cardinal Albert Vanhoye, *Le letture bibliche delle Domeniche, Anno C* (Rome: Apostolato della Preghiera, 2014), 216.

Part 2

Arguments from Christian Experience and from Scripture

Galatians 3:1–5:12

Three Quick Arguments for Faith over Works of the Law

Galatians 3:1–18

After a sharp conclusion to the first part of the letter (2:21), Paul begins the second part with words that sting: "O stupid Galatians! Who has bewitched you?" (3:1). He follows up with a series of †rhetorical questions about his readers' Christian experience to support his insistent statement about †justification in 2:16. The Galatians did not receive the Spirit as a consequence of doing the works required by the †law, but as a consequence of believing in the †gospel when it was preached to them (3:2–5). Finally, Paul confirms their experience with a scriptural argument based on the example of Abraham (3:6–14) and the promises made to him long before the law was given (3:15–18).

An Argument from Christian Experience (3:1–6)

¹O stupid Galatians! Who has bewitched you, before whose eyes Jesus Christ was publicly portrayed as crucified? ²I want to learn only this from you: did you receive the Spirit from works of the law, or from faith in what you heard? ³Are you so stupid? After beginning with the Spirit, are you now ending with the flesh? ⁴Did you experience so many things in vain?—if indeed it was in vain. ⁵Does, then, the one who supplies the Spirit to you and works mighty deeds among you do so from works of the law or from faith in what you heard? ⁶Thus Abraham "believed God, and it was credited to him as righteousness."

OT: Gen 15:6
NT: Rom 10:17; 1 Cor 1:23; 12:10

The second part of the letter begins with a kind of volcanic eruption. As he was explaining that no one is †justified by works of the †law in 2:15–21, Paul was thinking of the Galatians who were foolishly taking the opposite position and rejecting the generous gift of God, thus making Christ's death futile (see 2:21). In 3:1 Paul explodes. He vehemently reproves the Galatians and quickly poses an urgent series of five †rhetorical questions.

In verse 6 Paul confirms the implicit answer to his rhetorical questions, in effect supplying the response the Galatians ought to give. The Galatians should respond, "We received the gifts of God not by practicing the law—we did not even know the law—but by receiving the proclamation of the gospel with faith." Paul notes that such a spiritual experience corresponds to what Scripture says about the foundation of Abraham's relationship with God: "Abram put his faith in the LORD, who attributed it to him as an act of righteousness" (Gen 15:6). The testimony of Scripture verifies the pattern of the Galatians' spiritual experience.

3:1   Paul's words here are harsh. Instead of saying "brothers and sisters" or "beloved ones," Paul uses their regional name, **Galatians**, and precedes it with the pejorative adjective **stupid** or foolish, the opposite of wise.[1] The perspective is identical to that of the reproof at the beginning of the letter (1:6), and the reasons are the same. What Paul expressed there with the verb "amazed" he now expresses with a question that emphasizes the irrationality of the Galatians' position: **Who has bewitched you?** What sorcerer has befuddled your minds? The Galatians' attitude is not at all in line with the †gospel proclamation they received, which highlighted the love of Christ manifested by his passion and death "for our sins" (1:4; 2:21). Paul's preaching, in fact, was wholly concentrated on "Christ crucified" (see 1 Cor 1:23). His language is literally graphic: **Jesus Christ was publicly portrayed** (Greek *prographō*) **as crucified** before their eyes, as if to say, "We painted a picture for you of Jesus' passion and death." Contemplating Christ on the cross should have guarded the Galatians from wandering off the right path and kept them focused on what it is that brought them salvation.

3:2   With a kind of †rhetorical flourish, Paul presents himself as an inquirer who wants **to learn** something from them, something so important that it should be sufficient to resolve the whole issue: **Did you receive the Spirit from works of the law . . . ?** The Galatians surely knew the answer, because Paul refers to an experience they had at the beginning of their Christian life. Something

---

1. Other instances of the same word in Scripture include Prov 17:28 †LXX; Sir 21:19; 42:8; Rom 1:14; 1 Tim 6:9; Titus 3:3. Jesus uses it to reprove the unbelief of the two disciples on the road to Emmaus (Luke 24:25).

happened that had made it clear that they had received the Spirit, although Paul does not specify how that was manifested. In Gal 4:6 he mentions a form of charismatic prayer, and it is likely that the Galatians experienced speaking in tongues and prophecy from the beginning of their lives as Christians.[2] In 5:22–23 Paul lists the "fruit of the Spirit," new qualities that appear in the lives of those who allow themselves to be led by the Holy Spirit: "love, joy, peace," and so on. However the Spirit manifested his presence among the Galatians, it was something evident, a fact that no one contested.

The point needing clarification is something else. What did the Galatians have to do to receive the Spirit? Paul poses only two alternatives: "works of the law" or **faith in what you heard**. We see here again the two alternatives presented by Gal 2:16 concerning the basis of †justification.

The Galatians have no choice but to respond to the questions Paul asks by saying, "We received the Spirit by faith in what we heard and not by works of the law." As pagans they did not even know the †law of Moses, and the requirement of keeping that law was not the message that Paul brought to them. Thus they had not fulfilled the works required by the law. They only needed to hear with †faith the proclamation of salvation through the crucified and risen Christ.

With his typical boldness Paul leads the Galatians to recognize that Christian life begins not with doing but with hearing and believing. Traditional ethical teaching says, "It is not enough to listen; conduct is what counts." Jesus had reasserted this principle in the conclusion of his Sermon on the Mount (Matt 7:24–27; see Luke 6:47–49). The Letter of James presents the same perspective (James 1:22–25). Paul himself speaks this way in Rom 2:13, and his exhortations are often along this line (Gal 6:3–4, 9–10; 2 Thess 3:6–13). Although generally valid, when it comes to entry into Christian life this traditional rule does not apply. At the beginning, the fundamental disposition necessary is a receptive one, to believe in the good news, to accept God's gracious gift of justification in baptism. The indwelling Holy Spirit is a divine gift and not the result of any human work. Once the Holy Spirit has been received, then conduct based on faith and the power of the Spirit becomes possible (see Gal 5:6, 16, 25).

Paul denounces the contradictory position the Galatians manifest by their **3:3** wanting to place the †law at the foundation of their lives. **Are you so stupid? After beginning with the Spirit**, whom they received by hearing with †faith, they should have followed through on a path that was consistent with that

---

2. Acts attests to such experiences in connection with Christian initiation (Acts 8:14–19; 10:45–46; 19:6), while Paul's letters mention charisms as a normal aspect of the life of his churches (Rom 12:6–8; 1 Cor 12; 14; 1 Thess 5:19–21).

What Does Paul Mean by "Faith"?

BIBLICAL BACKGROUND

When Paul speaks of the †faith that †justifies (Gal 2:16) and of the "faith in what you heard" that resulted in the Galatian Christians receiving the Holy Spirit (3:2, 5), he is not describing mere mental assent to doctrine (see commentary on 2:20). Instead he is referring to a †grace-enabled response to preaching, an inspired conviction that Jesus really is the Son of God who died for our sins, rose from the dead, and is coming again to give us eternal life in the kingdom of God. It is characterized by personal trust *in* God and *in* Jesus; a confidence in all that they have promised, including the promise of the Holy Spirit; and a willing surrender to all that God may ask, what Paul elsewhere calls "the obedience of faith" (Rom 1:5; 16:26).

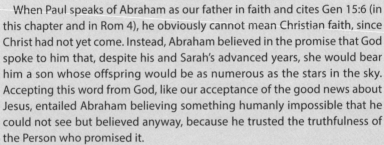

When Paul speaks of Abraham as our father in faith and cites Gen 15:6 (in this chapter and in Rom 4), he obviously cannot mean Christian faith, since Christ had not yet come. Instead, Abraham believed in the promise that God spoke to him that, despite his and Sarah's advanced years, she would bear him a son whose offspring would be as numerous as the stars in the sky. Accepting this word from God, like our acceptance of the good news about Jesus, entailed Abraham believing something humanly impossible that he could not see but believed anyway, because he trusted the truthfulness of the Person who promised it.

The word "faith"[a] belongs to the vocabulary of personal relationship. The word is used to refer both to the trust or confidence that someone places in another person and to the faithfulness or trustworthiness of that other person. A sound relationship is characterized by faith and faithfulness on the part of both parties. Faith in God or in Jesus first means placing our trust in him, believing his promises in Scripture and in the †gospel, and entrusting our lives to him. At the same time, Christian faith entails faithfulness to God—Father, Son, and Spirit—that is expressed in loyalty and obedience (see the sidebar, "'Faith in Christ' or 'the Faithfulness of Christ'?," p. 86).

a. Greek *pistis*.

beginning, keeping their attention on Jesus crucified and risen, continuing to put faith in their union with Christ as the foundation of their right relationship with God. Instead they are trying to advance on a different basis, keeping the law of Moses, and therefore they are **now ending with the flesh**. By means of this powerful antithesis, Paul wants them to understand that people who put their trust in the works of the law are trusting in their own strength, which is only human and †fleshly and bound to fail (Jer 17:5–6). Furthermore, several precepts of the law that the †Judaizers are urging on them are fleshly in another sense—namely, they pertain only to the body: circumcision (see Gen 17:10–13; Lev 12:3; Gal 5:2–6) and prohibitions of various foods. These are likely the specific observances Paul has in mind, because they erect a barrier between Jewish and †Gentile Christians.

Paul asks, **Did you experience so many things in vain?** The spiritual ex-   3:4
perience of the Galatians had been very rich. The verb translated "experience" can refer to every kind of experience, including those that are painful.[3] In 1 Thessalonians Paul speaks of the Thessalonians "receiving the word in great affliction, with joy from the holy Spirit" (1 Thess 1:6). It is likely the Galatians had similar experiences—which would count for nothing on the path they are choosing, because relying on the works of the †law creates an obstacle to the action of the Holy Spirit (Gal 2:21; 3:3). The next phrase is obscure: **if indeed it was in vain!** This NABRE translation expresses Paul's hope that the Galatians will not continue on that misguided path and their Christian life can be salvaged.[4]

Then Paul says, **Does, then, the one who supplies the Spirit to you and**   3:5
works mighty deeds among you do so from works of the law or from faith in what you heard? Here Paul sums up the argument in verses 2–4 but introduces a new element. Paul speaks not only of the initial gift of the Spirit received in the past but also of the Galatians' continuing relationship with God, who generously supplies the Spirit and works mighty signs and wonders in the community of believers. Paul speaks often of miracles in the life of the Church (Rom 15:19; 1 Cor 12:10, 28, 29); here he is so confident of his readers' experience of the Holy Spirit and the Spirit's miraculous power that he uses this remarkable fact to make the point that this activity of the Spirit stems from †faith in the †gospel rather than observance of the †law of Moses.

Although, strictly speaking, verse 6 begins a new scriptural argument (3:6–14)   3:6
for faith as the basis of justification, it follows closely what has just been said about the gift of the Spirit.

Paul quotes Gen 15:6 (**Thus Abraham "believed God, and it was credited to him as righteousness"**) to confirm from Scripture what he has just shown

---

3. Elsewhere in the NT, this verb (Greek *paschō*) is commonly translated "suffer," leading the ESV to render this phrase, "Did you suffer so many things in vain?"

4. Another possibility would be to interpret the phrase as "if *only* it was in vain," hinting that his readers' present course could result in a situation that is worse than before (see Gal 5:4). A person who has received †grace and has then been unfaithful to it falls to a lower condition than the person who has not yet received grace. "The last condition of that person is worse than the first" (Matt 12:45; see 2 Pet 2:20–22).

the Galatians from their experience—namely, that the basis of Christian life is hearing with †faith rather than observing the †law. According to Gen 15, God did not command Abraham anything in that encounter; rather, God made him a promise of descendants more numerous than the stars in the sky, something that would have been hard for an elderly, childless man to believe! It was an unconditional promise: Abraham was not given any law to keep or task to accomplish. The only question was whether he would have faith in God's word, and Abraham believed God. Similarly for the Galatians, at the time of their conversion all they needed to do was to believe the word of God that was spoken to them, and that is what they did.

What is the connection between "righteousness" in Gen 15:6 and †justification for a Christian? First, as we mentioned earlier, the terms used in the Greek are forms of the same word: to be justified (*dikaiomai*) is to be judged or made righteous (*dikaios*; see the sidebar, "What Does It Mean to Be Justified?," pp. 82–83). But there is more. In Scripture "righteousness" is more than conformity to a standard of conduct: it describes a relationship between persons. One who is righteous before God is one whose attitude and actions make a harmonious relationship with God possible. Thus Gen 15:6 means that Abraham's faith placed him in harmony with God. Although Paul greatly deepens the biblical teaching on the significance of faith, his teaching is firmly rooted in the Old Testament.[5]

As a consequence of faith, Abraham was accounted righteous, and as a consequence of faith, the Galatians received the Spirit. This raises a question. Is there a connection between these two gifts, justification and the Spirit? The issue is so clear to Paul that he does not feel the need to make it explicit. The Holy Spirit is received in the same way that righteousness was credited to Abraham *because justification (being made righteous) and the gift of the Spirit are intrinsically linked.* To demonstrate that "a person is not justified by the works of the law but through faith" (Gal 2:16), Paul shows that the gift of the Spirit is received by hearing with faith and not by works of the law. Then to confirm this he has recourse to a text that does not mention the Holy Spirit but speaks of "righteousness" (Gen 15:6). In this way Paul reveals his conviction that it is

---

5. E.g., Isa 7:9; 12:2; 28:16. Although Paul's teaching is grounded in the Jewish Scriptures, under ordinary circumstances it would not have occurred to Jews in Paul's day that Gen 15:6 could suggest an opposition between faith and works. For instance, 1 Macc 2:52 takes the phrase from Gen 15:6 that God "credited [it] to him as righteousness" and refers this statement to the incident in which Abraham was commanded to sacrifice Isaac (Gen 22), in which his obedience was understood as faith in action (see James 2:21). The erroneous teaching in Galatia, however, enables Paul to grasp a deeper meaning in Gen 15:6—namely, the priority of believing, of the act of faith, over other actions that necessarily follow. Both interpretations of Gen 15:6 are biblical; understood properly in their contexts, they complement rather than contradict one another.

the Holy Spirit who justifies believers (made explicit in 1 Cor 6:11).[6] Justification is not a merely judicial act by God; it entails the impartation of spiritual power that enables a person to live a new way of life that is pleasing to God. The external manifestation of the Holy Spirit through visible gifts is evidence of the Spirit entering into believers and justifying them.

Reflection and Application (3:2–5)

Paul's argument in Gal 3:2–5 raises questions about the experience of the Holy Spirit in the Church today. Paul takes for granted that the Galatian Christians were aware of having powerfully experienced the Spirit at the time of their conversion. If Paul were to ask the members of your parish, "Does he who supplies the Spirit to you and works miracles among you do so by works of the law, or by hearing with faith?" (3:5 RSV), would anyone understand his question? Or would people respond, "What miracles?" or "What do you mean, 'supplies the Spirit'?"

Because most Catholics were baptized as infants and confirmed while still very young, and because few come to the sacraments of initiation seeking or expecting to experience the Holy Spirit, many have not experienced receiving the Spirit as a life-changing event. Although they received the grace of the Holy Spirit through baptism and confirmation, many did not experience the full fruitfulness of the sacraments at the time because the dispositions of faith, repentance, understanding, and desire were lacking (see Catechism 1131).[7] For some, the dispositions conducive to the full fruitfulness of the sacraments come later, perhaps through a movement in the Church or through participation in a vital parish.

Recent popes have encouraged Catholics to seek and cultivate the work of the Spirit in their lives, both for the sake of their own relationship with God and for the sake of the Church's mission. On the eve of Pentecost 1998, St. John Paul II exhorted the faithful,

Today, I would like to cry out to all of you gathered here in St. Peter's Square and to all Christians: Open yourselves docilely to the gifts of the Spirit! Accept

6. After naming patterns of unrighteous conduct that exclude a person from the kingdom of God, Paul declares: "That is what some of you used to be; but now you have had yourselves washed, you were sanctified, *you were justified in the name of the Lord Jesus Christ and in the Spirit of our God*" (1 Cor 6:11, italics added).

7. See Ralph Martin, "The Post-Christendom Sacramental Crisis: The Wisdom of Thomas Aquinas," *Nova et Vetera*, English ed., 11, no. 1 (2013): 57–75.

gratefully and obediently the charisms which the Spirit never ceases to bestow on us! Do not forget that every charism is given for the common good, that is, for the benefit of the whole Church.[8]

On Pentecost 2008, Pope Benedict XVI encouraged Christians, "Let us redis-cover, dear brothers and sisters, the beauty of being baptized in the Holy Spirit; let us recover awareness of our Baptism and our Confirmation, ever timely sources of grace."[9] In 2014, Pope Francis spoke to almost fifty-three thousand people gathered in the Olympic stadium in Rome for the national conference of the Italian Renewal in the Spirit movement: "You . . . have received a great gift of the Lord. You were born of the will of the Spirit as 'a current of grace in the Church and for the Church.' . . . I expect from you that you share with all, in the Church, the grace of Baptism in the Holy Spirit."[10]

The good news is that God is still eager to supply his Spirit to his people and to work miracles among us. Jesus' words in Luke 11:9–13 explain how and provide a promise on which to base expectant faith: "Ask and you will receive; seek and you will find; knock and the door will be opened to you. . . . If you then, who are wicked, know how to give good gifts to your children, how much more will the Father in heaven give the holy Spirit to those who ask him?"[11]

Scriptural Argument: The Faith of Abraham and Blessing for the Gentiles (3:7–14)

[7]**Realize then that it is those who have faith who are children of Abraham.
[8]Scripture, which saw in advance that God would justify the Gentiles by faith, foretold the good news to Abraham, saying, "Through you shall all the nations be blessed." [9]Consequently, those who have faith are blessed along with Abraham who had faith. [10]For all who depend on works of the law are under a curse; for it is written, "Cursed be everyone who does not**

8. See "Holy Father's Speech for the World Congress of Ecclesial Movements and New Communi-ties," May 27, 1998, http://www.vatican.va/roman_curia/pontifical_councils/laity/documents/rc_pc_laity_doc_27051998_movements-speech-hf_en.html.

9. See *Regina Caeli*, Solemnity of Pentecost 2008, May 11, 2008, at https://w2.vatican.va/content/benedict-xvi/en/angelus/2008/documents/hf_ben-xvi_reg_20080511_pentecoste.html.

10. "Pope Francis' Comments and Address at Charismatic Renewal Convention," ZENIT, June 3, 2014, available at https://zenit.org/articles/pope-francis-comments-and-address-at-charismatic-renew al-convention/.

11. Programs such as the Life in the Spirit Seminar, the Alpha Course, and ChristLife have helped approximately 150 million Catholics to experience the power of the Holy Spirit by fostering the disposi-tions that enable the grace of the sacraments to be released and by prayer with the laying on of hands.

persevere in doing all the things written in the book of the law." [11]And that no one is justified before God by the law is clear, for "the one who is righteous by faith will live." [12]But the law does not depend on faith; rather, "the one who does these things will live by them." [13]Christ ransomed us from the curse of the law by becoming a curse for us, for it is written, "Cursed be everyone who hangs on a tree," [14]that the blessing of Abraham might be extended to the Gentiles through Christ Jesus, so that we might receive the promise of the Spirit through faith.

OT: Gen 12:3; 15:6; Lev 18:5; Deut 27:26; Isa 53:4–5; Hab 2:4
NT: Rom 1:17; 4:16; 1 Cor 1:18–25; Eph 1:13
Catechism: only Jesus perfectly fulfills the law, 578, 580; Abraham's offspring, 706

After verse 5 Paul stops posing †rhetorical questions. From 3:6 to 4:7 we have a doctrinal argument based on texts from the Old Testament. It is not easy to follow the logic of his presentation, because Paul is passionate and does not take time to indicate all the steps in his thinking. In addition, he does not always complete one topic before beginning another but moves unexpectedly from one to another and then returns to an earlier subject because his arguments are intertwined. For example, the topic of sonship appears in 3:7, suddenly disappears, and then returns as an aside in 3:16, only to be taken up again in 3:19, 26, 29.

Paul's doctrinal presentation here (3:7–14—although it actually begins with 3:6) concerns the relationship between †faith and †law, and those are the words that appear most frequently. One can seek to base one's relationship with God on either faith or law, but not both. Paul shows that these two principles are mutually exclusive and that the only valid principle is faith.

Having just quoted Genesis about Abraham (3:6), Paul draws a surprising conclusion: **Realize then that it is those who have faith who are children of Abraham**. The reference to those who have †faith (literally, "those who are *from* faith") continues the theme of the previous section and refers to people whose relationship with God is based on faith. They stand in contrast to "all who depend on works of the †law" (literally, "those who are *from* works of the law," 3:10). The second part of the sentence, however, introduces a new theme, that of being children of Abraham. Paul will return to it later using different language, speaking of the offspring or "descendant" of Abraham in 3:16, 19, and 29. Only then will it be clear why Paul brought it up, but we will state it right away: the underlying question is, Who gets to share in Abraham's †inheritance? For first-century Jews, Abraham's inheritance did not just refer to the land of Israel but also symbolized the blessings of the age to come (see the

3:7

sidebar, "What Is Abraham's Inheritance?"). The question of who shares in this inheritance was probably raised by the †Judaizers. Since God's promises were made to Abraham and his children, the inheritance will be given to them, not to others. Consequently, the decisive question was, How does a person enter into Abraham's family? According to Gen 17:13–14, for males the indispensable means of participating in the †covenant is circumcision, which brings with it the obligation to observe the law of Moses. In this way the position of the Judaizers—that †Gentile Galatian believers needed to be circumcised—was firmly established. Paul is in a hurry to refute that argument, and for this reason he immediately declares that faith rather than circumcision and works of the law is what makes people children of Abraham.

What kind of relationship with Abraham is Paul talking about when he speaks of Abraham's "children"? In the Bible there are a variety of literal and metaphorical senses in which people can be referred to as the children of someone else. What kind of children is Paul talking about? For instance, the Wisdom books often use the term "son" to refer to a disciple of a teacher of wisdom (see, e.g., Prov 1:8, 10, 15). In Hebrew thought, "son of" or "child of" can mean one who resembles or acts like another. Jesus calls his opponents children of the devil, because their acts and intentions are like the devil's (John 8:39–44). The context indicates that Paul has in mind a sonship of imitation: Abraham believed; whoever believes is like Abraham and is a son or daughter of Abraham in that sense. In Romans, Paul will insist that believers are children of Abraham because their faith is like his (see Rom 4:11–12, 16–18).

The question remains, however, whether a sonship of imitation, a kind of spiritual sonship, is enough to give a person access to the inheritance of Abraham. The Judaizers maintained it did not. They could argue that Scripture strongly insists on the necessity of a physical link. In the very promise God gave Abraham in Gen 15, it was specified that the heir would not be a foreigner but that "your own offspring will be your heir" (Gen 15:4). So Paul's declaration in this verse that those who have faith are the sons and daughters of Abraham is not yet sufficient to settle the matter. Consequently, the Apostle will return to the question of Abraham's children later and will take pains to show also a physical link between Abraham and Gentile Christians (see Gal 3:16, 29). For the moment, however, he simply affirms that faith makes people children of Abraham, without exploring this in detail.

3:8   Paul now shifts his focus to consider another link between †Gentiles and Abraham. He quotes God's promise to Abraham: **Through you shall all the nations** (or "all the Gentiles") **be blessed.** Instead of focusing on the *problem*

What Is Abraham's Inheritance?

In ordinary English usage the word "†inheritance" refers to property that is transferred to someone upon the death of the owner. When inheritance is spoken of in the Bible, however, the emphasis falls less on the transfer of ownership and more on the manner in which property is possessed by the one who inherits—that is, on its being the permanent possession of an individual or family.

God promised the land of Canaan to Abraham and his descendants as their permanent possession (Gen 15:7, 18; Exod 32:13), and Scripture speaks of this promised land as Israel's inheritance (Deut 1:38; 4:21; Josh 11:23) and each tribe or family's allotted portion as their inheritance (1 Kings 21:3; NABRE, "heritage").

By the time of Jesus many Jews understood that the promise of "the land" to Abraham and his descendants encompassed not only Canaan but ultimately the whole world at the end of history (Rom 4:13; see Matt 5:5; the Hebrew word for the "land" also means the "earth"). The first Christians understood that God began to fulfill his promise by bestowing the whole world on Abraham's descendant, †Messiah Jesus, the king and embodiment of faithful Israel (Matt 28:18; Gal 3:16), who will take full possession of the earth when he returns in glory. Jews and †Gentiles who believe in Christ have become coheirs through their union with him in †faith and baptism (Gal 3:26–29). They will enjoy the fullness of the inheritance at the resurrection, when they fully possess eternal life in the kingdom of God. In the meantime, many of the benefits of the inheritance—life, righteousness, peace, joy, blessing (Rom 14:17)—are available now through the gift of the Spirit, "the first installment of our inheritance" (Eph 1:13–14; see 2 Cor 1:22).

---

of establishing a relationship between Gentiles and Abraham that the †Judaizers' position presupposed, Paul presents a positive perspective. He is able to do this easily because the first statement in the Bible about the relationship between "the †nations" and Abraham is positive. At the very beginning of Genesis's account of the story of Abraham, the Bible records God's promise: "All the families of the earth will find blessing in you" (Gen 12:3). This promise is repeated several times, with the word "families" replaced by "nations" (Gen 18:18; 22:18; 26:4), the same word commonly translated "Gentiles."

Paul interprets Gen 12:3 in a surprising way. Although †justification is not even mentioned, Paul introduces his quotation of Genesis by declaring that Scripture **saw in advance that God would justify the Gentiles by faith**. Thus

Paul identifies the blessing promised to the nations with their justification by
†faith.

To understand Paul's thinking here, it is necessary to remember that blessing
in the Bible never refers merely to good wishes. Rather, God's blessing always
entails his bestowing some real benefit. Consequently, "All the families of the
earth will find blessing in you" (Gen 12:3) promises that the Gentiles will participate in some way in Abraham's privileged relationship with God.

To clarify this relationship, Paul implicitly links Gen 12:3 with Gen 15:6,
which he quoted at Gal 3:6 above ("Abraham 'believed God, and it was credited
to him as righteousness'"). In Gen 12:2, God says to Abraham, "I will bless
you." It is not yet an actual blessing but only a promise of blessing. Paul sees the
first fulfillment of this promise in Gen 15:6, which affirms that God counted
Abraham's faith as righteousness. And this blessing of righteousness is based
not on any work of Abraham's but on the fact that he believed in the word of
God. The person who obtains a good and right relationship with God in Gen
15:6 is "Abraham who had faith" (Gal 3:9); he does not rely on his own ability
to accomplish something but on the absolute trustworthiness of God.

Since the blessing promised to the Gentiles is a share in Abraham's relationship with God (Gen 12:3), that blessing will consist in God's accounting them
righteous through faith, just as he did for Abraham. This explains how Paul can
declare that the promise in Gen 12:3 was prophetic of God's plan to justify the
Gentiles through faith (Gal 3:8). His declaration is based on the relationship of
these two texts (Gen 12:3; 15:6) and on the experience of his apostolic ministry
among Gentiles, which manifested the fulfillment of the ancient promise. God's
promise that "all the families of the earth will find blessing in you" (Gen 12:3)
meant that they would come to share in Abraham's harmonious relationship
with God, and this was perfectly fulfilled when the forgiveness of sins and all
the other benefits of justification were offered to all nations through faith in
Christ, who died for the salvation of all. Paul thus recognizes Gen 12:3 as an
early announcement of his †gospel: God **foretold the good news to Abraham**,
or more literally, "God evangelized Abraham in advance."

3:9   Paul's conclusion reinforces the point: **Consequently, those who have faith
are blessed along with Abraham who had faith**. Since in Gen 15:6 the one who
is blessed by God is Abraham, who believed, the way to share in his blessing
is to be a believer like him.

3:10   At first glance one might think that Paul changes the subject between verses 9
and 10, since the vocabulary is completely different. In reality, however, there
is a close connection expressed through antithesis. "Those who have faith" in

verse 9 stand in contrast to **all who depend on works of the law** in verse 10. Those who "are blessed" (v. 9) stand in contrast to those who **are under a curse** (v. 10). With this contrast Paul returns to his polemic against the †Judaizers, who want to impose the †law of Moses on the Galatians.

Paul distinguishes two mutually exclusive categories. On one side are those who have †faith, whether they are Jews or †Gentiles, and are blessed with Abraham. On the other side are all those who rely on the works of the law, whatever their ethnic origin, who are under a curse. It is clear that Paul is warning about the perilous situation of the Judaizers and the Galatians who are inclined to follow them.

A few nuances in the text should be noted. Paul does *not* say, "Those who keep the law are cursed," which would directly contradict the Old Testament (e.g., Deut 28:1–14). Rather, he says, "all who depend on [literally, are *from*] works of the law are under a curse." The difference is crucial.

The phrase to be "*from* works of the law" reveals the crux of the issue, which has to do not with one's behavior but with the principle on which one hopes to be saved. It is possible to practice the law without depending on the works of the law. The issue is the starting point of one's relationship with God. From what, or on what basis, do I seek to be accepted by God? From my works in keeping with the law? Or from my faith in the person and work of Christ? Paul's warning in verse 10 is aimed at those who make their conduct the foundation of their relationship with God.

Paul also avoids saying that followers of the law are cursed. He says they "are under a curse," which is a more nuanced statement. Paul would not say that the law curses those who observe it, because that would be false. The law promises them multiple blessings (see Deut 28:1–13). However, Paul is pointing out that the law contains the threat of curses and that people who live under the regime of the law find themselves exposed to that danger.

To prove his point, he quotes Deut 27:26, which concludes a series of no less than twelve curses. Paul quotes from the †Septuagint version, which gives the verse a broad scope by its use of two words that express completeness: **Cursed be *everyone* who does not persevere in doing *all* the things written in the book of the law** (italics added).[12] Incurring curses is practically inevitable for those who live under the law, for according to the text, to avoid a curse one needs to be faithful to all the numerous prescriptions of the law. James 2:10 observes, "Whoever keeps the whole law, but falls short in one particular, has

---

12. The Septuagint says, "all the words of this law" (Deut 27:26 †LXX), but Paul has replaced "words of this law" with "things written in the book of the law," similar to the wording in Deut 29:19, 20, 26.

become guilty in respect to all of it" (see also Gal 5:3). To maintain continual, perfect observance of the whole law seems humanly impossible. Paul's argument is forceful.

3:11–12   If verses 11–12 were skipped, the reader could pass smoothly from verse 10 to verse 13, since both verses talk about curses. According to verse 10, the †law sets out a curse, and according to verse 13 Christ has set us free from this curse. However, in between, Paul felt the need to return to the theme of †justification and to give scriptural proof of what he asserted in 2:16 but did not demonstrate—namely, that the law does not bring justification. The proof he offers is also useful to complete the discussion on the blessing and the curse. If the law is incapable of making a sinner righteous, it will not be able to bring blessings to anyone, since the law promises blessing only to righteous people who keep God's commandments (Deut 28:1–2).

His demonstration occurs in a long sentence that contrasts the principle of †faith with the principle of works. We can express the logic of the sentence in this way: "It is clear that no one can be made righteous before God (i.e., justified) by the law, because the righteous †live on the basis of *faith*, whereas the law operates on the basis of *works*."

Paul's argument is based on a contrast of two statements in the Old Testament that share the phrase "shall live":

You shall therefore keep my statutes and my ordinances, *by doing* which a man *shall live*. (Lev 18:5 RSV [italics added])

Behold, he whose soul is not upright in him shall fail, / but the righteous *shall live by* his *faith*. (Hab 2:4 RSV [italics added])

These verses establish different foundations for life. According to Leviticus the foundation is keeping the law, doing rather than believing, while for Habakkuk the foundation is faith, from which comes righteousness.[13] This contrast of foundations serves to demonstrate Paul's thesis that there is a fundamental difference between the principle of law and that of faith, and since righteousness comes through faith, it cannot be attained by relying on the law.

Paul has distinguished two different approaches to relationship with God. On one side there is that of the law, in which people attempt to establish their worth

13. Many texts in the Old Testament insist on the necessity of performing certain actions in order to live (e.g., Deut 4:1; 6:24; 30:16; Neh 9:29; Ezek 20:11). The seeming contradiction between what many Old Testament texts say about the law and the lesson Paul draws from Hab 2:4 remains to be resolved. Paul addresses it in Gal 3:19–4:7.

on the basis of their own works but cannot get beyond their limitations. On the other side there is that of faith, in which people transcend themselves since they renounce trusting in what they can do and accept instead the foundation God offers, which is Christ the Son of God, who died and rose for our salvation.

From this we can see that the system of the law is not only a dangerous system because of the risk of a curse if one does not succeed at keeping all the requirements of the law. It is also intrinsically defective because it confines human beings within the limits of their own striving. Paul summons his readers to make a clear choice.

Verses 13–14 express the mystery of redemption with typical Pauline bold-   **3:13–14**
ness. **Christ ransomed us from the curse of the law by becoming a curse for us**. The sentence is long and overloaded because Paul wanted to insert a proof from Scripture; it is paradoxical because redemption is achieved by someone "becoming a curse." One might think that someone who becomes a curse could contaminate others. How is it then that Christ, by becoming a curse, has thereby freed us from the curse? The paradox continues in the clause that follows. Christ became a curse so that **the blessing of Abraham might be extended to the Gentiles** through him. It seems completely illogical: blessing comes from a curse?

Paul's paradoxical description of Christ's achievement evokes amazement and wonder at the plan of God, which completely surpasses human invention. The meaning of the cross of Christ comes to our attention not as a carefully balanced philosophical insight but as a fact that overturns every merely human idea. It is the divine foolishness that is wiser than human calculations, a stumbling block to human wisdom; it is the divine weakness that alone is capable of bringing salvation, while all human acts of virtue taken together fail (see 1 Cor 1:18–25).

"Christ ransomed us." The Greek verb Paul uses[14] belonged not to the religious vocabulary of the †Septuagint but to the language of the marketplace. It meant "to buy back or to purchase"; "redeem" would be a more exact translation. Who is redeemed? The first-person plural "us" refers to Paul and his fellow Jews who were "bought back" from the curse of the †law because they were subject to it. However, the effect of this ransom is far-reaching: it was so that the blessing of Abraham might be extended to the †Gentiles. This shows that the situation of the Jews was decisive for all †nations. As long as they remained under the curse of the law, it was impossible for the blessing of Abraham to reach the nations. If, however, a way out could be found for the Jews, then a solution would be available for the Gentiles as well.

14. Greek *exagorazō*.

The boldest and most difficult point of Paul's declaration is the way this freedom from the curse of the law comes: it comes through Christ himself "becoming a curse." Paul offers scriptural proof from Deut 21:22–23, which concerns the practice of hanging the corpse of an executed criminal on a wooden pole in the sight of all to dissuade others from imitating his conduct: **it is written, "Cursed be everyone who hangs on a tree."**[15] Deuteronomy did not originally refer to crucifixion since the Israelites did not inflict that torture. However, the final state of a person whom the Romans crucified was the same: a corpse hanging on "a tree" (in Hebrew the same word means both "tree" and "wood"), and Jews of Jesus' day understood Deut 21:22–23 to speak of crucifixion.[16]

Paul does not include the words "of God" from the Hebrew text of Deut 21:23, nor does he include "by God" from the Septuagint. Paul's text suggests, then, that Christ took on himself the "curse of the law"—that is, the situation of a person guilty of the most serious crimes—but not the "curse of God." In Christ's case, the element of personal guilt that draws the curse of God is absent. Externally Christ became "a curse," but at the deepest level he was more than ever the Son united to the Father in obedience and love (see Gal 1:4). He took the curse on himself for others, "for us," and this radically changes the significance of Christ's being hanged on a tree and leads to a vastly more positive outcome (see Isa 53:4–5).

This result is defined in Gal 3:14 by two parallel clauses that complete one another. The first is so **that the blessing of Abraham might be extended to the Gentiles**. The second is **so that we might receive the promise of the Spirit** through †faith. In this way Paul suggests a close relationship between the blessing of Abraham and the promise of the Spirit. The two phrases that follow these clauses, **through Christ Jesus** and **through faith**, apply to both affirmations: the blessing of Abraham, which, as we have seen, is †justification, and the promised Spirit are received through Christ Jesus and through faith in him. At first glance Paul appears to indicate different recipients of these blessings. On the one hand, the *Gentiles* receive the blessing of Abraham, while on the other, *we* receive the Spirit. However, the difference is not as great as it seems, because the "we" includes both those Christians who belong to Israel by birth and those who are Gentiles ("the nations"). In fact, the beginning of the section (3:1–5) recalled that the Galatian Christians, who are Gentiles, have "received the Spirit."

15. The †Septuagint translates the verse a bit freely: "Whoever is hanged on a tree is *cursed by God*." Paul does not use the adjective "cursed" to characterize Christ; he uses the noun ("a curse") as the Hebrew text of Deut 21:23 does in its legislation.

16. See Joseph Fitzmyer, *To Advance the Gospel*, 2nd ed. (Grand Rapids: Eerdmans, 1998), 125–46.

The implication is that this marvelous result could not have been attained without removing the obstacle of the law, or more precisely, the curse of the law. The law was not an arbitrary imposition that could simply be ignored to find another path to salvation. The law revealed the true condition of human beings. It revealed that there was an obstacle to the attainment of the promised blessing—that is, human sinfulness. To save the human race, it was necessary for Christ to place himself in our predicament and find a way out. And he did so, paying the price of our redemption himself.

Reflection and Application (3:7–14)

It is hard for human beings to accept that they cannot save themselves, that they are not able to truly succeed simply by their own power. It is common, in fact, to see the opposite: to encounter people who think they can chart their course and achieve their life's goals all on their own without the help of other people or of God. Sometimes we Christians unconsciously adopt a similar attitude. We think that our self-discipline, our good habits, our devotional practices, and our determination to keep God's †law will see us through.

And yet human beings must choose between pride and love. If we try to save ourselves by trusting in our moral rectitude, doctrinal orthodoxy, or service to the Church or to the poor, we succumb to pride and are already defeated. St. Paul says very strongly: "All who depend on works of the law are under a curse," since the law says, "Cursed be everyone who does not persevere in doing all the things written in the book of the law" (3:10), and perfect observance is impossible for fallen human nature. What is true of the law of Moses is true of Christian standards of conduct as well. We fallen creatures need help, and those who accept help are on the path of the kingdom of love, since accepting being saved by Another opens a person to love.

In this way, †faith introduces us to love. This is a sequence that we can often use to our advantage. When we become aware of our weakness, when we fall short of our resolutions or fall into some sin, two reactions are possible. We can get upset with ourselves because we did not succeed, because we did not do that which we decided to do. This is our spontaneous reaction, but it is not helpful. Instead, we must take advantage of our weakness and of our stumbles to place our trust entirely in God. Rather than be surprised when we fall short, we ought to say to the Lord: "I did not rely sufficiently on you, and this is why I fell. I want to take the occasion of this fall to trust in you and not in myself."

In this way even our failures can help us progress in faith, in love, in humility, and in gratitude.[17]

Legal Argument: The Priority of the Promise over the Law (3:15–18)

---

[15]Brothers, in human terms I say that no one can annul or amend even a human will once ratified. [16]Now the promises were made to Abraham and to his descendant. It does not say, "And to descendants," as referring to many, but as referring to one, "And to your descendant," who is Christ. [17]This is what I mean: the law, which came four hundred and thirty years afterward, does not annul a covenant previously ratified by God, so as to cancel the promise. [18]For if the inheritance comes from the law, it is no longer from a promise; but God bestowed it on Abraham through a promise.

OT: Gen 12:7; 15:13, 18; Exod 12:40–41
NT: Rom 4:13
Catechism: Abraham's descendant, 706

Beginning with verse 15, the perspective changes. In the preceding section, Paul presented two possible principles on which to build one's relationship with God, either †faith or the †law, demonstrating that they are mutually exclusive and that the only valid principle is faith. Now the Apostle introduces a legal argument in the light of the history of salvation, which better allows us to understand the relationship between the two opposing principles.[18] Verse 16 is a digression that introduces a different line of argument, so we will treat it at the end of the exposition of these verses.

3:15   Now Paul introduces a new kind of argument. Instead of basing himself on the word of God, as in the preceding section (3:6–14), he now speaks **in human terms**, drawing on human experience. The Apostle clearly distinguishes between the two sources of knowledge. Reasoning based on human experience is not as compelling as a proof from Scripture (1 Cor 9:8), and at times Paul emphasizes the radical inadequacy of human reasoning (see 1 Cor 1:17; 2:1, 4). Here, however, he makes use of it. The Apostle is not willing to base the

17. Adapted from Cardinal Albert Vanhoye, *Il pane quotidiano della Parola: Commento alle letture feriali della Messa ciclo I e II* (Casale Monferrato: Piemme, 1994), 720–21.

18. Chronology takes on greater importance in this part of the argument and continues until 4:7 (see 3:17, 19, 23, 25; 4:1–4, 7).

content of Christian faith on human reasoning, but he is quite willing to put reason at the service of †faith.

In this instance Paul presents an argument based on legal principles and concerning a legal document—specifically a **will**—that has been **ratified**. The Greek word Paul uses, like English "will," means a person's final disposition of his or her possessions. In the †Septuagint the word used here for "will" (*diathēkē*) translated the Hebrew word for "covenant," in particular God's †covenant with his people.

After the testator dies, it is no longer legally possible to **annul or amend** the will's provisions. According to Genesis, God made Abraham certain solemn promises, referred to in Scripture as a covenant, which had the effective value of a will because the promises designate an †inheritance for Abraham and his posterity. Paul has in mind the account in Gen 15 in which God promises Abraham both a descendant who will be his heir and an inheritance. The account concludes, "On that day the Lord made a covenant [*diathēkē*] with Abram, saying, 'To your descendant I will give this land'" (Gen 15:18 †LXX).

Paul clarifies that this will was in force because God had ratified it (Gal 3:17). When Abraham asks God for a confirmation of his promises (Gen 15:8), God responds by carrying out a solemn ancient covenant †ritual, passing through animals that had been cut in half, making his commitment to Abraham irrevocable.[19]

Paul's argument unfolds in verses 17–18 in a clear and compelling manner **3:17–18** (we will comment on Paul's digression in v. 16 after examining these verses). If God made an irrevocable commitment, it was not possible to annul or modify it later. The **law** came too late, **four hundred and thirty years afterward**, Paul says, to **annul a covenant previously ratified by God, so as to cancel the promise**.[20] If receiving the †inheritance promised by God to Abraham's offspring depends on observing the †law of Moses, that would mean the law has nullified God's gift. If a man promises a woman a diamond necklace as an expression of his love, he cannot then ask her to pay for it! God's promise to Abraham was in the category of a generous gift. In Gen 15, God did not impose any obligation

19. See Gen 15:9–10, 17. According to ancient custom, the covenant parties passed between the slaughtered animals to invoke a curse on themselves should they ever violate the covenant (see Jer 34:18 for an example of God promising to enforce a covenant sealed in this manner). In the covenant with Abraham, only God passes between the animals, an expression of the Lord's unilateral commitment to fulfill this promise.

20. According to most English translations, which are based on the Hebrew text, 430 is the number of years that Israel was enslaved in Egypt (Exod 12:40). Paul, however, follows the †Septuagint version of that verse, which says that the period of 430 years includes both the time of the patriarchs in Canaan and the time of slavery in Egypt. Rabbinic tradition also calculates 430 years between God's commitment in Gen 15 and the departure from Egypt.

Figure 12. Moses by Lawrence the Monk (Piero di Giovanni; Italy, ca. 1408–10).

on Abraham as a condition for receiving the promised inheritance. The law of Moses cannot change that promise after it has been made, since that would be like sending someone a bill for a gift already given.

3:16   Now let us return to Paul's digression in verse 16, where he begins by recalling from Gen 15:18 that **the promises were made to Abraham and to his descendant**.[21] Paul inserts an explanation that is quite surprising. He observes that the word "descendant" (Greek *sperma*, "seed") is singular, not plural, and declares that this singular noun refers to **Christ**. This may seem contrived, because the singular, *sperma*, like the English "offspring," can have a collective meaning and describe all of a person's descendants. Nevertheless, Paul's interpretation

21. Other versions render the word translated "descendant" in v. 16 as "seed" (NIV), "offspring" (RSV, NRSV), or "progeny" (NJB).

has precedent. Greek authors usually employed *sperma* to refer to a singular descendant. More importantly, the biblical texts that speak of the promises made to Abraham *always* use the singular, while the offspring of other biblical characters are often referred to as "sons" in the plural.[22] For Paul this detail is full of significance because it corresponds to God's plan. The promises made by God to Abraham were meant to be fulfilled not through a diffuse progeny but through one particular descendant through whom all others would gain access to the blessings.

Thus in the story of Abraham, the focusing of the promises on one unique descendant is expressed in a striking manner. The promise to Abraham in Gen 15:18 is not a direct promise of an innumerable multitude of sons but a promise of a single son at the right time, who then would become a multitude. When Abraham is lamenting his lack of heirs, God responds, "Your own offspring will be your heir" (Gen 15:4). The story that follows shows that Isaac is that unique son; Ishmael is excluded (see Gen 21:10, 12). God puts Abraham to the test, asking him to sacrifice his only son (see Gen 22:2, 12, 16). The obedience of Abraham, who did not withhold his beloved son, resulted in having his only son returned and in receiving a solemn confirmation of the promises (see Gen 22:17–18). Isaac too received not the promised †inheritance but only another confirmation of the promise to Abraham for his posterity (see Gen 26:3–4). Thus the story was progressing toward another descendant of Abraham who would truly be the heir capable of conveying that inheritance and blessing to all. This other "unique son" is Christ.

Paul's interpretation of the promise to Abraham of a unique descendant is therefore not arbitrary, provided it is situated in the larger context of Scripture and is not presented as the exclusive meaning of Gen 15:18. The other aspect of the promise—a multitude of descendants—far from being denied, will be maintained and powerfully illuminated in Gal 3:29.

The theological import of Gal 3:1–18 is immense. It provides a biblical model of how Christian doctrine is to be proved, in that Paul's theological argument is founded on three distinct elements: (1) the decisive event of Christ's passion and the resurrection, (2) the spiritual experience that results from the proclamation of this event, and (3) the testimony of Scripture. The argument includes three short sections that support Paul's affirmation in 2:16 that †justification comes by †faith rather than by works of the †law. The first argues on the basis

---

22. For example, "Aaron and his sons" appears fourteen times in Exod 29. However, quite a few OT texts use *sperma* in the collective sense of offspring (e.g., Gen 19:32, 34; 24:60; Lev 21:15; Num 14:24).

of the Galatians' experience of faith (3:2–5). The other two make scriptural arguments. One points to the righteousness credited to Abraham because of his faith, combined with the promise that the †nations would find blessing in him (3:6–14); in it the Apostle contrasts the dynamism of faith with the system of the law, showing that they are mutually exclusive. The other demonstrates by a legal argument that God promised to bestow the inheritance on Abraham's descendant long before the law of Moses existed (3:15–18).

The Temporary Role of the Law, the Extraordinary Benefits of Faith

Galatians 3:19–29

After explaining the precedence of the promise over the †law because it came first (3:15–18), Paul now examines the function of the law and its relationship to †faith in Christ. He shows that the law had only a temporary role and now must yield its place to faith in Christ. Now that faith has come, we have become children of God in Christ Jesus, the offspring of Abraham, and heirs to the promise made to Abraham.

The Purpose and Origin of the Law (3:19–20)

---

¹⁹**Why, then, the law? It was added for transgressions, until the descendant came to whom the promise had been made; it was promulgated by angels at the hand of a mediator. ²⁰Now there is no mediator when only one party is involved, and God is one.**

OT: Exod 20:19
NT: Acts 7:38, 53; Rom 4:15; 5:13–14, 20; Heb 2:2

In verses 15–18, Paul showed that the †law could not change what God had already   **3:19** promised to Abraham. God's promises were fully valid before the promulgation of the law and remained valid after it. The question naturally arises, **Why, then, the law?** Paul says, **It was added**. In saying the law was *added*, he is taking a position against some Jewish traditions which held that God created the †Torah, the law,

Diverse Biblical Perspectives on the Law of Moses

BIBLICAL BACKGROUND

Not only does Paul challenge conventional Jewish understanding about the possibility of †justification through the †law of Moses; he seems to suggest that the law comes from angels rather than God (Gal 3:19–20), and he describes Israel's subjection to the law as slavery to the †elemental powers (4:3).

Paul is not the first biblical author to express reservations about the law, at least as it was commonly understood. Deuteronomy anticipates Israel's failure to keep the law, implicitly pointing to its failure as an institution and announcing a future day when God will circumcise the hearts of the Israelites (Deut 30:6). The prophets and some psalms question the value of sacrifices prescribed by the law apart from an obedient heart.[a] At the same time they anticipate the replacement of the written law by foretelling God's intention to inscribe his statutes on human hearts (Jer 31:33–34; see 2 Cor 3:3).

Speaking with some Pharisees, Jesus sets aside the law's regulation of divorce (Deut 24:1–4) by saying, "Because of the hardness of your hearts Moses allowed you to divorce your wives, but from the beginning it was not so" (Matt 19:8). In this conversation, both the Pharisees and Jesus attribute the content of the legislation about divorce to Moses, rather than directly to God. Jesus likewise calls into question the adequacy of the law as a guide for conduct with his antitheses in Matt 5:21–48, where he repeats five times, "You have

before everything else and used it as his instrument in creating the world.[1] Paul follows biblical history, in which the law does not appear until after the exodus and thus occupies a secondary position in relation to the promise made to Abraham.

The purpose that Paul ascribes to the law is surprising: it was added **for transgressions**. If Paul had used the word "sins," the phrase could mean that the law had been instituted *because* people were sinning and they did not know the right path. However, the word "transgress" means to act contrary to a law, so transgressions cannot exist before a law has been promulgated (Rom 4:15 RSV).

So the law was instituted "for transgressions." On the face of it, this is a paradoxical statement. A law is established to be obeyed, not to be transgressed. What does Paul mean? He certainly does not mean that people were innocent before the law and that God imposed on them a law that was impossible to keep in order to make them fall and then condemn them. This would be sadistic and contrary to God's love for human beings and his hatred of sin. Rather, Paul is

---

1. Some sages identified Torah with preexistent wisdom (Sir 24:1–23; *Pirkei Avot* 6.10).

heard that it was said . . . [citing the law or its common interpretation], but I say to you . . . [explaining his own teaching, addressing inner attitudes, or clarifying God's intention]."

Nevertheless, other biblical texts affirm the divine origin of the law of Moses and its enduring significance. The prophets constantly call Israel to keep God's law (Mal 3:22), while the psalmist praises its excellence (Pss 19:8–12; 119). Paul says, "All scripture is inspired by God and is useful for teaching" (2 Tim 3:16), undoubtedly including the law of Moses; he cites the law as a source of instruction in numerous instances (1 Cor 9:8–10; Eph 6:1–3; 1 Tim 1:8–11). In Rom 7:12 he declares that "the law is holy, and the commandment is holy and righteous and good." Jesus insists that he has come not to abolish the law but to fulfill it, and that "until heaven and earth pass away, not the smallest letter or the smallest part of a letter will pass from the law" (Matt 5:17–18).

Would Paul or Jesus *deny* that the †Torah, the law of Moses, came from God? Never! Many biblical texts firmly teach this truth. Rather, drawing attention to the mediating role of angels (Gal 3:19), a particular angel, or Moses, instead of God himself, is a way of indicating that something other than the written law of Moses should be prioritized—namely, what God has accomplished in Christ. Paul's teaching in Galatians that explains the function of the law to reveal sin and the law's temporary role until the coming of Christ helps us make sense of the diverse perspectives on the law expressed in the New Testament.[b]

a. Pss 40:7–8 [see Heb 10:5]; 51:16; Isa 1:11–17; Mic 6:6–8.
b. Gal 3:19, 21–25; 4:1–7; see also Rom 3:20; 5:13–14; 7:1–25.

convinced that before the law people were already in a state of sin (see Rom 5:13–14). The purpose of the law was *to transform sins into transgressions.* That way, the law could make sin obvious and reveal the true human condition, since sin is very capable of camouflaging itself. The law also reveals that sin deserves punishment by defining penalties for various transgressions.

Paul at once clarifies that the negative function of the law was not intended to be permanent but applies only to a temporary stage in salvation history. The goal was the fulfillment of the promise. The law counted only **until the descendant came**, the privileged offspring (Gen 12:7; 15:18) **to whom the promise had been made**, whom Paul identifies as Christ in Gal 3:16.

The sentence continues with two statements about how the law was instituted that have the effect of distancing the law from God. Paul makes his point so briefly that the interpretation of this verse is difficult and far from certain (one scholar, drawing on the number found in 3:17, laments that there are 430 different interpretations of this verse!). Although Exod 31:18 speaks of God himself giving the tablets of the law to Moses, Paul follows Jewish traditions, reflected elsewhere in the New Testament, in declaring that the law **was promulgated by angels**, meaning either that angels functioned as intermediaries to transmit the law or that they were its authors.[2] The direction of Paul's thought favors the second alternative: the law was instituted by the angels, in contrast to the promises that God made directly to Abraham (Gal 3:16–17).

Paul adds that the law was given **at the hand of a mediator**. The obvious first candidate who comes to mind as the mediator is Moses. However, the Bible presents Moses as a mediator between God and the people (Exod 20:18–21; Deut 5:5, 22–31), not as a mediator between angels and the people. Here Paul seems to be speaking about a particular angel who represents the group of angels who established the law and communicates its regulations to Moses (Acts 7:38, 53).

3:20   Paul continues: **Now there is no mediator when only one party is involved, and God is one.** If "mediator" here means a representative of a group, a mediator of this kind cannot be directly speaking for God, because God is not a group. Although he refrains from stating it explicitly, Paul seems to be implying that God was involved only indirectly in the giving of the †law (see the sidebar, "Diverse Biblical Perspectives on the Law of Moses," pp. 120–21).[3]

What Law Can and Cannot Do (3:21–22)

---

[21]Is the law then opposed to the promises [of God]? Of course not! For if a law had been given that could bring life, then righteousness would in reality come from the law. [22]But scripture confined all things under the power of sin, that through faith in Jesus Christ the promise might be given to those who believe.

NT: Rom 3:9–20; 11:32; Gal 2:19–20
Catechism: the role of the law, 1963–64

2. Interpreters differ about which meaning is intended. Other biblical texts that confirm the role of angels in the giving of the law include Deut 33:2–4 †LXX; Acts 7:38, 53; Heb 2:2. The book of *Jubilees* (1:27–2:1, second century BC) explicitly attributes to an angel the task of dictating the law to Moses. Philo of Alexandria, a Jewish philosopher, and Josephus, a Jewish historian, both writing in the first century AD, recount similar traditions (Philo, *On Dreams* 1.143; Josephus, *Jewish Antiquities* 15.136).

3. Some scholars who find "the idea that Paul might be trying to distance God from the giving of the law . . . problematic" offer another interpretation of 3:20. The presence of Moses as a mediator in the giving of the law entails a human involvement that reveals the inferiority of the law to a promise given directly by the one God (see Douglas J. Moo, *Galatians*, BECNT [Grand Rapids: Baker Academic, 2013], Kindle loc. 6462).

Paul now returns to the relationship between †law and promise, which he began   **3:21**
to speak about in 3:15–18, and views it from a new angle: **Is the law then opposed to the promises [of God]? Of course not!** Although the law is inferior
to the promises, there is a unity to God's plan that includes both the law and
the promises.

In principle there are two possible ways the law could be "opposed to the
promises." The first would be if the law could impose requirements on people
as the necessary condition for the fulfillment of the promise. Paul has already
presented a strong legal argument why the law cannot do that (3:15–18). The
other possible way the law could be opposed to the promises would be if the
law replaced the promises, making them irrelevant, by delivering the benefits
promised to the patriarchs.

Paul writes: **For if a law had been given that could bring life, then righteousness would in reality come from the law**. Paul clearly regards this hypothetical statement as contrary to fact. In the next verse (v. 22) Paul presents
the fact that disproves the possibility that righteousness comes from the law:
"But scripture confined all things under the power of sin." Therefore *no* law has
been given that is capable of bringing life.

Before we examine Paul's rebuttal, it is worth considering why he raises
the question of whether the law is able to bring life. Paul assumes that to
make people righteous, it is necessary to "bring life"—literally, "to make alive."
This is a verb that the New Testament often uses to refer to resurrection and
salvation.[4] The Apostle has reflected on how a person can become righteous
before God, and his answer is radical. Because human beings are sinners and
sinners must die, they stand in need of a completely new life. Even dying
solves nothing for a sinner, unless his or her death somehow can lead to a
new life of union with God. Righteousness is found only in receiving new
life. Paul has understood that righteousness is obtained this way and only this
way (2:19–20). God's promise of blessing to Abraham (3:14) was in the end
a promise of resurrection—that is, the regeneration or re-creation of human
beings who are righteous and blessed.

From this perspective Paul asks, "Is the law capable of giving new life?" The
answer is of course no. The law is capable of bringing death to sinners, of punishing them, but it is not capable of bringing them life. Although the law has a
positive role of revealing what pleases God (3:24; 4:2), it works on people only
from the outside; it is not a principle of life. The law says what human beings

4. John 5:21; Rom 4:17; 8:11; 1 Cor 15:22, 36, 45.

should do but does not give them the power to do it. It does not change people on the inside; it leaves people where it found them, as sinners. The conclusion is clear: the law is incapable of giving life. It therefore does not convey righteousness and thus cannot take the place of the promise.[5]

3:22   To describe the situation under the †law, Paul declares that **scripture confined all things under the power of sin**.[6] This refers back to what was said in verse 19 about the law being given "for transgressions"—that is, to make sin obvious as violations of God's will revealed in the law. Later Paul will explain this more explicitly in his Letter to the Romans and cite many biblical texts, especially from the Psalms, to demonstrate that all human beings are under the dominion of sin, including those who live under the law (Rom 3:9–20).

A law that confined human beings under the power of sin was negative, but God's purpose was positive: to allow **the promise** to take effect by means of †faith in Christ. The law was incapable of resolving the problem of sin. The promised blessings of the †inheritance come not through observance of the law but **through faith in Jesus Christ**, or "through the *faithfulness* of Christ" as this Greek phrase (*pistis Christou*) can also be translated (see the sidebar, "'Faith in Christ' or 'the Faithfulness of Christ'?," p. 86). Nevertheless, the necessity of faith *in* Christ is clearly affirmed, since the next phrase states that the promise is **given to those who believe**.

The Two Periods of Salvation History (3:23–29)

---

[23]**Before faith came, we were held in custody under law, confined for the faith that was to be revealed. **[24]**Consequently, the law was our disciplinarian for Christ, that we might be justified by faith. **[25]**But now that faith has come, we are no longer under a disciplinarian. **[26]**For through faith you are all children of God in Christ Jesus. **[27]**For all of you who were baptized into Christ have clothed yourselves with Christ. **[28]**There is neither Jew nor Greek, there is neither slave nor free person, there is not male and female; for you are all one in Christ Jesus. **[29]**And if you belong to Christ, then you are Abraham's descendant, heirs according to the promise.**

NT: Rom 6:3–14; 8:14–19; 11:32; 1 Cor 12:13; Gal 4:4–7; Eph 2:14–15; Col 3:11

---

5. Paul already implied in 3:11–12 that the law does not bring life by citing Habakkuk to the effect that "the one who is righteous by faith shall live," and citing Deut 27:26 to say that those who do not do all the things written in the law are cursed.

6. The expression "all things" here could refer merely to all people, but in Rom 8:20, 22, Paul speaks of all creation being subject to the consequences of sin.

Catechism: the role of the law, 708, 1963–64; unity in the body of Christ, 791; baptism and justi-
    fication, 1227, 1243, 1445
Lectionary: 3:26–28: Christian Initiation; Baptism of Children

Now Paul more explicitly takes up the distinction hinted at in verse 22 between
two periods of salvation history: the time of the †law and the time of †faith.
Verses 23–24 describe the situation during the time of the law, and verses 25–29
describe the situation initiated by the coming of Christ.

Paul personifies †faith here, portraying it as someone who was due to come   **3:23**
and has finally arrived: **Before faith came, we were held in custody under law,
confined for the faith that was to be revealed**. The Apostle is an imaginative
teacher who knows how to make his instruction concrete and memorable. He
often personifies abstract realities such as sin (Rom 5:12; 7:8–9), death (Rom
5:12, 14; 1 Cor 15:54–56), and the †law (Rom 5:20; 7:1; Gal 3:24). The Greek
verb translated "held in custody," meaning "guarded" or "protected," confirms
that confinement under the law had a positive rather than a negative purpose.[7]
Although the law was powerless to keep a person from sinning, it was a great
gift to Israel to know God's ways, and it was a protection for society, at least
in principle, to be guarded by that truth (Exod 33:13; 34:1–28; Ps 147:19–20).
When Paul says "we" here, he again refers to himself and his fellow Jews, who
were subject to the law of Moses.

In this verse Paul speaks of the coming of faith as a unique event. He is not
referring to the faith that rises in the hearts of believers, an event that is not
unique, because it happens every day. Instead, Paul has in mind a change in
the spiritual situation of the human race that resulted from a particular event
at the center of history—the death and the resurrection of Jesus.

With his distinction between the two time periods and his attribution of faith
only to the second, Paul could seem too negative about the first. He could even
seem to contradict himself, since at the beginning of the chapter he emphasized
Abraham's faith (Gal 3:6, 9), but here he says Abraham lived in the period "before
faith came." It is clear that Paul's distinction between two periods is not intended
in an absolute sense. The time preceding Christ was not a time in which faith
was completely absent. Rather, faith was a flower that had not yet blossomed.
More precisely, faith had not yet been "revealed" because its foundation had
not yet been laid. That happened at Calvary. Through his cross and the resurrection, Jesus became the foundation of faith (1 Cor 3:11; see 1 Pet 2:4–6). By

---

7. The other New Testament uses of "held in custody" are positive and protective (2 Cor 11:32; Phil
4:7; 1 Pet 1:5). Likewise the next verb, "confined" or "enclosed," need not have the sense of "imprisoned"
that some translations give it.

virtue of his victory over sin and death—a victory obtained by his accepting death for the sake of love (see Gal 1:4; 2:20)—Christ was manifested as entirely worthy of our faith and was presented by God for all to believe in (Acts 2:36; 17:31; Rom 1:4; Heb 3:1–6). This is how faith was fully revealed.

There exists a notable difference between the faith of Abraham and the faith of Christians. For Abraham the perspective was one of waiting. Abraham's faith was faith in a promise about the future: "I will bless you; I will make your name great, so that you will be a blessing" (Gen 12:2). But for Christians, faith rests on a foundation that has already been laid. Our faith entails entrusting ourselves to Christ, who has now been revealed, and accepting his redemptive work that is already accomplished. The blessing is now in effect for us. †Justification has been fully realized, thanks to the gift of the Holy Spirit. A great change has taken place, and Paul is conscious of living in a privileged era.

3:24   The idea of being guarded or protected by the †law leads Paul to introduce a different but related metaphor: **the law was our disciplinarian**. This translation is perhaps overly negative; other translations include "guardian" (ESV) and "custodian" (RSV). The Greek word *paidagōgos* refers to a slave charged with supervising children and escorting them to meet the teacher from whom they would receive instruction. This meaning fits Paul's purpose, since his next words are **for** (literally, "unto") **Christ**. The NJB says it well: "The Law was serving as a slave to look after us, to lead us to Christ." This metaphor for the law bears connotations of supervision and restriction that are potentially unpleasant, as well as the positive idea of movement toward the Master. The law, Paul says, existed solely for the purpose of escorting Jews like himself to Christ, so **that we might be justified by faith**.

3:25–26   **Now that faith has come**, believers no longer depend on the †law to lead them to their Teacher: **we are no longer under a disciplinarian**. In fact, **through faith** our spiritual condition has changed completely. Here Paul passes immediately to the highest dignity conferred on those who believe

Walters Art Museum, CC0

Figure 13. Pedagogue and child (Greek terracotta, third or second century BC).

126

in Christ—namely, the dignity of being **children of God** (literally, "sons of God" [see the sidebar, "Understanding 'Children of God,'" p. 128]). This dignity is not restricted to those of Jewish descent; †Gentile Christians enjoy this privilege as well. Paul is eager to affirm this, so he jumps from the first-person plural in verse 25—"we [Jews] are no longer under a disciplinarian"—to the second-person plural in verse 26: **you** [Gentiles] **are all** children of God. This transition shows the Apostle's firm conviction that the change in the spiritual situation of Jews has brought with it the possibility of a similar change for all human beings.

Being a child of God does not exclude the need for teaching, but it does exclude being subject to the "disciplinarian," the law of Moses, since the sons and daughters of God **in Christ Jesus** participate in the glorious sonship of their risen †Lord.[8] Later in Galatians (5:13–26) Paul will indicate what replaces the law as the guide to Christian conduct.

Paul speaks of baptism as the means by which believers enter into this very **3:27** close relationship with Christ: **For all of you who were baptized into Christ have clothed yourselves with Christ**. Baptism is the concrete expression of adherence to Christ in †faith. Paul virtually identifies faith with baptism in these verses, illustrating that Christian faith is not only assenting to a creed or having a religious experience. Faith follows the pattern of the incarnation and therefore involves the body as well. Baptism expresses and brings about the incorporation of the whole believer—body, soul, and spirit—into the body of Christ. Paul will explain in Rom 6:3–14 how baptism unites believers to Christ's bodily death and resurrection, both in the present and in our ultimate future.[9] Baptism actualizes faith in Christ.

In this way baptism differs radically from circumcision. It is not just a rite but a means of truly joining the lives of two persons, the believer and Christ. While circumcision leaves a permanent, visible mark on the body that indicates belonging to a particular nation, baptism leaves no mark of nationality and is offered to people of every nation.

In speaking of baptism Paul does not say "baptized *in* Christ"; he literally says, "baptized *into* Christ." In other words, Christ is not the *element in which* a believer is immersed but rather the *person to whom* the believer is united through baptism. Immersion happens "in water" (see Matt 3:11) and "in the

8. Verse 26 could be translated differently. The NIV renders it, "In Christ Jesus you are all children of God through faith." The phrase "in Christ Jesus" can modify either "children of God" or "faith." It is not necessary, however, to choose between them: believers are children of God *in* Christ Jesus *through faith in* Christ Jesus.

9. In Rom 6:5 Paul uses the analogy of grafting a branch onto a tree: "For if we have *grown into union with him* through a death like his, we shall also be united with him in the resurrection" (italics added).

Understanding "Children of God"

**BIBLICAL
BACKGROUND**

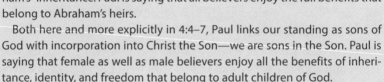

The NABRE, along with many contemporary translations, uses "child" and "children" in Gal 3:26 and 4:6–7, where the Greek says "son" and "sons." This inclusive translation is appropriate, since Paul clearly intends to include both male and female Christians and elsewhere uses the terms "sons of God" and "children of God" interchangeably (Rom 8:14–19). On the other hand, the words "child" and "children" often refer to minors, while Paul's emphasis is on adult children (see Gal 4:1–2). Here Paul probably uses "sons" since it more readily conveys the idea of being the heirs of Abraham's †inheritance. Paul is saying that all believers enjoy the full benefits that belong to Abraham's heirs.

Both here and more explicitly in 4:4–7, Paul links our standing as sons of God with incorporation into Christ the Son—we are sons in the Son. Paul is saying that female as well as male believers enjoy all the benefits of inheritance, identity, and freedom that belong to adult children of God.

Spirit" (see Matt 3:11; 1 Cor 12:13), but because of the union it effects, it is baptism "*into* Christ."

Baptism produces not only a change in relationship but also a change in one's being that Paul describes with the verb "to clothe": you have "clothed yourselves with Christ." This statement is a bit perplexing. How is it possible "to clothe oneself" with another person? The expression could be misunderstood as merely an external, superficial change: changing clothes does not transform a person. But here, as in certain Old Testament passages, "clothing oneself" expresses a change that redefines a person's life. For example, in a text that Paul may have had in mind, Isaiah writes:

> I will rejoice heartily in the LORD,
>   my being exults in my God;
> For he has clothed me with garments of salvation,
>   and wrapped me in a robe of justice [righteousness]. (Isa 61:10; see
>   Ps 132:16)

To be clothed in Christ brings a profound transformation (1 Cor 6:11).

3:28   Being clothed with Christ is so profound that it reaches the most important part of a person's identity and transforms it. Paul has the boldness to proclaim that **in Christ Jesus** the religious difference between Jew and Greek, the civil difference between slave and free, and finally the sexual difference between male and female no longer exist. Paul indicates the context in which these differences do not matter with the phrase "in Christ Jesus": in our relationships with the risen †Lord, these distinctions are no longer important.

The first distinction that Paul denies—**There is neither Jew nor Greek** (here referring to †Gentiles)—is the one he is most interested in. The other two are added to reinforce the first. The contrast is not on the cultural level, since then the pairing would be "Greeks and non-Greeks" as in Rom 1:14, where those of Greek culture enjoy preeminence and are listed first. Here the distinction is religious, so the preeminence belongs to the Jews. As members of the chosen people, Jews rightly considered themselves favored by God (see Rom 2:17–20; Eph 2:11–12). For a Jew like Paul to dare to declare that this fundamental religious difference no longer existed was extremely audacious. To many Jews and to the †Judaizers this assertion would have seemed to be the height of religious subversion. It is not surprising that Paul's apostolate encountered fierce opposition.

However, even the religious distinction of the Old Covenant between Jew and Gentile is overcome in Christ, since whoever is united to the risen Jesus through †faith belongs to a new category, that of "a new creation" (Gal 6:15; see Eph 2:13–19), which is equally accessible to Greek and Jew since the only condition to enter it is faith in Christ, who died and rose.

The second distinction Paul denies, **neither slave nor free person**, primarily concerns civil rather than social standing (otherwise Paul would have said "neither slave nor master"). The distinction between slaves and free citizens was fundamental to the entire organization of society in the Greco-Roman world. Free persons enjoyed a range of political and civil rights; slaves were deprived of rights and dignity. To deny this distinction was as subversive as denying a religious distinction between Jew and Gentile.

Paul mentions the slave first in this pairing because he wants to emphasize that in the Church and Christ's kingdom this standing that is unworthy of a human being has been overcome. Baptized into Christ, every believer enjoys full human dignity because the risen Christ is the perfect man. The human vocation, which according to Gen 1:26 is to exercise dominion over the earth, has been fulfilled in the risen Jesus, the Lord of the universe, to whom Christian slaves are now united.

It is worth noting, however, that Paul rejects not only slavery but also the status of the free person. He does not say, "There are no more slaves; everybody is free!" as one might expect. Instead he says, "There is neither slave nor free person." He explains this in more detail in 1 Cor 7:22, where he says, "The slave called in the Lord is a freed person in the Lord, just as the free person who has been called is a slave of Christ." Paul's point of view is not that of a social reformer correcting injustices. His perspective is deeper. Paul is focused on defining the status of human beings in Christ. He says that from that vantage point the civil status of the individual in the Roman Empire has no relevance since it does not exist in Christ. Of course, this perspective leads to a profound change of attitude, which is illustrated in Paul's letter to Philemon about the slave Onesimus, whom he describes as "no longer as a slave but more than a slave, . . . a beloved brother" (Philem 1:16 RSV). The recognition that in Christ there is "neither slave nor free person" would ultimately lead Christian societies to eliminate that civil distinction and to emancipate slaves.

The third and last denial of a distinction is the boldest of all because it concerns sexual differences. The wording of this statement is a bit different: instead of using "neither" and "nor" to deny a distinction, Paul says, there is **not male and female**. His point is to draw a contrast with Gen 1:27 and 5:2, which say "male and female he created them." Paul has the audacity to say, "There is no male and female." Paul is convinced that God has begun a new creation in Christ that is truly different from the first; human beings gain entry to this new creation through faith and baptism (Gal 6:15; 2 Cor 5:17). A clear implication of Paul's words is that the differences that existed in Judaism between males and females in religious matters (e.g., circumcision and temple access) are eliminated in Christ.

Paul's denial of a difference between male and female in Christ recalls the words of Jesus in the synoptic Gospels about the kind of existence people will have after the resurrection. When the Sadducees ask Jesus about the marital status of a woman who had been married to seven husbands, Jesus tells them, "At the resurrection they neither marry nor are given in marriage but are like the angels in heaven" (Matt 22:30). While Jesus refers to life after the resurrection, Paul refers to the present situation of Christians. Believers already participate in the life of Christ, who died and was raised. Paul seems to be saying that, since after death marriage and sexual union will cease to exist and humans will be "like the angels in heaven," in some sense at the deepest level of Christian identity, there is already "not male and female."[10]

10. Most Catholic interpreters, including St. John Paul II in his theology of the body, do not understand Jesus to mean that the distinction between male and female will cease in the age to come. One exegete puts it this way: although gender distinctions remain (1 Cor 11:2–16), "It is not any outward mark that distinguishes one before God . . . but faith. Distinctions of race, class, and sex have been dissolved by the new creation that has occurred in Christ. . . . In this world, racial, social and sexual differences painfully separate people from each other, but for those who form the new ⁺eschatological person they

It is obvious that this denial of distinction does not apply from the point of view of biology, psychology, and family life. Paul knows that marriage continues in the present age and that baptism does not suppress sexual desire. For this reason he gives considerable pastoral attention to sex and marriage in his writings.[11] It is worth noting that Paul did not say, "There is no man or woman." In 1 Cor 11:11 Paul says, "Woman is not independent of man or man of woman *in the Lord*" (italics added). Therefore, even *in the Lord* Paul recognizes a distinction between men and women and affirms their mutual interdependence. Men and women need each other to receive the †grace of Christ in its fullness.

Immediately after Paul's forceful denial of distinctions among Christians at the deepest level, he explains the absence of distinctions by an equally powerful affirmation: **for you are all one in Christ Jesus**. In verse 26 Paul referred to a plurality of sons and daughters: "You are all children of God in Christ Jesus." This could lead to thinking of God's children as a scattering of individual sons and daughters. But there is only one Christ. If all are clothed in Christ, since Christ is not divided, all are one in Christ. In this way the plurality of the children of God (v. 26) is shown to be a unity after all. The divine sonship of Christians is possible only in the unique Son, and for that reason all are one in him.

When Paul refers to the unity of all believers, he does not use the neuter form of the adjective "one," as Jesus does in the Gospel of John when he prays for his disciples, "May they all be one" (equivalent to "one thing," John 17:21; see 17:11, 23). Instead Paul uses the masculine form of "one" when he says, "You are all one in Christ Jesus." Why? In Eph 2:15–16 Paul declares that Christ has abolished the †law that had created the separation between Jews and Gentiles, "that he might create *in himself one new man* in place of the two, . . . and might reconcile us both to God in one body" (RSV, italics added). The Greek word translated "man" is *anthrōpos*, which means "human being" and includes both sexes. All the baptized thus form one single *anthrōpos*; they exist only "in Christ Jesus."

Nevertheless, the unity of all believers must not be confused with the person of Christ; there is a mystery here that is not easily understood. Elsewhere Paul uses the expression "body of Christ" to indicate the distinction: "Now you are Christ's body, and individually parts of it" (1 Cor 12:27). In Ephesians and Colossians he will speak of Christ as the head of the body, which is the Church.[12]

---

cannot deny one full access to God's people" (Frank J. Matera, *Galatians*, Sacra Pagina [Collegeville, MN: Liturgical Press, 1992], 143, 146–47).

11. See 1 Cor 6:9–7:40; Eph 5:3–6, 21–33; Col 3:18–19; 1 Thess 4:3–8.

12. Eph 4:15–16; 5:23; Col 1:18; 2:19.

The inclusion of Christians "in Christ" to form "one new man" helps explain the nature of our sonship in Christ and the unity it entails.

With verse 28 Paul concludes a topic he began in verse 25, explaining how it is that through faith Christians are not under the law. The reason is that thanks to faith we have become children of God by being incorporated into the risen Christ, the glorified Son of God.

3:29   Paul draws now a final conclusion: **And if you belong to Christ**—literally, "if you are of Christ"—**then you are Abraham's descendant, heirs according to the promise**. At first sight, this verse seems a strange conclusion to the discussion. Paul proclaimed that all believers are "children of God" in verse 26, and then he explained that point in the next two verses.[13] In verse 29, the concluding sentence, we would expect a further development of this thought. Instead we descend to an inferior level, from rejoicing in being "children of God" to rejoicing in being "the descendants of Abraham." If a person is already a child of God, what does it matter if one is a descendant of Abraham?

Paul does not deny this priority, but he has a good reason for wanting to emphasize that baptized believers are descendants of Abraham. Paul wants to finish the topic introduced in 3:7, where, after recalling Abraham's †faith, he said, "It is those who have faith who are children of Abraham." We pointed out at the time that this sudden affirmation was not yet adequately demonstrated. Before doing so Paul moved on to other questions.

A bit later Paul touched again on the topic of the offspring of Abraham. Observing that Genesis speaks of the posterity of Abraham with a singular term, "descendant" (literally, "seed"), Paul specified that this word applies to Christ (Gal 3:16). This remark seems inconsistent with 3:7, which speaks of the "children" of Abraham in the plural. How are these statements to be reconciled?

Paul provides the key in the verse we are considering. The offspring of Abraham is at the same time both singular and very numerous. Abraham's descendant is unique in that he is Christ alone; yet his offspring is numerous because it includes all who are "in Christ." Abraham's innumerable offspring remain singular because all the baptized are "one in Christ Jesus" (v. 28).

Paul has now completed his proof that "those who have faith . . . are children of Abraham" (3:7). They are not his children by a mere metaphorical sonship based on imitation or a similar spiritual outlook. A metaphorical sonship would not suffice to satisfy the promises of Genesis, which require physical descent: "Your own offspring will be your heir" (Gen 15:4). But whoever believes in

13. On the translation of "sons" as "children," see the sidebar, "Understanding 'Children of God,'" p. 128.

Christ does have a kind of physical relationship to Abraham because through baptism he or she is truly incorporated into Christ, a physical descendant of Abraham. Believers are inserted into Christ not simply by receiving the communication of a message to which they adhere mentally, but also by means of a communication of the life of his body. Christ acts in and through his resurrected body, descended from Abraham, to gather all who believe into himself. Through baptism Jesus acts to assimilate believers both spiritually and physically to the same body that died and gloriously arose.

The Galatians were concerned with ensuring their relationship with Abraham so as to secure their claim on the promises made to Abraham and thus share in his †inheritance. The †Judaizers claimed that circumcision, mentioned in Gen 17:9–14, was indispensable. But Paul demonstrates conclusively that faith in Christ completed by baptism gives believers the closest possible ties to Abraham, ties that are stronger than any that could come through circumcision. Thanks to faith and baptism, believers are joined to Christ, and since Christ is the unique descendant to whom the promise applies, all Christians are Abraham's offspring, "heirs according to the promise." Paul's demonstration is now complete. It was a bit tumultuous and not easy to follow, but it provides a compelling argument.

Reflection and Application (3:27–28)

Equality in Christ. Paul's declaration that "there is not male and female" (3:28) is often cited as the basis for Christian feminism, and with good reason. Paul affirms that at the deepest level of Christian identity, that of our union with Christ and †justification, there is no distinction on the basis of one's sex. This affirmation provides solid biblical testimony that woman and man have an equal dignity in Christ.

Some feminists want to go further and invoke this text regarding the ministerial priesthood. They say that since "there is not male and female" in Christ, priestly ordination should be conferred on women as it is on men. Is this a valid argument?

The answer depends on whether or not ministerial priesthood is located at the level at which Paul denies that any distinction exists. It is certain that Paul's denial of a distinction between male and female in Christ does not apply to every aspect of human existence and Christian life. Otherwise, one would need to say that marriage is impossible for a Christian man and woman since "there is not male and female" in Christ.

The context clearly indicates that Paul's denial of distinctions concerns what is most fundamental to Christian life—namely, justification by †faith and incorporation into Christ through baptism. The Apostle affirms absolute unity and equality at this level for every believer. It does not follow from this that differences disappear in other dimensions of Christian life. For instance, Paul insists that respecting differences in charisms is indispensable. "Now the body is not a single part, but many" (1 Cor 12:14) with diverse functions (12:15–17).

If we ask where ministerial priesthood fits, the answer comes to us in that same chapter of 1 Corinthians. Paul locates roles of authority and ministry in the Church not at the level of fundamental unity but rather at the level of necessary diversity: "God placed the parts, each one of them, in the body as he intended" (1 Cor 12:18). Then Paul asks, "Are all apostles? Are all prophets?" (12:29).

It is thus clear that ministerial priesthood does not belong in the category of things for which Paul denies distinctions; it follows that the claim that Gal 3:28 requires the priestly ordination of women is not valid. Nevertheless, Gal 3:28 provides a solid basis for the participation of all believers—women as well as men, laity as well as clergy—in the most important aspect of Christian priesthood, namely, the offering of our lives through Christ to God out of love and the transformation of that offering by the action of the Holy Spirit. This spiritual worship, this liturgy of life, is a fundamental aspect of Christian life and a direct result of our justification by faith (Rom 12:1–2).

Adoption as Sons and Daughters of God

Galatians 4:1–11

Along the way to the surprising conclusion of Gal 3:28–29 that †Gentile believers have become Abraham's descendants and heirs through baptism into Christ, Paul made another extraordinary declaration that he did not explain: "For through faith you are all children of God in Christ Jesus" (3:26). Paul now returns to this topic, perhaps feeling the need to balance the impression left in 3:29, where he seemed to emphasize being Abraham's heirs more than being sons and daughters of God. Paul now explains how we have become children of God and speaks of the scarcely imaginable intimacy with Jesus and the Father that this entails. He begins again from the perspective of salvation history.

Adoption and Inheritance (4:1–7)

[1]I mean that as long as the heir is not of age, he is no different from a slave, although he is the owner of everything, [2]but he is under the supervision of guardians and administrators until the date set by his father. [3]In the same way we also, when we were not of age, were enslaved to the elemental powers of the world. [4]But when the fullness of time had come, God sent his Son, born of a woman, born under the law, [5]to ransom those under the law, so that we might receive adoption. [6]As proof that you are children, God sent the spirit of his Son into our hearts, crying out, "Abba, Father!" [7]So you are no longer a slave but a child, and if a child then also an heir, through God.

OT: Job 14:1–2

NT: John 1:14; Rom 8:3, 9, 14–17; Phil 2:7; Col 2:8, 20

Catechism: fullness of time and Annunciation, 484; the law, Jesus, and redemption, 580; baptism and adoption, 1265; relationship with God and the Spirit, 683, 1695

Lectionary: 4:4–7: Mary Mother of God; Common of the Blessed Virgin; Presentation of Lord's Prayer

The structure of this passage resembles that of the sections that immediately precede it. The word "heir" in the first verse links this section to the last verse of the previous one (3:29), while the words "heir" and "slave" in the first and last verses frame 4:1–7 as a distinct unit. As in 3:15–18, Paul starts this unit with a familiar legal custom, this time concerning the status of minor children (4:1–2), and he uses it to illuminate the progression of salvation history (4:3–7). As in 3:23–29, Paul distinguishes two successive and contrasting periods within that history, one of subjection (4:3) and one of freedom (4:4–7).

4:1–2   After celebrating the fact that believers are Abraham's heirs (3:29), Paul returns to consider the earlier situation of Jews under the †law and introduces a new comparison: **as long as the heir is not of age, he is no different from a slave**. In the first century, an heir, usually the eldest son, could not exercise the legal rights of an heir while he was still a minor. Saying that there was *no* difference between a minor heir and a slave is an exaggeration to make a point, since the heir was not obliged to work the way slaves were. Paul is comparing the minor child's inability to make his own decisions to the slave's lack of freedom. This is particularly striking since in principle, even during his minority, the heir was **the owner of everything**. This principle can be seen in the parable of the prodigal son, when the father says to the older son, "Everything I have is yours" (Luke 15:31). However, an heir who is still a minor cannot freely dispose of his goods; **administrators** manage them for him. Nor can the minor heir do as he chooses, since he is **under the supervision of guardians**.[1] The use of a plural in these titles emphasizes his dependence and limited freedom: lots of other people make decisions for him.

The situation, however, is not destined to last. Its time limits are indicated at the beginning and end of the sentence in two slightly different ways. At the beginning, when Paul uses the phrase "as long as the heir is not of age," he indicates that the heir's status of submission will not end until he is an adult.

---

1. According to some scholars, Paul's discussion assumes that the situation being presented involves a minor son whose father has died, leaving the child in the control of guardians until he reaches his majority. An adult heir's use of the family property was still subject to the father as long as he lived unless the father distributed all or part of the †inheritance (see Luke 15:12). But Paul is concerned with only one point of comparison, the adult child's freedom from administrators and guardians.

However, at the end of the sentence, Paul speaks of **the date set by his father**. From what we know of first-century practice, the age of majority was often determined by law rather than the decision of the father. However, the Apostle is not focused on being legally precise, but is setting up his application of this comparison to salvation history, where everything depends on the Father's decision (see Gal 4:4–5).

Paul's comparison (4:3–7) emphasizes a clear distinction between two time **4:3** periods. The first period is that of childhood, **when we were not of age**, or of slavery, when we **were enslaved**. Childhood and slavery serve as metaphors for an earlier period in salvation history. When Paul uses the first-person plural "we," he clearly refers to himself prior to his conversion along with his fellow Jews. Whether or not Paul includes the †Gentile Christians of Galatia is uncertain, but not so important. To affirm that Jews "were enslaved to the †elemental powers" was a bold new statement. It was customary for Jews to view pagan Gentiles in this way. The Gentiles served idols of gold, silver, iron, and wood (see Deut 29:17), so they were slaves to the elements. However, to say such a thing about Jews, who took pride in worshiping the true God, was potentially offensive; the fact that Paul includes himself among those enslaved softens the blow.

What are **the elemental powers of the world**—literally, "the elements of the world"—whose control was weighing down Paul and his fellow Jews? This phrase is not common in the New Testament and is found again only in Col 2:8, 20. The same Greek word for "elements" (*stoicheia*) refers to the elements that compose the earth (2 Pet 3:10, 12) and to basic elements of Christian teaching (Heb 5:12). What would it have meant to Paul's readers in Galatia? Some exegetes think Paul is referring to the †law of Moses as elementary principles of religious instruction; but the phrase that follows, "of the world," does not fit that interpretation. Other scholars think Paul refers to spiritual beings—principalities and powers that govern the universe—as in Eph 6:12 (here NABRE's "elemental powers" and RSV's "elemental spirits" suggest this interpretation), but the only clear uses of this Greek word with that meaning occur in a period later than the New Testament. A third possibility is the most likely since it was the most common use of this Greek word in Paul's day—namely, that it refers to the four elements that Greek thinkers regarded as composing the physical world: earth, water, air, and fire.[2] Although obedience to the law was the way Israel expressed submission to God, Paul is saying that subjection to the law entails a subjection to the world in its material dimension. In the verses that follow,

---

2. It is used this way in Wis 7:17; 19:18; *4 Maccabees* 12:13; Philo; Josephus; and the Apostolic Fathers.

Paul describes the Galatians' observance of "days, months, seasons, and years," a religious calendar governed by the movements of the sun and moon, as subjection to the elements (Gal 4:9–10). In Colossians, Paul characterizes dietary rules as submission to the elements of the world: "If you died with Christ to the elemental powers [elements, *stoicheia*] of the world, why do you submit to regulations as if you were still living in the world? Do not handle! Do not taste! Do not touch!" (Col 2:20–21).[3]

Paul understands that †faith in Christ raises a human being to a completely new level, bringing a person into a relationship with God in the Spirit through faith and in love—a life that is no longer governed by regulations concerning the elements of the physical world. Paul realizes that under the Old Covenant the religion of Israel was more rudimentary. Even circumcision is only an external physical rite. The regulations of the Mosaic law made Israel subordinate to physical elements that compose the world; from that point of view it kept the Jews in a spiritual situation analogous to that of the Gentiles. While Paul clearly exaggerates the similarity of Israel's religion to that of Gentiles to make his point, we see in Paul's reevaluation of the †ritual commandments of the †Torah his boldness in expressing the radical newness of life in Christ in comparison with the Old Covenant.

Other passages in the New Testament point in a similar direction. According to the Gospel of Mark, Jesus relativized certain prescriptions of the law that dealt with ritual purity and acceptable foods (Mark 7:3–8, 15–23), placing his focus on the heart. Likewise, the Letter to the Hebrews speaks of the inadequacy of the sacrifices of the Old Covenant, which sufficed only for "the purification of the flesh" (Heb 9:13 RSV) and could not truly purify consciences but were only of temporary value (9:8–14, 23–24). The coming of Christ changed everything, making possible a new kind of relationship with God.

4:4–5   Paul now describes the second period of salvation history. His description of the former period in verse 3, "when we were not of age," contrasts with a solemn phrase that indicates the special importance of the new period: **when the fullness of time had come** (see Mark 1:15).

The divine initiative consists in **God** sending **his Son** so that we could become his children. It is clear that this is a preexisting Son who is **sent** by God, not a human being like everyone else whom God adopts.[4] Furthermore, in verse 6

---

3. An analogous contrast between the ceremonial laws of the Old Covenant and the new reality in Christ is found in Heb 9:9–14, where Old Testament laws are described as "regulations concerning the flesh, imposed until the time of the new order" (Heb 9:10; see 13:9).

4. When the subject of adoption surfaces in v. 5, it refers to the adoption of Christians, not to the Son, who was sent. The sentence (vv. 4–5) makes no sense if the Son, who was sent, has the same status as the people who are adopted by God as a result of his coming.

Paul expresses a clear parallel between the sending of the Son and the sending of the Spirit. Since clearly the Spirit preexists with God, the parallel confirms that the Son also preexisted with him before being sent.

The coming of the Son is presented not as something glorious but rather as humbling in two respects: the Son of God is (1) **born of a woman** and (2) **born under the law**. The phrase "born of woman" was often used in Jewish literature to highlight human fragility. For instance,

> Man born of woman
>> is short-lived and full of trouble,
> Like a flower that springs up and fades. (Job 14:1–2)[5]

The fact that the Son was "born under the †law" brings him down another step. The Son of God is sent not only to be born as a man but also as a man subject to an external norm. How extraordinary! Nevertheless, according to Paul, these two marks of lowly status are the paradoxical means for the Son's obtaining two very positive results. First, the Son of God was subject to the law in order **to ransom**—that is, to redeem or free—**those under the law**; second, he was born of woman so that all who are likewise born of woman **might receive adoption** as children of God—thus explaining Paul's earlier declaration that "through faith you are all children of God" (Gal 3:26).

What is the key to this amazing paradox? How can these humiliations of the Son of God produce such a positive outcome? As regards freedom from the law, Paul explained in 2:19–20: "Through the law I died to the law, that I might live for God. I have been crucified with Christ; yet I live, no longer I, but Christ lives in me." Christ submitted himself to the law to the point of undergoing the penalty of death on our behalf. However, he found a way to undergo death to produce new life. By accepting the death imposed by the law with perfect filial obedience (1:4) and an extraordinary love for his brothers and sisters (2:20), Christ freed himself from the law and likewise frees those who unite themselves to him through †faith (see Rom 7:1–4).[6]

The key to the second paradox, that the Son of God was born of a woman in order to obtain divine adoption for us, involves events of Jesus' birth, which are not something that Paul explains elsewhere. Light on this point comes to us from the passages in Matthew and Luke that explain "how the birth of Jesus Christ came about" (Matt 1:18) in an altogether unique way. His mother Mary,

---

5. See also Job 15:14; 25:4. In the *Hymns* of †Qumran, "born of woman" is placed in parallel with "creature of clay" (1QH 13:14–15; 18:12–13).

6. Paul attributes this result both to faith and to baptism (Rom 6:3–10).

a virgin, "was found with child through the holy Spirit" (Matt 1:18). Paul's way of speaking of Jesus' birth agrees with the Gospels, since he presents Christ both as the Son of God and as born of a woman, without the least mention of the participation of a human father (Matt 1:20, 23; Luke 1:27, 35). By God's decision it was Mary alone who gave to Jesus his †flesh, his human nature.

"Adoption" is a legal term mentioned only five times in the Bible.[7] The closest parallel to this text is Rom 8:15–17, a passage that explains how Paul understands divine adoption:

> You did not receive a spirit of slavery to fall back into fear, but you received a spirit of adoption, through which we cry, "*Abba*, Father!" The Spirit itself bears witness with our spirit that we are children of God, and if children, then heirs, heirs of God and joint heirs with Christ.

In Paul's understanding, adoption in Christ is not merely a change in legal status that brings no change to the adopted person. Rather, it is a decisive divine intervention that communicates the life of God through participation in the sonship of the risen Christ: "It is no longer I who live, but Christ who lives in me" (Gal 2:20 RSV). That life of sonship, of living as God's sons and daughters, is animated by the Holy Spirit, whom Paul speaks about in the next verse.

The Apostle uses the first-person plural **we** to speak of those who may receive adoption, in contrast to the third-person plural of "those under the law," referring to Jews. This "we" whom God adopts includes all who believe in Christ, regardless of origin, whether Jewish or †Gentile.

4:6   While verse 5 indicates that God's purpose in sending his Son was our freedom and adoption as sons, verse 6 declares that this purpose has already been achieved: **As proof that you are children, God sent the spirit of his Son into our hearts.**[8] "Spirit" is not capitalized in this translation (NABRE) because the focus is on Christ's spirit, his inner life, being sent into our hearts. Nevertheless, the parallel text in Romans makes clear that the spirit of Christ *is* the Spirit of

---

7. Rom 8:15, 23; 9:4; Gal 4:5; Eph 1:5.

8. Most English translations say, "*Because* you are children . . . ," instead of "As proof that you are children. . . ." Both translations are possible, although they express different relationships between sonship and the gift of the Spirit. In the more common translation, believers are adopted as children, and then, because of their adoption, God sends them the Spirit. However, the NABRE translation interprets adoption and bestowal of the Spirit as simultaneous, since receiving the Spirit is what makes us adopted sons and daughters and is therefore a sign of that relationship. This was the interpretation of the Greek Fathers of the Church and is more in keeping with Paul's teaching on this subject in Romans (Rom 8:15–17) and thus more likely his meaning here.

God (Rom 8:9–11). God responds to the believer's †faith with the gift of the Spirit, who makes the believer a son or daughter of God.

By using the same verb "to send," Paul expresses a relationship between the sending of the Son and the sending of the Spirit. Two similar divine actions are placed in parallel: "God sent his Son. . . . God sent the spirit" (Gal 4:4, 6). The context shows an even closer relationship between the two—namely, that the gift of the Spirit was made possible by the redemptive obedience of Christ. Other passages in the New Testament confirm this perspective (Gal 3:13–14; John 16:7; Acts 2:33).

Instead of speaking simply of the Holy Spirit, Paul uses a phrase that is very original and found only here in the whole Bible: "the spirit of his Son." The phrase complicates the sentence, and some ancient manuscripts simplify it by omitting "of his Son." However, the logic of the passage requires the complexity because it is explaining how God has made us his sons and daughters thanks to the sending of the Son and the Spirit. In order for us to become God's children, the Father himself must act. An action by the Son alone would not be sufficient. It would not be sufficient if God sent only his Holy Spirit to us, as he did to various individuals in the Old Testament (e.g., Judg 13:25; 1 Sam 16:13; 19:20), because the Spirit alone would not establish a *filial* relationship. This is why Paul says, "God sent the spirit *of his Son*," who cries, "Abba, Father!" The Spirit is in an intimate relationship with God the Father, who sent him, and with the Son, to whom he belongs. Believers are thus brought into intimate relationship through the Spirit, in the divine Son, with God the Father himself.

The Old Testament records two analogous instances of God transferring the spirit of one person to another. In the book of Numbers (11:17, 24–25), God takes some of the spirit that was on Moses and bestows it on seventy elders of Israel; in 2 Kings 2:9–10 Elisha receives a double portion of the spirit of Elijah. In neither of those cases, however, does God establish the person as his son; rather, he gives him the capacity to carry out a mission: governing in the case of the seventy elders, prophecy in the case of Elisha.

Readers might wonder if "the spirit of his Son" means the same thing as "the Spirit of God." Although this passage does not explicitly say so, the parallel text in Rom 8:14–17 leaves no doubt, since there the children of God are led by "the Spirit of God" (Rom 8:14). The context makes clear that when Paul speaks of the indwelling of the Spirit in the hearts of believers, he does not distinguish between "the Spirit of God" and "the Spirit of Christ" (Rom 8:9). Elsewhere Paul clearly affirms that the Spirit of God is given to believers (1 Cor 3:16; 6:19; 1 Thess 4:8). We can therefore conclude that "the spirit of his Son" in verse 6 is identical to "the Spirit of God."

Is Everyone a Child of God?

BIBLICAL
BACKGROUND

Although both St. Paul and St. John speak of the fact that Christians have become children of God as an extraordinary †grace, it is common to hear people refer to every human being as a child of God. What does Scripture teach?

To begin with, Genesis presents Adam, who represents humanity as a whole in God's image and likeness, as God's son (see Gen 1:27; 5:1–3), and the Gospel of Luke confirms this perspective in its genealogy of Jesus (Luke 3:38). It is therefore legitimate, biblically speaking, to speak of all human beings as God's children.

Scripture also speaks in a particular way about the people of Israel as God's son (Exod 4:22–23; Hosea 11:1) and about the Israelites as "sons and daughters" (Deut 32:19; Isa 43:6).

God promises a special relationship of sonship to the kings who descend from David: "I will be a father to him, and he shall be a son to me" (2 Sam 7:14). Although this promise, famously expressed in Ps 2:6–9, applied in some measure to all the Davidic kings, it found its complete and ultimate fulfillment in Jesus, the †Messiah.

Jesus revealed that his own relationship to God as Son was something altogether new and of a different order from any other sonship. On the one hand, he was the human son of God by being the son of David, by embodying Israel in himself (Hosea 11:1), and by being the Son of Man[a]—that is, Adam's preeminent descendant. On the other hand, Christ was the preexistent divine Son, who was with the Father from all eternity.[b]

Jesus' coming into the world made possible a new kind of relationship with God that comes by divine power, through †faith in Jesus, rather than by

This does not mean that the difference in the terms is unimportant. Rather, it is rich with doctrinal content. "The spirit of his Son" reveals that the way the Holy Spirit comes to us is through the redemptive self-emptying of the Son of God.

The Spirit of the Son of God sent into our hearts makes us sons and daughters of God and expresses that filial relationship by crying out within us, **"Abba, Father!"** This way of addressing God is found three times in the New Testament, the first time on the lips of Jesus during his agony (Mark 14:36) and the other two times linked to the prayers of Christians (Gal 4:6; Rom 8:15). It stands out because it consists of an Aramaic word, *Abba*, accompanied by its translation. "Abba" was a way of addressing one's father within a family setting in Judaism. It was not customarily used to address God. However, according to Mark 14:36, ordinary human generation (John 1:12–13). While John speaks of this new divine sonship as being born of or begotten by God,[c] Paul uses the analogy of adoption to describe it[d] but indicates that it entails far more than a change of legal status, since God has sent "the spirit of his Son into our hearts" (Gal 4:6; see also Rom 8:15).

Nonetheless, the New Testament points to an even more wonderful future relationship with God as his sons and daughters. Paul speaks of an "adoption" that we await, "the redemption of our bodies" (Rom 8:23). For John that future intimacy with God goes beyond the marvelous current condition of being God's children in whom his seed[e] is present (1 John 3:9). He says, "Beloved, we are God's children now; what we shall be has not yet been revealed. We do know that when it is revealed we shall be like him, for we shall see him as he is" (1 John 3:2).

To sum up, while every human being is a child of God, created in his image and likeness, and Israel is God's son through God's †covenant with the patriarchs, baptized Christians have been adopted by God and made his children in a far deeper way. We have received in our hearts the Spirit of God's only begotten Son, who makes possible an extraordinary intimacy with the Father (to know him as "Abba," Gal 4:6) and with Christ himself (to become "one spirit with him," 1 Cor 6:17). An even greater intimacy with the Father, Son, and Holy Spirit awaits us when Christ returns (1 Cor 15:28; Eph 2:7).

a. Hebrew *ben adam*.
b. Matt 11:27; John 1:1–14; 3:12; 5:19–20; 6:38; 10:30; 14:9–11; 16:28; Phil 2:5–11; Col 1:13–16; Heb 1:2.
c. 1 John 2:29; 3:9; 4:7; 5:1, 4, 18.
d. Rom 8:15; Gal 4:5; Eph 1:5.
e. Greek *sperma*; RSV, "nature."

Jesus addressed God as "Abba" in Gethsemane, demonstrating his awareness of the unique intimacy of his relationship with God (see Matt 11:27; Luke 10:21–22; John 10:30, 38). The first Christians, including the Galatians, were aware of having received the Spirit in their hearts when they came to believe in Christ. They were so strongly aware of being united through the Spirit in Jesus' filial relationship with the Father that they could address God in the same familiar way. Both here and in Rom 8:15, Paul presupposes that his readers are familiar with this Aramaic word, indicating that even Greek-speaking †Gentile Christians had adopted the practice of using "Abba" in prayer to address God as their Father. This intimacy with God through the Spirit of his Son, with the privilege of addressing God as Father in familiar terms as his beloved children, is available to all who are baptized believers in Jesus.

4:7   Paul concludes, **So you are no longer a slave but a child**—literally, "son." What exultation there is in these words! Paul employs the second-person singular "you," which would have caught the original readers' attention; it emphasizes that this conclusion applies to every single Christian. This status of being a son or daughter stands in marked contrast to the condition of slavery described in verse 3. Becoming God's children puts an end to subservience and confers on us the highest possible dignity. The Spirit of adoption frees Christians from fear and makes it possible for us to grow in God's likeness (Rom 8:15; 2 Cor 3:17).

But there is more! Sonship brings the right of †inheritance: **and if a child then also an heir, through God**. The gift of the Spirit we have received is proof of our access to the inheritance promised to Abraham's offspring (Gen 12:7; Gal 3:29), but even this gift is not the whole inheritance. It is only a down payment, "the first installment of our inheritance" (Eph 1:14; see 2 Cor 1:22; 5:5). The situation of Christians is full of hope, since it entails receiving an inheritance from God himself (see the sidebar, "What Is Abraham's Inheritance?," p. 107). With this final clarification, Paul communicates complete assurance to the Galatians, freeing them from the fear aroused by the †Judaizers of being excluded from the promised inheritance.

Reflection and Application (4:1–7)

The fact that God has made us sons and daughters is a truth that can take our breath away once we grasp it. Neither fear nor shame nor feelings of inferiority nor insecurity need to weigh down those who know that they are God's children, sons and daughters in Christ. Those who struggle with these emotions can find strength by meditating on or memorizing some of these verses (e.g., Gal 4:4–7; Rom 8:14–17). Although we are called to humility and service like Jesus, the truth is that we Christians are all royalty, princes and princesses, children of the greatest King!

Another striking truth in these verses is that God the Father has shared with us the Spirit that he and his Son Jesus share. In that way we have been brought into communion, an intimate relationship, with the Trinity—we share the same Spirit, the same inner life, as the Father and the Son, although not in the same way. It is what Jesus promised in the Gospel of John: "Whoever loves me will keep my word, and my Father will love him, and we will come to him and make our dwelling with him" (John 14:23). The Father and the Son dwell in us by means of their Spirit, whom we have received.

Although Paul presupposes that his readers have an experiential knowledge of God as Father, we know that not all Christians today share that experience. Many need to learn this truth through meditation on God's word or through inspired preaching or teaching that brings the message home, or through prayer to be filled anew with the Holy Spirit.

Some people have obstacles to experiencing the fatherhood of God, due to negative experiences of their human fathers. By God's grace, and sometimes with the help of counseling or healing prayer, these brothers and sisters can also come to experience God as Father. The first step is to make a conscious choice to listen to and believe what the word of God says about our objective standing as sons and daughters, and about the kind of Father that God is.[9] Alongside that act of faith, which bears repeating until it becomes a habitual way of thinking, we can count on the Holy Spirit to gradually make this fact a reality in our experience. We can cooperate with this work of the Spirit by continually asking the Father to send the Holy Spirit to fill our hearts. Jesus' promise in Luke 11:9–13 reassures us of the outcome:

> I tell you, ask and you will receive; seek and you will find; knock and the door will be opened to you. For everyone who asks, receives; and the one who seeks, finds; and to the one who knocks, the door will be opened. What father among you would hand his son a snake when he asks for a fish? Or hand him a scorpion when he asks for an egg? If you then, who are wicked, know how to give good gifts to your children, how much more will the Father in heaven give the holy Spirit to those who ask him?

Concluding Exhortation: Do Not Return to Slavery (4:8–11)

---

[8]At a time when you did not know God, you became slaves to things that by nature are not gods; [9]but now that you have come to know God, or rather to be known by God, how can you turn back again to the weak and destitute elemental powers? Do you want to be slaves to them all over again? [10]You are observing days, months, seasons, and years. [11]I am afraid on your account that perhaps I have labored for you in vain.

OT: Isa 37:19
NT: 1 Cor 8:4; Gal 4:3; Col 2:16; Heb 7:18
Catechism: liturgical observance of days and seasons, 1163–73

9. See, e.g., Exod 34:5–7; Ps 103:8–18; Isa 49:13–16; Matt 5:44–48; 6:25–33; 7:7–11; John 14:8–10; 16:26–27; Eph 3:14–21.

Paul's Nuanced View of the Law

BIBLICAL BACKGROUND

Paul's clear declarations in Galatians and Romans that Christians are freed from the †law[a] have led some interpreters to regard Paul as antinomian, a teacher who completely rejects law. But other statements in Paul's letters reveal a great appreciation for the law. How can we reconcile these seemingly contradictory positions?[b]

First, it will help to review what Paul says against law. Paul insists that no one can be put right with God by works of the law (Gal 2:16), that "all who depend on the law are under a curse" (3:10). The law cannot give life (see 3:21). Rather than coming directly from God, the law of Moses "was promulgated by angels at the hand of a mediator" (3:19), and its purpose is to reveal sin (3:19, 22; Rom 3:20; 5:20; 7:7–13). The law leaves people enslaved to the elements, or "†elemental powers," of this world (Gal 4:3, 8–10). God intended it only as a temporary guardian for Israel until the coming of Christ, of †faith, of the Spirit, and of adoption as sons and daughters (3:23–25; 4:1–3; Rom 10:4). Those who seek to be †justified on the basis of the law are "separated from Christ" and have "fallen from grace" (Gal 5:4).

In other passages, however, Paul expresses a very high regard for law and even describes Christian life as "keeping God's commandments" (1 Cor 7:19). He says the law of Moses is "spiritual" (Rom 7:14), "holy and righteous and good" (7:12). He seems to have continued to observe the law in some respects (see the sidebar, "Did Paul Keep the Law of Moses?," pp. 174–75). He expects his readers to exceed the ethical requirements of the law of Moses by living in the Spirit[c] (Gal 5:16, 18, 22–26; Rom 8:4, 13–14) and keeping the commandment to "love your neighbor as yourself," which fulfills the whole law (Gal 5:14; Rom 13:8–10). Paul respects the law of Moses as divine revelation and cites it as his authority for doctrinal teaching (Gal 3:6–9, 16–18; 4:21–31), church practice (1 Cor 9:9; 1 Tim 5:18), and moral instruction of †Gentile Christians (Eph 6:2–3). He indicates that the law remains in force against gross violations of morality and says that this understanding fully accords with "the glorious gospel . . . with which I have been entrusted" (1 Tim 1:8–11). Far from being antinomian, Paul condemns "lawlessness" (2 Cor 6:14; Titus 2:14) and insists that unrepented serious sin will exclude a person from the kingdom of God (1 Cor 6:9–10; Gal 5:19–21; Eph 5:5). Paul himself does not hesitate to give authoritative instructions and rules for his churches when circumstances call for it (1 Cor 11:16, 33–34; 14:26–40; 2 Thess 3:6, 10–12).

How then do we understand Paul's sharp critique of the law? First, it is helpful to realize that Paul's passionate teaching in Galatians does not aim to present a perfectly balanced systematic exposition of all that he understands about the law, but rather to combat an error that threatens the †gospel. Second, when Paul refers to the "law,"[d] the term can refer to the law of Moses (the Pentateuch), to the entire Scriptures, to other traditional teaching, or even to some controlling entity (e.g., "the law of sin," "the law of the spirit," and "the law of my mind" in Rom 7:23–8:2). Consequently, it is always necessary to consider the context to understand precisely what Paul means by "law" in each instance.[e]

In Galatians and the early chapters of Romans, Paul is addressing the basis of justification—that is, the foundation of a relationship with God. Judaism held that the right foundation consisted in accepting the law of the †covenant at Sinai. The first Jewish Christians continued to observe the law of Moses while also believing in Christ.[f] Following this pattern, the †Judaizers wanted to require Gentile Christians to keep the law of Moses as an essential element of Christian life. The Apostle Paul realized that this position undermined the gospel and was incompatible with God's plan for gathering Gentiles into the people of God.[g] There cannot be two different foundations for a right relationship with God—the death of Christ on the one hand and the law of Moses on the other (Gal 2:21–3:1).

Paul also rejects every human claim to establish one's relationship with God on the basis of ethical conduct—the idea that "if I keep the moral law, I am just before God, and God must recognize me as righteous." Thinking like this not only contradicts what Scripture says about the universality of sin[h] but also makes justification, a person's relationship with God, depend on human effort and accomplishment, and that leads to boasting rather than gratitude and dependence on God (Matt 5:3; Eph 2:8–9). Neither the law of Moses nor striving to keep the moral law can establish a person in a right relationship with God. The only foundation is †grace received through faith in Christ.

a. Gal 2:19–20; 5:18; Rom 6:14–15; 7:1–14.
b. For more, see Cardinal Albert Vanhoye, *The Catholic Priest as Moral Teacher* (San Francisco: Ignatius, 1990), esp. "The Apostle Paul as Moral Teacher and Guide," 21–38. Also see the sidebar, "Law in Catholic Tradition," pp. 196–97.
c. Gal 5:16, 18, 22–26; Rom 8:4, 13–14.
d. Greek *nomos*; Hebrew *torah*.
e. See the great variety of uses in Rom 7:12–8:8, and note that the Greek word translated "principle" in Rom 7:21, 23 is also *nomos*, "law."
f. Acts 10:14; 21:20.
g. James and the Jerusalem Council reached the same conclusion (Acts 15:13–29).
h. Ps 143:2; Gal 2:16; Rom 3:9–20, 23.

Having ended his theological argument against looking to the †law of Moses for †justification, the Apostle now speaks directly to the Galatians to make them see the stark contrast between the doctrine he has just expounded and their present way of thinking. The fact is that the Galatians are no longer slaves but sons and daughters of God. However, their current mentality is a return to slavery, a foolish and indefensible reversal that is highlighted by Paul's impassioned question in verse 9: "Do you want to be slaves . . . all over again?"

4:8   Their slavery in the past was a consequence of ignorance: they **did not know God**—a truly deplorable condition. The book of Wisdom proclaims, "Foolish by nature were all who were in ignorance of God" (Wis 13:1). Not knowing the true God, the Galatians, like other †Gentiles in the Greco-Roman world, were slaves to false gods, to idols, a servitude not fitting to human beings, who are of infinitely greater value than gods of wood, stone, or metal, which are incapable of helping those who worship them (see, e.g., Ps 115:4–7; Isa 44:9–20; Jer 10:3–5).

4:9–11   The time of ignorance for the Galatians is now over. Paul's preaching has revealed to them the true God, the Father of Jesus Christ. They **know God, or rather**, they are **known by God**. Paul uses the verb "know" not in the sense of mere intellectual understanding but in the biblical sense of having a personal and experiential relationship with someone. This explains why the Apostle felt the need to correct his initial expression, "You have come to know God," and substitute a passive verb, "You have come . . . to be known by God." The active voice could have implied that people are able, through their own power, to come into relationship with God. Paul instead wants to emphasize that their relationship with God is a result of God's initiative, an initiative of love (see Rom 5:8).

God's gift of a personal relationship with himself is liberating. However, the Galatians have actually taken on a new slavery by accepting a teaching that obliges them to observe numerous legal prohibitions. From the context we know that Paul is talking about Jewish observances. The surprising thing is that by speaking of turning back, Paul presents their adherence to the †law of Moses as a return, although a partial one, to paganism. The Galatians were likely convinced of just the opposite. They thought that submission to the law constituted progress in their relationship with God. Paul asserts that they are going backward: **How can you turn back again . . . ? Do you want to be slaves . . . all over again?**

This is a return not to the worship of idols but to submission to **weak and destitute** "elements" (literal translation)—that is, the world in its material, physical aspects—a submission that Paul views as common to both Judaism and paganism (see commentary on 4:3). As an example of this slavery, Paul points out the observances of the Jewish religious calendar, governed by the movements of the sun and moon. The first word, **days**, refers specifically to observance of the Sabbath and perhaps other Jewish festivals (see Col 2:16). Although Sabbath observance is prescribed in the Decalogue (Exod 20:8–11; Deut 5:12–15), Paul does not want this rule imposed on †Gentile Christians because it is a mark of Jewish identity, a commandment given to Israel but not to the †nations.[10] The Apostle similarly opposes the observance of other prescriptions from the law of Moses such as **months**, meaning monthly feasts at the new moon (see Num 10:10; 28:11), and **seasons**—the Feast of Unleavened Bread in the spring (see Exod 23:15; 34:18), the harvest feast in the summer (see Exod 23:16; 34:22), and the Feast of Booths in the fall (see Lev 23:33–36). Finally, Paul mentions the observance of **years**, probably the Sabbatical Year (see Exod 23:10–11; Lev 25:1–7). All of this constitutes a subjection again to "the elements" that was required of Israel for a time but that has no inherent value for an authentic relationship with God. The passion and resurrection of Christ have marked out another path, a path of freedom, and the Galatians are abandoning that path. If they persist in this misguided direction, Paul's work on their behalf will be ruined. The Apostle expresses that fear with sadness: **I am afraid . . . that perhaps I have labored for you in vain**.

To summarize, in the previous section (Gal 3:19–29) the Apostle examined the †law of Moses from the perspective of salvation history and showed that the law was intended to fulfill only a temporary function until †faith in Christ could replace it, with the result that believers in Christ are no longer under the law. In the present section (4:1–11) Paul reveals how the coming of Christ and the gift of the Spirit have made possible an extraordinarily intimate relationship with God for believers.

The former function of the law was to reveal the spiritual condition of human beings. As sinners, human beings transgressed the law, and their wickedness was thus exposed. The law can condemn the sinner to die, but it cannot impart a new life that conforms the person to God's standards of righteousness. However, this function of the law had a positive aspect: by revealing the wretchedness of the human race, it showed our desperate need for redemption and thus prepared for the coming of Christ. In that sense, the law led to Christ, just as the *paidagōgos* (3:24–25; NABRE: "disciplinarian"), the household slave charged with the supervision of children, brought them to their teacher.

Faith, on the other hand, is much more powerful than the law because it unites human beings to Christ, the Son of God, and makes them share in his divine sonship. Baptism brings about this participation because it unites all believers into one body in Christ. Whether a person is of Jewish origin or of Gentile origin makes no difference. Other differences between people, such as civil and sexual differences, likewise lose their importance and make no difference in regard

10. For more on Christian fulfillment of the Sabbath, see Catechism 2175–76.

to a person's union with Christ. This union inserts all believers into Abraham's line of descent and ensures access to the †inheritance promised to his offspring.

In 4:1–11 Paul explains the paradoxical way that God has accomplished his plan. God sent his Son to share the condition of the Jews, who were subject to the law, in order to free them from that condition. He sent his Son to share our human nature so that he could adopt us as his sons and daughters. The sign that this adoption has taken effect is the Spirit of the Son, whom God has sent into the hearts of believers.

The conclusion is clear. Believers are no longer a subject people; they are sons and daughters of God and therefore his heirs. For the Galatians to subject themselves to the law of Moses would be an irrational and harmful step backward.

Reflection and Application (4:8–11)

Observing days, months, seasons, and years. It might seem that Paul's criticism of the Galatians for "observing days, months, seasons, and years" could apply to the liturgical tradition of the Church. We Catholics observe Sunday as the Lord's Day, other feast days, seasons (Advent, Christmas, Lent, and Easter), and jubilee years as well. What is the difference between these observances and those that Paul condemns?

The decisive difference is that the Galatians' observance of Israel's religious calendar was based on the view that they were obliged to keep the †law of Moses in order to be in a right relationship with God; in other words, it had become a basis of their †justification. Paul is absolutely uncompromising on this point: "By works of the law no one will be justified" (2:16).

There is nothing wrong—in fact, there is much that is very helpful—about structuring the calendar to remember and celebrate God's great salvation in Christ. We know that the early Christians, including Paul, remembered Jesus' resurrection on the first day of the week by gathering on the Lord's Day (Acts 20:7; 1 Cor 16:2; Rev 1:10). The early Church also celebrated Easter, the Christian Passover, right from the beginning. Through the centuries the Church's liturgical calendar has grown and been revised from time to time. By the authority Christ gave to the apostles (Matt 16:19; 18:18; 1 Cor 11) and they passed on to the bishops, the Church has made a few elements of the liturgical calendar obligatory for Catholics: attending Mass on Sunday and a few annual feasts; fasting on Ash Wednesday and Good Friday. But the Church does not regard even these obligatory observances—not to mention the rest of the liturgical calendar—as practices that justify us before God, as the †Judaizers regarded the law of Moses. Rather, they are means by which the Church commemorates the works of the †Lord, especially the death and resurrection of Christ in the grace-filled mystery and communion of the Eucharist, to lift our minds to the things above (Col 3:1) and to grow together in the Lord (Heb 10:25).

A Personal Appeal

Galatians 4:12–20

Since the beginning of Gal 3, Paul has been presenting arguments. He has reasoned, discussed, and illustrated, using every kind of evidence: Sacred Scripture, the experience of Christian life, the history of salvation, and legal proofs. He has not spoken about himself, and his personality has vanished for the moment behind his doctrinal arguments.

Galatians 4:11, however, marks the reappearance of Paul's "I" as he expresses a fear about the outcome of his apostolate among the Galatians: "I am afraid . . . that perhaps I have labored for you in vain." Verses 12–20 continue this shift in perspective and are characterized by a highly personal tone. The first-person singular is used in nearly every verse. However, Paul is speaking not just about himself but about his relationship with the Galatians. The pronoun "you" appears fourteen times in these nine verses.

One could wonder why Paul brings his personal relationship with the Galatians into a doctrinal discussion. In 1 Corinthians he strongly rejects the cult of personality among Christian leaders and asks, "What is Apollos, after all, and what is Paul?" His answer is that they are merely servants through whom the Corinthians have believed (1 Cor 3:5). Nevertheless, Paul attaches great importance to his Christian disciples' faithfulness to him for the sake of their preserving the †faith in all its purity—and we see this beginning from his earliest letter, 1 Thessalonians (e.g., 2:7–12, 17–20). Paul is convinced that their adherence to Christ is closely linked to their relationship with him, their father in the faith (see 1 Cor 4:15–16). For this reason, Paul seeks to renew this relationship.

An Appeal to Remember Their Love in the Past (4:12–16)

---

[12]I implore you, brothers, be as I am, because I have also become as you are. You did me no wrong; [13]you know that it was because of a physical illness that I originally preached the gospel to you, [14]and you did not show disdain or contempt because of the trial caused you by my physical condition, but rather you received me as an angel of God, as Christ Jesus. [15]Where now is that blessedness of yours? Indeed, I can testify to you that, if it had been possible, you would have torn out your eyes and given them to me. [16]So now have I become your enemy by telling you the truth?

NT: Matt 10:40; 2 Cor 12:7–10; Gal 2:5

Paul begins this section of his letter by inviting the Galatians to reflect on an earlier stage in their relationship.

The first sentence is surprising, but not because Paul invites the Galatians   **4:12–13** to imitate him. Paul often urges readers to imitate his conduct; for example, in 1 Cor 11:1 he writes: "Be imitators of me, as I am of Christ." Giving a good example and inviting imitation is an important means through which Paul teaches the Christian way of life.[1] What is surprising is that Paul seems to say *he* has imitated the Galatians: **be as I am, because I have also become as you are**. However, Paul is not writing about his following the Galatians' pattern of Christian conduct but is rather summoning them to reciprocity in a personal relationship.[2] Although the letter is not explicit, the context suggests that Paul refers to his own renunciation of the privileges of being a Jew (see Phil 3:4–8) for the sake of his new †Gentile Christians. He asks now for a reciprocal act by the Galatians—that is, that *they* also would renounce the markers of Jewish identity (e.g., circumcision, kosher food, calendar observance) that they were in the process of accepting in a misguided attempt to share the religious standing of Jews.

All of a sudden the Apostle refers to the past, recalling that when he first visited the Galatians they were very generous and welcoming to him: **You did me no wrong**. The goal of this reminder of their good relationship in the past is obviously to urge the Galatians to remain attached to their apostle and his doctrine. That **physical illness** was the circumstance that forced him to stop in Galatia, and consequently to preach the †gospel there, indicates that Paul

---

1. See, e.g., 1 Cor 4:16; Phil 3:17; 1 Thess 2:7–12.
2. Paul invokes reciprocity in personal relationships in other texts, such as 2 Cor 6:11–13.

St. John Chrysostom on Paul's Pastoral Skill LIVING TRADITION

An astute pastor and great preacher himself, St. John Chrysostom, archbishop of Constantinople (397–407), notices how Paul pastors his Galatian flock.

See how again he addresses them by a name of honor ["brothers," 4:12], remembering to be gracious . . . for just as continual flattery ruins people, so a continuously severe mode of speech hardens them. Therefore it is good to maintain a balance everywhere. See how he defends what he has said, showing that it was not in mere indignation but in concern for them that he said what he has said. For since he has given them a deep cut he next injects this appeal like oil. And showing that his words did not come from hatred or enmity, he reminds them of the charity that they displayed toward him and carries on his argument ironically.[a]

a. John Chrysostom, *Homily on Galatians* 4.8–12, in ACCS VIII:61–62.

did not originally intend to evangelize in their region, but that Providence had a different plan.[3]

4:14–15   Paul's sickness was a **trial** for the Galatians, who could have been tempted to **show disdain or contempt** for Paul, whose body was in a pitiful condition, and to reject him. To "show contempt" is a translation of a verb that means "to spit" and perhaps hints at an ancient superstition. To protect themselves from certain diseases, people would spit when they saw a sick person. The Galatians did not have that kind of reaction to Paul; on the contrary, they were very hospitable, receiving him **as an angel**—that is, a messenger **of God**—even **as Christ** himself. Paul reminds them of **that blessedness of yours**. This probably refers to the happiness they felt at Paul's arrival: "We are blessed because we welcomed Paul! We have discovered a treasure!" At that time the Galatians showed extraordinary love toward Paul: **I can testify to you that, if it had been possible, you would have torn out your eyes and given them to me.** Paul's mention of eyes could mean that he had an eye disease (see 6:11), but does not prove it, since "tearing one's eyes out" was a figure of speech referring to an attitude of extreme generosity.

3. This fact is of interest for reconstructing Paul's journeys and supports the hypothesis that locates the addressees of the letter in what is commonly called north Galatia, a region populated mainly by immigrants from Gaul (see "Who Were the Galatians?" in the introduction, pp. 20–25). Acts describes Paul passing through Phrygia and Galatia without planning to evangelize there (Acts 16:6; 18:23), while his earlier evangelizing in south Galatia—in Pisidia and Lycaonia—was intentional (Acts 13:14–14:22).

Paul moves from this description of the idyllic past to the current state of the   **4:16**
Galatian church's relationship to him. He points to its complete inconsistency
with their previous attitude by an ironic question: **So now have I become your
enemy by telling you the truth?** The Galatians are now opposed to him and his
doctrine; some regard him as an enemy. Such a change of attitude is unjustified,
since they have nothing to accuse him of. It is completely unreasonable to consider the Apostle, who proclaimed the truth of salvation to them, as their enemy.

The Contrasting Motives of the Judaizers and Paul (4:17–20)

¹⁷**They show interest in you, but not in a good way; they want to isolate
you, so that you may show interest in them. ¹⁸Now it is good to be shown
interest for good reason at all times, and not only when I am with you.
¹⁹My children, for whom I am again in labor until Christ be formed in
you! ²⁰I would like to be with you now and to change my tone, for I am
perplexed because of you.**

NT: 1 Cor 4:15; Eph 4:13; Col 1:28; 1 Thess 2:7–8
Catechism: growing in Christ's likeness, 793–94

Paul continues his personal appeal by contrasting the motives of the rival teachers to his own parental love.

Without any transition, Paul abruptly introduces a third-person plural verb: **4:17**
They show interest in you. Although Paul does not say so explicitly, it is clear
that he is taking aim at the †Judaizers. He considers them his rivals because they
want to isolate the Galatians from him and to attach these †Gentile Christians
to themselves. Their motive, Paul says, is **so that you may show interest in
them**. Paul suffers because of that. His suffering is revealed by an omission: he
does not specify who it is that the rivals want to "isolate" the Galatians from.
Obviously, he is that person. He twice uses the Greek verb *zēloō*, translated as
"show interest in," which can also refer to the emotion of jealousy. In fact, the
situation does involve a competition for the affection of the Galatian Christians. When it comes to the faithful whom he fathered and raised in the †faith,
Paul is like a jealous lover. He uses the same verb to say to the Corinthians: "I
am jealous for you with a godly jealousy. I promised you to one husband, to
Christ, so that I might present you as a pure virgin to him" (2 Cor 11:2 NIV).

This verse begins with what may be a proverb: **Now it is good to be shown**   **4:18**
interest for good reason at all times. In other words, it is always fine to be courted

for a good purpose. But then the Apostle gets personal: **and not only when I am with you**. Despite the acceptance implied by his words, Paul may be hinting, like a wounded lover, that his beloved Galatians have been unfaithful in his absence. Or, if his words are taken at face value, Paul is saying that he does not object to the Galatians receiving the attention of others in his absence, provided that the reason, the goal, is positive—but in the case of the †Judaizing teachers, it is not.

4:19 The tone changes again, however, in verse 19, where Paul's affection resembles that of a mother (see 1 Thess 2:7–8), rather than a father or a lover: **My children, for whom I am again in labor until Christ be formed in you!** In a sublime expression of generous love, Paul places in a positive light the pain he suffers at the inconstancy and personal disloyalty of the Galatians. He wants his suffering to be for the benefit of their spiritual life, a means to their having a deeper union with Christ. Paul intends and believes that all the suffering he endures in his ministry is for the benefit of those entrusted to his care—a continuation of Christ's suffering for the sake of the Church (2 Cor 1:3–7; 4:11–12; Col 1:24).

4:20 Paul concludes this section by expressing the spontaneous desire of anyone who loves, the desire to be physically present to his loved ones: **I would like to be with you now** (see 1 Thess 2:17; 3:6–10). He wants to find a solution: **and to change my tone**. He senses that a letter will not be enough. A dialogue in person is needed to fully resolve the crisis in their relationship. Paul feels at a loss and says so: **I am perplexed because of you**. This poignant admission reveals his sincerity and deep affection.

Reflection and Application (4:12–20)

The Apostle's intense affection for the members of his churches, expressed in this heated correction of the Galatians, shines through in several of Paul's letters.[4] Although the mutual love between a pastor and his people, like every other affection, can assume unhealthy forms, it also has great potential for good. Receiving the †gospel cannot be detached from the people who communicate that message to us. For good or for ill, they represent what they teach. So when Paul is encouraging Timothy to hold fast to the message he has heard, he says, "Remain faithful to what you have learned and believed, because you know from whom you learned it" (2 Tim 3:14), referring both to himself and to Timothy's grandmother, Lois, and mother, Eunice (1:5; 3:14–15). Leading people to †faith and forming them in it establishes a spiritual family relationship. Paul writes to the Corinthians,

---

4. E.g., 2 Cor 2:2–4; 6:11–13; 7:2–7; Phil 1:3–4; 4:1; 1 Thess 2:7–12, 17–20; 3:8–10.

Diverse Insights into Paul's Change of Tone

LIVING TRADITION

It is interesting to see how two Church Fathers interpret what Paul says about changing his tone (Gal 4:20). St. John Chrysostom thinks Paul wants to express his grief more explicitly:

> Let me show you how impatient, how incensed he is, how he cannot bear these things. For such is love: it is not content with words but seeks also to be personally present. . . . *To change my tone,* he says, that is, to cry out and to make mournful noise and tears and to turn everything into lamentation. For in a letter it was not possible to show his tears and mourning.[a]

St. Jerome thinks that Paul desires the greater effectiveness of personal presentation and that love makes him want to be more severe:

> Holy Scripture edifies even when read but is much more profitable if one passes from written characters to the voice. . . . Knowing, then, that speech has more force when addressed to those who are present, the apostle longs to turn the epistolary voice, the voice confined within written characters, into actual presence.
>
> I used coaxing words to you just now, . . . but for the sake of that love which prevents me from allowing my sons to perish and stray forever I wish that I were now present—if the bonds of my ministry did not prevent me—and change my coaxing tone to one of castigation. It is not because of fickleness that I am now coaxing, now irate. I am impelled to speak by love, by grief, by diverse emotions.[b]

a. John Chrysostom, *Homily on Galatians* 4.20, in ACCS VIII:65.
b. Jerome, *Epistle to the Galatians* 2.4.20, in ACCS VIII:65–66.

Even if you should have countless guides to Christ, yet you do not have many fathers, for I became your father in Christ Jesus through the gospel. Therefore, I urge you, be imitators of me. For this reason I am sending you Timothy, who is my beloved and faithful son in the Lord; he will remind you of my ways in Christ [Jesus], just as I teach them everywhere in every church. (1 Cor 4:15–17)

Familial love is fitting for the Church. As human beings we don't want the truth to be packaged in mere propositions, but incarnated in people who believe and live what they speak about,[5] people who love us and whom we can love in return.

5. Pope Paul VI wrote, "Modern man listens more willingly to witnesses than to teachers, and if he does listen to teachers, it is because they are witnesses" (*Evangelii Nuntiandi* [Evangelization in the Modern World] 41).

We who are teachers need to remember that our relationship with those we lead is as much about love as it is about knowledge. We must remember that the family is the paradigm for relationships in the Church, as Paul's advice to Timothy illustrates: "Do not rebuke an older man, but appeal to him as a father. Treat younger men as brothers, older women as mothers, and younger women as sisters with complete purity" (1 Tim 5:1–2).

Leadership entails a responsibility not to let our conduct or teaching be the cause of any of the †Lord's little ones stumbling (Matt 18:6). While working on this chapter, Peter Williamson spoke with a young man who had recently withdrawn from a very fruitful role in youth ministry. The reason? The pastor whose ministry had powerfully influenced this man's life for good and who had contributed greatly to his growth as a lay minister changed his position regarding the morality of homosexual acts. This led to a split in the community and left the young man torn and confused. The person who had been truth's best witness in his life now stood opposed to a truth taught by Scripture, Tradition, and the Church. The fact that the gospel produces bonds of affection and trust obliges leaders to conduct themselves as fathers and mothers, older sisters and older brothers, who are trustworthy, constant both in teaching and in right conduct.

Another Argument from Scripture

Galatians 4:21–31

At this point, not knowing what else to say to convince the Galatians (4:20), Paul quite possibly stopped dictating the letter for a while. Soon, however, his inventive mind found yet another argument from Scripture. Perhaps his mention of labor pains (4:19) led him to think about motherhood. Reflecting on the story of Abraham (Gen 16–22), Paul considers the significant difference between the situation of Sarah, a mother who was free, and Hagar, a mother who was a slave. Paul returns to the theme of Abraham's descendants (see Gal 3:7, 16, 29) and of Christian freedom (see 4:1, 9), but from a new angle.

Two Sons, Two Covenants, and Two Mothers (4:21–27)

²¹Tell me, you who want to be under the law, do you not listen to the law? ²²For it is written that Abraham had two sons, one by the slave woman and the other by the freeborn woman. ²³The son of the slave woman was born naturally, the son of the freeborn through a promise. ²⁴Now this is an allegory. These women represent two covenants. One was from Mount Sinai, bearing children for slavery; this is Hagar. ²⁵Hagar represents Sinai, a mountain in Arabia; it corresponds to the present Jerusalem, for she is in slavery along with her children. ²⁶But the Jerusalem above is freeborn, and she is our mother. ²⁷For it is written:

> "Rejoice, you barren one who bore no children;
>   break forth and shout, you who were not in labor;

> **for more numerous are the children of the deserted one
> than of her who has a husband."**

OT: Gen 16:1–6, 15; 17:3–8, 15–19; 18:10–14; Exod 24:7–9; Ps 87; Isa 54; 66:7–13
NT: Rom 6:14
Catechism: the Church and the Jerusalem above, 757

The way Paul interprets the Old Testament in the light of Christ shows both insight and a wonderful creativity. Paul sees in Ishmael's slave mother and in Isaac's freeborn mother a prefiguring of two contrasting religious situations, one of subjection to the †law of Sinai and one of Christian freedom. This kind of †typological exegesis is very different from historical-critical exegesis—which aims exclusively at the literal sense, the meaning that the human author was expressing—yet it is very important for the Christian tradition, which approaches Scripture as God's inexhaustible word and recognizes the Bible's multilayered richness.

4:21   Paul's opening words draw his readers into the discussion: **Tell me, you who want to be under the law, do you not listen to the law?** His question plays with two biblical meanings of the word "law," legislation and divine revelation. The Galatians wanted to submit to Mosaic legislation, but they should have been more attentive to the †law as divine revelation. Paul is saying that if they had done so, they would have understood that there was no reason to renounce their Christian freedom, since the law or †Torah, as a revelation of God's plan, announces its own termination as a legal system. Paul discerns this prophetic meaning through some features of the story of Abraham that concern his descendants, as set forth in Gen 16–21.[1]

4:22–23   Here the Apostle sets forth what he considers the relevant facts and then gives a †typological commentary on them in verses 24–28. Paul's presentation of the facts is straightforward: **Abraham had two sons**, Ishmael and Isaac. Paul's focus, however, is on the contrasting descriptions of the mothers—one a **slave woman** (Hagar) and one a **freeborn woman** (Sarah)—and on the difference in the two sons' births. One son was **born naturally** (Ishmael), without any special intervention by God (see Gen 16:3–4), but the other was born **through a promise,** since the birth of Isaac depended on God's miraculously overcoming Sarah's infertility (see Gen 17:16–19; 18:10–14).

Paul's description of Isaac's mother corresponds to the biblical account: Sarah (earlier named Sarai, Gen 17:15) was a free woman, and Hagar was her slave

---

1. Paul does not refer to Gen 25:1–6, which would complicate the perspective he is presenting. That text speaks of other sons of Abraham by Keturah, whom Abraham married after the death of Sarah.

The Fourfold Meaning of Jerusalem

LIVING TRADITION

St. John Cassian (360–435), monk and theologian, taught the fourfold sense of Scripture using the example of Jerusalem:

> One and the same Jerusalem can be understood in a fourfold way: historically as the city of the Jews, allegorically as the church of Christ, †anagogically as the heavenly city of God, which is the mother of all, and †tropologically as the human soul, which is often upbraided or praised under this name by the Lord.[a]

So a Christian might pray for "the peace of Jerusalem" (Ps 122:6) on behalf of the Church, of which Jerusalem is a †type, or look forward in hope for the descent of the heavenly Jerusalem (Rev 21:2), or accept exhortations to Jerusalem in Isa 52 or 54 as words of personal encouragement.

a. John Cassian, *Conferences* 14.8.4, in ACCS VIII:69–70. Cassian, like Paul in Gal 4:24, uses "allegory" to mean "type."

(see Gen 16:1–2, 6). The word "freeborn" is not found in the Genesis account, but Paul adds it because it is very important for his argument, which is based on the contrast between "slave" and "free." The second contrast, between being born "naturally" and being born "through a promise," accurately reflects the biblical account, but again Paul introduces language that is not found in Genesis to help him make his point clear.

Paul began this section with two symmetrical sentences that contrasted **4:24–26** Abraham's sons—born of a slave versus born of a free woman, and born naturally versus born through a promise (vv. 22–23). However, when it comes time for his †typological explanation, which he refers to as **allegory**,[2] he shifts his focus. The attention is no longer on the two sons but on the two mothers (vv. 24–27). In addition, the symmetry that is clear-cut in verses 22–23 becomes less precise. After mentioning **two covenants**, Paul refers only to one, which he characterizes as **from Mount Sinai, bearing children for slavery**. We would expect Paul to describe the other †covenant, the one that comes from Calvary and bears children for freedom. However, Paul moves in another direction

2. Paul does not distinguish between "allegory" and "type." Allegory attributes meanings that are other than the plain sense to persons, objects, or actions that appear in a narrative (e.g., Christ's interpretation of the parable of the sower in Matt 13:18–23). Types are persons, places, institutions, and events in Scripture that prefigure later realities in salvation history. For example, Adam is a "type" of Christ; manna is a "type" of the Eucharist. Although in Gal 4:24 Paul presents a typological exegesis of biblical persons, places, and events, he calls it "allegory."

because he wants to clarify immediately what stands in contrast to **the present Jerusalem**, which he has just mentioned.

Paul contrasts **the Jerusalem above**, which is **freeborn**, to "the present Jerusalem" in slavery. Paul's thought here, as is often the case, is highly original. He parallels the covenant[3] at Sinai with the slave woman Hagar, because this covenant imposed submission to the †law (see Exod 24:7–8), which Paul criticized above as a kind of slavery (see Gal 4:3). The idea that the law brought slavery stands in contrast to the Jewish traditions, some expressed in Scripture (Ps 119:45, 96), that presented law as a safeguard of true freedom, a perspective shared with Greek thought. While Paul may be exaggerating to make a point, what brought him to his innovative position of depicting the law as a kind of slavery was the discovery of something much better—namely, the wonderful spiritual freedom that comes through a loving relationship with Christ (see Gal 2:19–20). Whoever enters this relationship is guided by the Spirit and no longer needs the law. Such a person is "not under the law but under grace" (Rom 6:14; see commentary on Gal 5:18, 22–23).[4]

To support his claim about the typological correspondence between the covenant at **Sinai** and the biblical **Hagar**, Paul adds a geographical fact: Sinai is **a mountain in Arabia**, the country of Hagar's descendants. Such a detail obviously provides not logical proof but symbolic confirmation of the connection of Mount Sinai with Hagar.

Paul links the covenant of Sinai to "the present Jerusalem," which consists of the Jews who do not believe in Christ *and* †Judaizing Christians whose †faith lacks consistency because they consider the law of Sinai as foundational for Christian life.

In contrast to "the present Jerusalem," one would expect "the *future* Jerusalem." Instead Paul says "the Jerusalem above," indicating a contrast of level, not simply of time—a qualitative rather than a chronological contrast. By its unbelief, the present Jerusalem, which symbolizes the part of Judaism that did not accept Jesus,[5] belongs to "the present evil age" (1:4) and is still a slave to "the †elemental powers" of the world (4:3, 9). In contrast, the other Jerusalem, established by Christ's resurrection, belongs to the "new creation" (6:15) that lies in the future but is already present, that belongs not to the world here below

---

3. See the explanation of the meaning of covenant at 3:15.

4. For balancing perspectives, see the sidebar, "Paul's Nuanced View of the Law," pp. 146–47, and the reflection that follows it.

5. Acts indicates that many Jews, including "thousands" in Jerusalem (Acts 21:20), did believe in Jesus. But it seems the majority of Jews, and certainly most of the religious and political leadership of Jerusalem, did not believe, either during Jesus' lifetime or afterward (Acts 22–23).

Figure 14. Jebel Musa, the traditional location of Mount Sinai.

but to the world above. Since it is located "above," the new Jerusalem is not subject to the limitations of this world: Christ "gave himself for our sins that he might rescue us from the present evil age" (1:4). As for the earthly Jerusalem, it is natural for it to be subject to a particular legal system because it is an earthly city located in the world below and belonging to this age. On the other hand, the Jerusalem above, in line with its nature, is independent of any earthly ties to a particular nation and is characterized by openness to all (3:28). Christians belong to this new Jerusalem; they are her children, conceived through her preaching and born in her through baptism.

What is the connection between "the Jerusalem above" and the Church? Paul does not explicitly say, leaving the matter open for discussion. The fact that the Church exists as an earthly reality argues against her being simply identical to the Jerusalem above. One could say that "the Jerusalem above" refers to the transcendent dimension of the Church; it is a way of expressing the fact that, while the Church is in the world, it is not of it (see John 17:15–16). Her children already possess heavenly citizenship due to their union with the risen Christ, who has ascended into heaven (Eph 2:6; Phil 3:20; Col 3:1–4).

By saying that the heavenly Jerusalem is **our mother**, Paul includes believers of every national origin, Jews like himself, the Galatian Christians who are not Jews, and so many others.

Jerusalem, Mother of All Nations

BIBLICAL BACKGROUND

Besides Isa 54, from which Paul quotes, two other Old Testament texts speak strongly of Jerusalem as the "mother" or origin of God's people, and both refer to the future inclusion of †Gentiles among God's people. Isaiah 66 speaks of the miraculous birth to Zion (another name for Jerusalem) of a son, of a nation, and of children in a single moment (Isa 66:7–8), and then speaks of God gathering all †nations to himself (66:18–23).

The other passage is Ps 87:

> On the holy mount stands the city he founded;
>   the Lᴏʀᴅ loves the gates of Zion
>   more than all the dwelling places of Jacob.
> Glorious things are spoken of you,
>   O city of God.

> Among those who know me I mention Rahabᵃ and Babylon;
>   behold, Philistia and Tyre, with Ethiopia—
>   "This one was born there," they say.
> And of Zion it shall be said,
>   "This one and that one were born in her";
>   for the Most High himself will establish her.
> The Lᴏʀᴅ records as he registers the peoples,
>   "This one was born there."

4:27   To account for the heavenly Jerusalem's extraordinary fruitfulness, Paul quotes a prophecy from Isa 54:1:

> Raise a glad cry, you barren one who never bore a child,
>   break forth in jubilant song, you who have never been in labor,
> For more numerous are the children of the deserted wife
>   than the children of her who has a husband.

In its original context this prophecy concerns Jerusalem at the time of the exile, when the city was like a **barren** woman since she did not have inhabitants and appeared to be abandoned by God, her husband, after the destruction of the temple. In contrast, Babylon, a pagan city, was like a very happy woman. Supported by her god, as it must have seemed to her people, she enjoyed power and prosperity and ruled over an immense empire.

The prophecy predicts a reversal of this situation. All of a sudden, the **deserted one** will become a mother surrounded by **numerous** children, meaning that Jerusalem will be repopulated and even overpopulated because the people

> Singers and dancers alike say,
>   "All my springs are in you." (RSV)
>
> What is remarkable about this psalm is that it speaks of Gentile nations that were once enemies of Israel as people who have come to know God, and even as people who were born in Zion, who have come to celebrate Jerusalem as the source of their life, their "springs" of water.
>
> A notable New Testament vision also speaks of the origin of the new people of God. In the book of Revelation, John reports seeing "a great sign . . . in the sky, a woman clothed with the sun" (Rev 12:1). The woman who wears a crown of twelve stars symbolizes Zion, who miraculously gives birth to a son (Isa 66:7) "destined to rule all the nations" (Rev 12:5). Since the people of God of the Old and New Testaments are continuous, the woman is also the Church, whose children are identified as "those who keep God's commandments and bear witness to Jesus" (Rev 12:17). Mary, the actual "woman" of whom Jesus the †Messiah and Son of God was born, represents and embodies Zion and is a †type of the Church. She is honored in the Catholic Church as "the mother of Christians," a fitting title, since Mary is the mother of the Son of God, in whom baptized believers have received adoption as God's sons and daughters (Gal 4:4–6).
>
> a. Here "Rahab" refers to Egypt (see also Isa 30:7).

in exile will return from all the †nations with their children born in exile. The prophet describes this extraordinary and miraculous influx in Isa 49:12, 18–23; 60:4; and 66:8–13. In the chapter quoted by Paul, the prophet says, "You will spread out to the right and to the left, / and your descendants will possess the nations" (Isa 54:3 NRSV).

By quoting this text from Isaiah, Paul indicates that it had not been completely fulfilled by the return from exile in the fifth and sixth centuries BC. In fact, the return had been rather modest and limited, so that after the return, the prophecy still retained its value as a promise for the future. Jews in the period of the Second Temple generally agreed on this point and based their expectation of the future glorious restoration of Jerusalem on this prophecy and others like it (e.g., Tob 13:10–18). Paul discerns that the prophecy looks beyond the material restoration of the earthly city of Jerusalem to the decisive stage of God's plan in which a spiritual city (the Church) is established that is accessible to all nations. The Apostle thus applies the prophecy to this new Jerusalem: it might appear to be like a barren and abandoned woman, since it does not yet have the shape or structure of a normal city, yet God gives it a stupendous fruitfulness. Composed initially only of Jews—ensuring its continuity with ancient Jerusalem—it now takes possession of the nations (Isa 54:3) through the conversion of many peoples.

Reflection and Application (4:21–27)

A person might wonder whether birth from "the Jerusalem above" (4:25–27) is merely a metaphorical way of referring to the spiritual birth of Christians in contrast to the natural descent of the Jewish people from Abraham. Although spiritual birth is clearly one implication of having "the Jerusalem above" as our mother, the contrast between two Jerusalems ("present Jerusalem" and "Jerusalem above") has broader implications. Other New Testament texts elaborate on the "Jerusalem above." Hebrews 12:22–24 contrasts the spiritual situation of Christians with that of Israel at Mount Sinai under the Old Covenant and says this:

> You have come to Mount Zion and to the city of the living God, the heavenly Jerusalem, and to innumerable angels in festal gathering, and to the assembly of the firstborn who are enrolled in heaven, and to God, the judge of all, and to the spirits of the righteous made perfect, and to Jesus, the mediator of a new covenant, and to the sprinkled blood that speaks a better word than the blood of Abel. (ESV)

The text identifies Mount Zion with the heavenly Jerusalem, the place where God dwells and Christ is with him on the throne—a reality to which Christians on earth "have come." Other passages in Hebrews exhort readers to "approach" God's throne with confidence (Heb 4:16; 10:19–22). As the body of Christ on earth, the Church is the temple of God on earth (1 Cor 3:16), the place where his Spirit dwells, although that temple is still under construction (Eph 2:19–22; 1 Pet 2:5). As God's dwelling on earth, it overlaps with heaven, God's true dwelling, which Hebrews identifies as the heavenly Jerusalem. This helps to explain how Christian worship, and above all, the Mass, is a participation in the liturgy of heaven. Believers have access to God's temple in heaven through Christ and in the Holy Spirit. Other Pauline texts also refer to the real but hidden present access of Christians to the life of heaven.[6]

Visions in the book of Revelation depict Christians on earth worshiping in God's temple (Rev 11:1–2) and singing as they follow the Lamb on the heavenly

6. See Rom 5:2; Eph 1:3; 2:4–6, 18; 3:12; Col 3:1–4.

Mount Zion (14:1–5). The visions foretell that the fullness of God's kingdom will come to pass when the heavenly Jerusalem, the holy of holies of the temple built and indwelt by God, descends from heaven and is established on the new earth (21:1–3, 10–23).[7]

Paul's reference to the "Jerusalem above" who "is our mother" in Gal 4:26 is the earliest New Testament text that refers to the extraordinary spiritual reality that is our origin, our present place of worship, and our future destiny.

Implications for Christian Identity (4:28–31)

---

[28]Now you, brothers, like Isaac, are children of the promise. [29]But just as then the child of the flesh persecuted the child of the spirit, it is the same now. [30]But what does the scripture say?

"Drive out the slave woman and her son!
For the son of the slave woman shall not share the inheritance
with the son"

of the freeborn. [31]Therefore, brothers, we are children not of the slave woman but of the freeborn woman.

OT: Gen 21:1–13
NT: Rom 9:8; 11:28–29; Gal 3:29; 4:3; 5:11

After his joyful quotation of Isaiah, Paul returns to the connection between believers and Isaac, who was born "through a promise" (4:23). The †Gentiles' conversion to †faith in Christ fulfills the promise contained in Isaiah's prophecy (Isa 54:1, quoted in Gal 4:27) and so many other prophecies of the Old Testament, beginning with the promise in Gen 12:3 that all the families of the earth will be blessed (see Gal 3:8).[8] Paul's Gentile Christian readers are thus **like Isaac, . . . children of the promise**. **4:28**

They should remember, however, that as in the case of Isaac, they cannot expect that their situation will be tranquil. Ishmael, Abraham's son by the slave Hagar, did not leave Isaac alone. Although the NABRE translation of Gen 21:9 **4:29**

---

7. There is no temple in the new Jerusalem because the city itself is the place of God's dwelling (1 Kings 6:19–20; Rev 21:22). The fact that it is the holy of holies is indicated by its being a perfect cube with equal length, width, and height like the original holy of holies (Rev 21:16). For a fuller explanation of these texts from Revelation, see Peter S. Williamson, *Revelation*, CCSS (Grand Rapids: Baker Academic, 2015).

8. Other prophecies that the Gentiles will join Israel in worshiping God include Pss 22:28; 67:3–6; 72:17; Isa 2:1–3; 52:10; 66:18–21; and many more.

simply says that Ishmael was "playing" with Isaac, other translations (including the †Septuagint) interpret the Hebrew verb to mean playing as an expression of mockery or hostility. Paul follows that interpretation, which allows him to make yet another comparison with the situation of the Christians, this time with those who were being **persecuted** by some Jews (Gal 5:11).[9] Referring to Ishmael as **the child of the flesh** (literally, "the one born according to the †flesh") in order to reinforce Ishmael's connection with the Jews, Paul uses a contrasting expression for Isaac, **the child of the spirit** ("the one according to the Spirit"), to underscore the parallel between Isaac and Christians. He contrasts natural birth with birth brought about by the action of the Holy Spirit.

4:30   Sarah, vexed by Ishmael's conduct toward Isaac, appeals to Abraham: **Drive out the slave woman and her son!** (see Gen 21:10–12). God himself tells the patriarch to listen to Sarah. Paul thus presents Sarah's request as an authoritative word from Scripture and an expression of God's will. The Galatians should break with the †Judaizing Christians so that there will be no ambiguity about †justification—that is, about the basis of membership in the Church. †Gentile Christians ought not to make compromises to gain admission to synagogues in the hope of sharing in Israel's †inheritance. In fact, the inheritance will be given not to the children born according to the †flesh but to the children born of the promise—namely, Jews and Gentiles who believe in Jesus.

4:31   Paul's interpretation of Genesis shows him to be rather audacious, since by it he severs the bond between the majority of the Jews—those who have refused to believe in Christ—and their ancestor Isaac and associates them instead with Ishmael, the ancestor of a †Gentile people that was not in a †covenant relationship with God. Conversely, the Apostle affirms that the Galatians, who have no racial ties with Abraham, "like Isaac, are children of the promise" (4:29) and **children not of the slave woman but of the freeborn woman**. Paul thus sets forth a striking paradox. At the same time it is important not to overstate his position. Paul does not say that the non-Christian Jews *are* children of Hagar; he says only that they belong to the covenant of Sinai, which was prefigured in the person of Hagar.[10]

Paul distinguishes two possible ways to be children of Abraham. One is "according to the †flesh"—namely, through natural descent without any spiritual

9. Acts of the Apostles indicates that Jews who did not accept Jesus were the primary persecutors of Christians in the earliest days of the Church (e.g., Acts 5:17–40; 6:8–14; 7:54–58; 8:1; 12:1–4; 13:45–50; 14:2–6, 19; 21:27–28; 23:12–14). There is, however, no indication that Jews were persecuting Christians in Galatia; Paul may be referring to persecution of himself by †Judaizers (see Gal 5:11).

10. Paul provides a more complete and nuanced account of God's relationship with the Jews who do not believe in Christ in Rom 9–11, where he affirms that "the gifts and the call of God are irrevocable" (Rom 11:29) and foresees a day when "all Israel will be saved" (Rom 11:26).

union with the patriarch—and the other "according to the spirit," which involves a spiritual union. The authentic descendants for whom the †inheritance is reserved are obviously the ones who are spiritually united to Abraham (see 4:30; Rom 9:6–13). This union is obtained by adhering in †faith to God's plan, which was accomplished in Christ. The Jews who refuse to believe in Christ break their spiritual bond with Abraham and thus place themselves in the situation prefigured by Ishmael. On the other hand, every person who believes in Christ, the son of Abraham through the promise, is spiritually united to Abraham and is grafted into his authentic line of descent (see Rom 11:17). This applies first of all to Jews, but it also applies to non-Jews, because the decisive factor that connects a person to the promise is his or her spiritual response of faith in Christ.[11]

Reflection and Application (4:28–31)

From the very beginning, Christians have identified with Israel, God's chosen people. Every morning in the Liturgy of the Hours, the Church prays the Song of Zechariah (Luke 1:68–79), which, in the translation of the liturgy, begins, "Blessed be the Lord, the God of Israel; he has come to his people and set them free." Likewise when Christians pray the Psalms, we pray them identifying with Israel (sometimes referred to as Jacob) and with Jerusalem. The New Testament confirms the perspective that the Church is an †eschatologically expanded Israel, gathered around its †Messiah. Romans 11:17–24 speaks of †Gentiles, wild olive branches, being grafted into the cultivated olive tree of Israel. Ephesians 2:11–22 speaks of the reconciliation between Jew and Gentile achieved by Christ's death on the cross. It explains how Gentile believers, who were once complete outsiders, have become members of God's household and are being built into a temple where God dwells by his Spirit. First Peter, sent to predominantly Gentile communities of Christians in Asia Minor, addresses the recipients as sojourners of the "dispersion" (*diaspora*), a term used to refer to Jews living outside the land of Israel (1 Pet 1:1). The same letter refers to its Gentile Christian readers by terms previously used only of Israelites—"a chosen race, a royal priesthood, a holy nation, a people of his own" (2:9). And it exhorts them to "maintain good conduct among the Gentiles" (2:12)—"Gentiles" in this context referring to pagans, people who are not part of God's people. This close identification of

---

11. Earlier, in Gal 3:28–29, Paul showed that adherence to Christ secures not only a spiritual union with Abraham but also a physical connection, since believers have become members of the body of Christ, who is *the* descendant of Abraham, par excellence.

the Church with Israel led some early Christians to think that Gentile converts should keep the †law of Moses, a misunderstanding that Paul firmly rejects.

A question that the New Testament does not address is what this means for the relationship of Christians to Jews who do not believe in Jesus, especially those born generations after the leadership of the Jewish nation rejected the Messiah. Some Christians answer this question with a theology that regards the Church as the replacement for Israel. But that does not do justice to the texts that indicate God will never give up on his chosen people Israel (e.g., Isa 49:15; Rom 11).[12] The best answer to this question is the one that recognizes God's relationship both with Israel and with the Church. The patriarchs and the ancient writings that we call the Old Testament do not belong exclusively to either Jews or Christians; they are our common heritage. Christians respect Jews as our older brothers in the †faith of Abraham. It is our desire and prayer that one day they will attain the full purpose God has in mind for them by coming to faith in Jesus, the Messiah of Israel, so that they too may share in the †inheritance promised to Abraham's descendants.

---

12. The Catholic Church teaches about God's continuing special relationship with the Jewish people in Vatican II's *Nostra Aetate* (Declaration on the Relation of the Church to Non-Christian Religions) 4.

Concluding Summons to Live as Free People

Galatians 5:1–12

Now the Apostle draws practical conclusions not only from his final scriptural argument (4:21–31) but also from the whole doctrinal section (3:1–4:31). Galatians 5:1–12 is a tumultuous passage containing an exhortation (5:1), a warning (5:2–4), and a doctrinal statement (5:5–6), followed by a reprimand (5:7), a reassurance (the first part of 5:10), a prediction of judgment (the second part of 5:10), a personal defense (5:11), and a final declaration against the troublemakers (5:12).

Stand Firm in Freedom (5:1–6)

¹For freedom Christ set us free; so stand firm and do not submit again to the yoke of slavery.

²It is I, Paul, who am telling you that if you have yourselves circumcised, Christ will be of no benefit to you. ³Once again I declare to every man who has himself circumcised that he is bound to observe the entire law. ⁴You are separated from Christ, you who are trying to be justified by law; you have fallen from grace. ⁵For through the Spirit, by faith, we await the hope of righteousness. ⁶For in Christ Jesus, neither circumcision nor uncircumcision counts for anything, but only faith working through love.

NT: John 8:32; Acts 15:10; Rom 2:25; 7:6; 2 Cor 3:17; Gal 6:15; James 1:25; 2:18–20
Catechism: why the law cannot save, 578; freedom through Christ and the Spirit, 1741; the new law, 1972; faith, 162, 1814

Paul has just shown from Scripture that the true identity of his Christian readers is as "children not of the slave woman but of the freeborn woman." Now he urges them to †live in accord with their status as free people, warning that the path of circumcision and †justification through the †law is completely incompatible with life in Christ.

5:1   Paul makes clear that the Christian status of **freedom** has as its origin a specific intervention by Christ in the past: **Christ set us free**. This proclamation of freedom, unique in the New Testament except for John 8:36, uses new terminology for what Christ has accomplished, expressed elsewhere by "ransom" (Gal 3:13; 4:5), "rescue" (1:4), and similar words. The difference between "set free" and the other terms is that the others focus on the negative aspect, the bad situation or evil from which we have been delivered. "Set free" emphasizes the positive, referring to the excellent standing that we have received, corresponding to our dignity as sons and daughters of God. Although the †covenant established at Mount Sinai was granted to people who had been freed from slavery in Egypt, it nevertheless brought them into a servitude to the †law that Paul compares to slavery (4:24–25). Through his death and resurrection, Christ has conferred true freedom on believers and has brought us to a higher kind of spiritual existence, where the law is no longer in charge as a disciplinarian or guardian (3:23–25; 5:22–23) and we are free (2 Cor 3:17). Paul will explain the purpose of this freedom in the next section (Gal 5:13–26).

Having established this fundamental principle, Paul immediately speaks of its practical consequences in a very important exhortation. In it we can recognize two of the goals that the Apostle pursues in this letter: (1) a defense of his †gospel, the gospel of freedom, and (2) a struggle against the †Judaizing propaganda that led the Galatians into slavery. **Stand firm**—that is, firmly attached to the gospel of freedom—**and do not submit again to the yoke of slavery**. Since the redemptive work of Christ consisted in obtaining freedom for us, whoever wants to benefit from this work needs to guard his or her freedom. A clear choice must be made between the freedom established by Christ and religious slavery.

It is interesting to note that the original Greek says to not submit again to a "yoke" of slavery—without the definite article. This widens the scope of this prohibition beyond a warning against submitting to the Mosaic law. Christians should not submit themselves to *any* religious teaching that entails a similar slavery. There is an incompatibility between relying on Christ and relying, not only on the Mosaic law, but on any religious system or rule of piety or conduct that claims to determine a person's standing with God. While rules of life can

Figure 15. Ancient surgical instruments used for circumcision.

fulfill an important function for individuals and communities, they can never be allowed to substitute for the only true foundation of a right relationship with God—that is, †faith in Jesus and in his death and resurrection.

In the verse that follows, however, Paul returns to the case of the Mosaic law, the issue in question, and affirms the absolute incompatibility between Christian life and †justification by the law.

Here the Apostle resumes speaking in the first-person singular in the fatherly   **5:2** tone with which he addressed the Galatians in 4:19–20: **It is I, Paul, who am telling you**. He first takes aim at circumcision—the means by which men were initiated into the †covenant, the characteristic mark of Jewish identity, and the most important expression of †justification through the †law in the eyes of the †Judaizers. **If you**, Christians of other nationalities, **have yourselves circumcised, Christ will be of no benefit to you**. Christ removed the barrier between Jews and †Gentiles (see 3:28; Eph 2:14–16) and placed a love in the hearts of believers that transcends barriers (Rom 5:5).

Paul combats an illusion that could have led the Galatians to an acceptance   **5:3** of circumcision. They may have thought that undergoing this rite would be sufficient and would not entail further obligations. Paul disabuses them of that misunderstanding by solemn testimony: **I declare to every man who has**

Did Paul Keep the Law of Moses?

BIBLICAL
BACKGROUND

A person might assume from what Paul says here in Galatians and elsewhere[a] that, since turning to Christ, he no longer practiced the †law of Moses and dissuaded other Jews from doing so as well. That is exactly what many interpreters have concluded, but there are some strong reasons to believe that is not the case.[b]

As Galatians makes crystal clear, Paul absolutely denies that a person can be †justified—put in a right relationship with God—through observing the law of Moses, and therefore he is utterly opposed to †Gentile Christians being circumcised and taking on the Jewish law. It is also clear that Paul associated freely and ate with Gentiles, which contradicted traditional Jewish interpretations of the law (although not the written law itself), and perhaps took other liberties for the sake of evangelization (1 Cor 9:20–21).

However, other indications in his letters and Acts suggest that in most respects Paul continued to live as an observant Jew. Immediately after winning the argument at the Jerusalem Council that Gentiles need not be circumcised (Acts 15), Paul circumcises Timothy—whose mother was Jewish (2 Tim 1:5) and whose father was a Gentile—on account of the Jews in that region (Acts 16:3). A little later, Paul makes a Nazirite vow, a voluntary act of piety spelled out in the law (Acts 18:18; Num 6:5–9, 18); other references in Acts and 1 Corinthians suggest that Paul continued to observe Israel's feasts (Acts 20:16; 27:9; 1 Cor 5:7; 16:8).

The strongest indication that Paul continued to keep the law occurs in Acts when Paul arrives in Jerusalem with alms for the Jewish Christian community there. James, the leader of the Jerusalem church, informs him,

> Brother, you see how many thousands of believers there are from among the Jews, and they are all zealous observers of the law. They have been informed that you are teaching all the Jews who live among the Gentiles to abandon Moses and that you are telling them not to circumcise their children or to observe their customary practices. (Acts 21:20–21)

himself circumcised that he is bound to observe the entire law. This meant, among other things, that †Gentile Christians would need to distance themselves from their own culture to live a Jewish way of life.

5:4   The Apostle moves on to the Galatians Christians' underlying motive for circumcision: **you who are trying to be justified by law**. For them, circumcision was the first step in the direction of seeking to be accepted as righteous by God on the basis of one's own works performed in conformity to the †law. Paul has repudiated that way of thinking with great insistence (three times in

James advises Paul to demonstrate publicly that the rumor is false by joining some local Jewish Christians who have just made a Nazirite vow:

> Take these men and purify yourself with them, and pay their expenses that they may have their heads shaved. In this way everyone will know that there is nothing to the reports they have been given about you but that you yourself live in observance of the law. (Acts 21:24)

Paul does exactly as James suggests, refuting the false report that Paul is teaching Jews to abandon the law of Moses. Some interpreters think that in doing so Paul acted merely for the sake of expediency. But for Paul to deliberately give public evidence to a lie that he was living "in observance of the law," when he was not, would contradict what we know of Paul's character and would make him guilty of something worse than the inconsistency for which he reproves Peter in Gal 2:11–14.

What seems most likely is that Paul and the Jews in his churches continued to follow the law of Moses, but not to maintain a right relationship with God—in other words, not for justification, which Jews and Gentiles alike receive through †faith in Christ. Rather, the †Torah taught the way of life God gave Israel; Paul and other Jewish Christians loved their heritage (see Rom 9:4–5) and did not think that the arrival of the †Messiah and the inclusion of the Gentiles meant that they should cease to live as Jews! Also, when they kept the law Jewish Christians followed the Christ's authoritative interpretation of it[c] rather than the dominant Pharisaic interpretation, "the tradition of the elders," which Jesus rejected (Matt 15:2–8; Mark 7:3–8; see the sidebar, "Paul's Nuanced View of the Law," pp. 146–47).

a. See Rom 3:19–4:25; 7:1–4; 8:1–4; 1 Cor 9:19–23; Phil 3:2–11.
b. This interpretation of Paul, in combination with the rivalry between Judaism and Christianity in its first few centuries, led to Church prohibitions against Jewish Christians observing the law of Moses. This had the tragic result of the loss of a corporate Jewish witness to the Messiah in the Church. In recent decades Messianic Jews and Hebrew Catholics have revived the earlier practice of following Jesus while continuing to observe a Jewish way of life.
c. See Matt 5:17–48; 12:1–8; 19:3–9; 22:15–40.

2:16) and has explained his reasons at length (2:17–21; 3:6–29). His warning here to those who persist in this error is very stark: **You are separated from Christ . . . ; you have fallen from grace**. Seeking †justification through the law breaks a person's relationship with Christ because it means that person is denying the effectiveness of the redemptive death of Christ. Paul said it in 2:21: "I do not nullify the grace of God; for if justification comes through the law, then Christ died for nothing." Instead of relying on the work of Christ, such people are relying on the conformity of their conduct to the requirements of the law. By this act they place themselves outside the sphere of †grace, outside the realm of the gratuitous love of God.

5:5   The Apostle contrasts this ruinous attitude to that of true believers—**Through the Spirit, by faith, we await the hope of righteousness**—recalling his readers' attention to the central positive themes of his letter: righteousness (i.e., †justification), †faith, and the Spirit. Now he adds hope, which corresponds to the theme of the †inheritance that Paul has touched on.[1] In the New Testament, hope is not merely a wish but a confident expectation of a future good. The phrasing here is surprising, however, because he refers to the object of Christian hope not as the "inheritance" but rather as "righteousness." Paul teaches in 2:16 and 3:24 and elsewhere[2] that the gift of righteousness—that is, justification—is received on the basis of faith *at the beginning* of Christian life. Yet here he says "we await" this gift at the end when Christ returns (see also 1 Cor 1:7; Phil 3:20). Paul is speaking about justification ("righteousness") differently from the way he speaks about it so far in Galatians. Instead, he speaks of justification as it was customarily employed in Judaism—namely, as a positive judgment about a person's standing that takes place after death: those who are judged righteous will enter into eternal life, while the unrighteous will go to eternal punishment (see Dan 12:2–3; Matt 25:46; John 5:29).[3] So Paul is saying that we Christians are waiting with confident expectation to be found righteous at the final judgment, when God judges people according to how they have lived (2 Cor 5:10).

What is interesting about this text is that Paul does not say that the final judgment depends on works—as the traditional Jewish and Christian understanding is expressed in other texts, including some written by Paul.[4] Instead he speaks of the role of faith and the Spirit, just as he does earlier in the letter, where he refers to the initial justification that places a person in a right relationship with God (Gal 2:16; 3:5–6, 11, 14; 4:4–7). Paul's position is consistent: having taught that faith and the Holy Spirit are the foundation of our justification and right relationship with God, he insists that they remain foundational for the whole edifice of Christian life. Just as Christian life begins with faith and the gift of the Spirit, it reaches its goal by the same means.

---

1. Gal 3:18, 29; 4:7, 30; 5:21; other texts explicitly link hope with the inheritance: Eph 1:18; 1 Pet 1:3–4.

2. See Rom 5:1, 9; 1 Cor 6:11.

3. Some interpreters do not think it possible that Paul would speak about final justification this way, and therefore they interpret the text as saying, "We await the hope that springs from righteousness." While possible, this translation seems forced. Besides, Paul clearly speaks of the relationship of righteousness to justification at the final judgment in Rom 2:5–16 and alludes to it in other texts (Rom 14:10; 1 Cor 4:3–5; 2 Cor 5:10).

4. See Matt 25:31–34; John 5:29; Rom 2:5–8; 2 Cor 5:10; James 2:14–26.

There exists an important difference, however, between initial †justification **5:6**
and final justification, which is indicated in verse 6, where Paul speaks of **faith**
working through love. In initial justification, †faith is not accompanied by works
for the simple reason that it has not been able to produce anything yet. Works
done previously did not have faith as their foundation and are thus excluded
as the basis of justification (see 2:16). However, after initial justification, faith
does not remain passive. Rather it manifests a powerful dynamism with which
the believer must actively cooperate. Otherwise, his or her faith could suffocate
and come to nothing. What counts for final justification is thus "faith working
through love."

Paul knows from experience that faith produces love, an active love. Faith is a
personal adherence to God, who has loved us to the point of giving his own Son
for all of us (Rom 5:8; 8:32); it is the embrace of Christ, who loved us and gave
himself over to death for us (Gal 2:20). By faith we receive the Holy Spirit (3:2,
14), whose first "fruit" is "love" (5:22; see Rom 5:5). The dynamism produced
by Christian faith is one of charity—that is, of love toward all. By contrast,
circumcision does not change the heart of the person. It is a rite that initiates a
person into a particular people, and it therefore can function as a barrier to the
universality of divine love. Paul, however, is not saying that noncircumcision is
any better, since it also leaves human beings in their sinful condition. Therefore
as regards justification before God, **neither circumcision nor uncircumcision**
counts for anything. Both conditions leave human beings in an unsatisfactory
position, with an inadequate kind of existence. It is necessary to be raised to a
higher plane, that of "faith working through love."

Reflection and Application (5:1–6)

The source of love. The only thing that matters is to lean on Jesus in †faith. The
source of love is not in us, and we delude ourselves if we think we are able to be
charitable on our own. Only in Jesus can we draw upon that source, because it
is he who is the fountain of life, of all good, and of the charity that draws us out
of our selfishness and moves us to give ourselves to others, purified deep down
by divine love (Rom 5:5; 1 John 4:7–10). Let us pray for the faith that makes
Jesus the sole foundation of our life and that transforms us by means of charity,
a gift that has already been given and that the Spirit can make fruitful in us.[5]

5. This reflection is drawn from Cardinal Albert Vanhoye, *Il pane quotidiano della Parola: Commento
alle letture feriali della Messa ciclo I e II* (Casale Monferrato: Piemme, 1994), 731–32.

Freedom in Christ. Paul declares triumphantly: "For freedom Christ set us free; so stand firm and do not submit again to the yoke of slavery" (Gal 5:1). We find a similar note sounded in the Gospels. Jesus introduces his preaching in Nazareth by saying,

> The Spirit of the Lord is upon me,
>   because he has anointed me
>   to bring glad tidings to the poor.
> He has sent me to proclaim liberty to captives
>   and recovery of sight to the blind,
>   to let the oppressed go free. (Luke 4:18; see John 8:31–32)

Jesus came to restore to the human race its full dignity, which is possible only in freedom. Christians are free, liberated by Jesus, and we must remain so, just as Paul admonishes the Galatians: "Do not submit again to the yoke of slavery" (Gal 5:1). We must therefore persist in exercising our liberty by continually liberating ourselves from the false freedom of following our own impulses, which easily degenerates into slavery. Here, however, St. Paul is not writing the Galatians about combating sin: neither circumcision nor keeping the †law of Moses is a sin or immoral in itself. Paul was fighting for the freedom of these Christians who were foolishly submitting to a yoke from which Christ had liberated them.

Christian freedom, as Paul will indicate (5:18), is to be led by the Holy Spirit. This freedom is a source of great joy and opens beautiful and unexpected vistas before us. In this interior freedom we see the material and moral slavery of so many brothers and sisters with eyes of mercy and compassion, and we find the courage to fight alongside them so that they may also be free, using all the means that the love and hope that spring from the †gospel suggest to us.[6]

Do Not Be Misled (5:7–12)

---

[7]You were running well; who hindered you from following [the] truth? [8]That enticement does not come from the one who called you. [9]A little yeast leavens the whole batch of dough. [10]I am confident of you in the Lord that you will not take a different view, and that the one who is troubling you will bear the condemnation, whoever he may be. [11]As for me, brothers, if I am still preaching circumcision, why am I still being persecuted?

---

6. Vanhoye, *Il pane quotidiano della Parola,* 727–28.

In that case, the stumbling block of the cross has been abolished. [12]Would that those who are upsetting you might also castrate themselves!

NT: 1 Cor 1:18–24; 5:6; 15:33; Gal 6:12

Having forcefully restated his position, Paul reprimands the Galatians one last time and has stern words for those responsible for the false teaching that threatens their relationship with God.

Paul begins with a compliment: **You were running well**. However, the fact that   5:7
he puts the verb in the past tense makes the compliment an implicit reproof. The sports metaphor of running a race, which the Apostle likes to use (1 Cor 9:24–27; Gal 2:2; Phil 2:16), serves here to describe the past fervor of the Galatians that has now disappeared. Paul's question aims at making the Galatians aware of the negative nature of the change that has occurred. Their former spiritual vigor has been **hindered** by someone; their admirable running has been interrupted to the point that they no longer obey [the] **truth**, the authentic †gospel. This passage is closely related to the beginning of the letter, where Paul reproaches the Galatians for following "a different gospel," which is not the true gospel of Christ, and for "forsaking the one who called" them (Gal 1:6).

Here Paul touches on the same issue, but with a new and more positive nu-   5:8–9
ance. The Greek does not say **the one who called you** in the past tense, as the NABRE has it (as in 1:6), but rather "the one who is calling you," in the present tense to indicate that God in his goodness *continues* to call the Galatians to communion with himself. Then Paul quotes a proverb: **A little yeast leavens the whole batch**. The proverb contrasts the small amount of yeast with the large quantity of dough that is affected.[7] Through this remark about the small amount of yeast, Paul may be seeking to minimize the number of those responsible for the Galatians' error, lessening the community's guilt. At the same time, he implies that they should get rid of the harmful yeast (1 Cor 5:5–7), just as Israel eliminated the old yeast at Passover time (Exod 12:15, 19; 13:7).

This possibility is strengthened as Paul, on the one hand, expresses confidence   5:10
regarding the response of the Galatians and, on the other hand, announces the future **condemnation** of the troublemaker. As to the response of the Galatians, Paul is **confident** that they **will not take a different view** from his. As regards the origin of the upheaval in the community, we see a difference here from Paul's

---

7. This proverb appears again in 1 Cor 5:6, where the action of the yeast also stands for something that is not positive but rather a pernicious fermentation, a "troubling" of the community (see Gal 1:7; 5:10). Jesus uses the metaphor of yeast both positively, to describe the growth of the kingdom (Matt 13:33), and negatively, to describe the influence of the teaching of the Pharisees (Matt 16:6, 11–12).

earlier affirmation about "some" who were disturbing them (1:7). In this passage Paul uses the singular, **the one who is troubling you**, and adds, **whoever he may be**, either indicating that he did not know the individual's name or that his condemnation focuses on the action rather than the particular person. His statement shows a desire to blame only the one person who is principally responsible for the whole situation and to be lenient with the other members of the community.

5:11   Paul returns to the main issue of circumcision in the final words of this section. He pushes back against what seems to be an audacious insinuation that Paul himself had no objection to the circumcision of †Gentile Christians and even taught it himself at times. Paul responds to this false claim with a fact that refutes it: he has been persecuted by the Jews (see 2 Cor 11:24, 26). If he were **still preaching circumcision**, he would not be **persecuted** by them at all.[8]

Now comes an abrupt declaration about the cross: **In that case, the stumbling block of the cross has been abolished**. In order to understand this statement, it is necessary to supply a few points that are implicit. If Paul had still been preaching circumcision, his preaching would have constituted a path of salvation different from and incompatible with the one opened up by the cross of Christ (Gal 5:2, 4). Teaching Gentile Christians to be circumcised would have denied the sole efficacy of the cross and encouraged people to avoid its offensiveness. From the human point of view, the cross is a stumbling block or offense[9] (see 1 Cor 1:17, 22–23), but it is an offense that absolutely must be retained, since the cross is the irreplaceable instrument of our salvation (see 1 Cor 1:24–25).

5:12   To demonstrate his opposition to circumcision in the clearest way, the Apostle ends with a harsh wish directed at those who were advocating it: **Would that those who are upsetting you might also castrate themselves!** Of course Paul does not mean this literally, but there are circumstances when strong language is fitting. In this case the truth of the †gospel and the very salvation of the Galatian Christians were under threat. In this way Paul definitively dismisses the †Judaizers who were causing havoc in his communities.

Summary of Doctrinal Presentation (3:1–5:12)

This exhortation (5:1–12) concludes the doctrinal section (3:1–5:12) of the Letter to the Galatians, in which the Apostle has laid out with stupendous depth his

---

8. Some Jews in Paul's day did preach conversion to Judaism through circumcision and observance of the †law of Moses (Matt 23:15; Acts 15:21), but Paul was not one of them.

9. Greek *skandalon*, from which comes the English "scandal."

theological teaching about the relationship between †law and †faith and about the mystery of Christ and its realization in the lives of believers. Above all he highlights the foundation of Christian life—that is, the free gift of †justification that results from adhering to Christ in faith—and the implication for the extension of the people of God among all †nations, namely, that †Gentiles need not live as Jews to belong to Christ.

The theological content in this section is very rich. The Apostle seeks to persuade the Galatians not to pursue justification, the divine blessing, or the †inheritance promised to Abraham's descendants by submitting to the law. By "law" Paul refers especially to the legislative system of the Jewish people and, in particular, the †ritual prescriptions of the law that functioned as markers of Jewish identity (circumcision, calendar, and dietary regulations). Nevertheless, what is said about the law applies to every other work by which a person might seek to justify or save himself or herself (see Eph 2:8–9). The only way forward is faith, which leads us to cling to Christ; it frees us from the curse of the law and brings us the blessing of the Holy Spirit.

Paul's first argument is that of the experience of Christian conversion (Gal 3:2–5). When the Galatians came to faith, they received the Holy Spirit, whose presence was clearly manifested by "mighty deeds" (3:5)—namely, miracles. In this powerful experience (3:4), the observance of the Jewish law played no part, for the simple reason that the Galatians did not know the law. At the beginning of their evangelization, Paul was not concerned to teach the law of Moses.[10] He preached only Christ and his paschal mystery. He proclaimed that Christ "gave himself for our sins" (1:4) and that he was "crucified" (3:1) and then "raised . . . from the dead" (1:1). The only thing required of the Galatians was to accept this message in faith. It was therefore inconsistent with the Galatians' Christian experience to attribute a saving importance to legal observances, especially those pertaining to the body, such as circumcision and dietary proscriptions. The Spirit had raised them to a higher kind of life (3:3; 4:9, 26).

This first argument is then confirmed and reinforced by arguments from Scripture, especially by reference to Gen 15:6, establishing a clear relationship between Abraham's act of faith and God's crediting it to him as righteousness

---

10. Eventually, of course, Paul's churches became thoroughly acquainted with the Jewish Scriptures (1 Tim 4:13; 2 Tim 3:16–17). Galatians itself and other New Testament books directed primarily to Gentiles (e.g., Mark, Luke, Acts, John, 1–2 Corinthians, Ephesians, 1–2 Peter, Revelation) require a deep familiarity with the Old Testament. It is likely that the early Christian congregations acquired this familiarity by following the synagogue practice of public reading and explanation of the Old Testament Scriptures.

Deep Magic in Narnia

Christian artists never tire of finding new ways to recall the mystery of Christ's saving death and resurrection. C. S. Lewis's *The Lion, the Witch, and the Wardrobe*, a novel for children of all ages, is a marvelous example.

Edmund has betrayed his friends to the Witch, a Satan-like figure. She asserts her claim to his life on the basis of the Deep Magic that God, the Emperor-Beyond-the-Sea, established. Addressing Aslan, the great lion who represents Christ in the Narnia novels, she says, "You at least know the magic which the Emperor put into Narnia at the very beginning. You know that every traitor belongs to me as my lawful prey and that for every treachery I have a right to kill."[a] Aslan acknowledges her claim and offers his own life in exchange for Edmund's, a substitution that the Witch gleefully accepts. She humiliates and finally slays the great lion on the Stone Table.

Later Susan and Lucy find the Stone Table broken and the lion's body gone. Aslan comes up behind them and speaks, arousing in them first fear and then great joy.

> "Aren't you dead then, dear Aslan?" said Lucy.
> "Not now," said Aslan. . . .
> "But what does it all mean?" asked Susan when they were somewhat calmer.
> "It means," said Aslan, "that though the Witch knew the Deep Magic, there is a magic deeper still which she did not know. Her knowledge goes back only to the dawn of Time. But if she could have looked a little further back, into the stillness and the darkness before Time dawned, she would have read there a different incantation. She would have known that when a willing victim who had committed no treachery was killed in a traitor's stead, the Table would crack and Death itself would start working backwards."[b]

a. C. S. Lewis, *The Lion, the Witch, and the Wardrobe* (New York: Collier, 1970), 138–39. Like every artistic representation of our redemption, this story presents only an analogy whose details should not be pressed for an exact correspondence.
b. Lewis, *The Lion, the Witch, and the Wardrobe*, 159–60.

(Gal 3:6). To obtain a right relationship with God, no work was required of Abraham beyond his receiving a word from God in faith. Abraham serves as a paradigm for non-Jews as well as Jews, since another passage in Scripture says that all the nations will be blessed in him (Gen 12:3; see Gal 3:8). Paul sees a profound connection between this blessing, justification, and the gift of the Spirit. In fact, justification is the initial blessing that opens the way for many other blessings. The one who makes justification effective is the Spirit (1 Cor

6:11), who then transforms believers' whole lives by placing them in an intimate relationship with the Son and the Father (see Gal 4:6).

To place one's trust in observing the law is deadly because the law curses and condemns those who do not conform to its prescriptions (3:10). On their own, human beings could not escape the curse of the law because they were sinners. Christ, however, has changed the spiritual situation of humanity because he has taken on himself the curse of the law in such a way that he freed us from it and has made his blessing overflow to us (3:13–14). The key to this paradox is that Christ became a curse "for us" (3:13)—that is, out of love for us (2:20) in perfect conformity to the will of the Father (1:4). When the curse is confronted and accepted by the One who did not deserve it and is endured purely out of obedience to the Father and love for his brothers and sisters, its effect is reversed. Instead of the alienation and death that belong to the curse, Jesus' death on the cross opens the way to reconciliation and life in communion. There is now the possibility of escaping the curse of the law. It consists in accepting with faith the redemption accomplished by the love of Christ, which is the realization of the promise of blessing made to Abraham for the benefit of his descendants and of all nations.

The connection between the law and the promise requires an explanation. Paul notes that the promise came before the law, so its validity does not depend on the law (3:15–17). The law can neither prevent the fulfillment of the promise nor bestow what was promised. The law cannot bestow justification, because it can only impose the sentence of death on a transgressor; it is not able to communicate new life or make the transgressor a righteous person (3:21).

The law does no more than reveal the dire situation of sinful humanity, causing people to pass from a more or less hidden state of guilt to a state of manifest transgression (3:19). This revelation of sin is, however, useful. By showing people their powerlessness, it can prepare them to welcome the Savior, thus clearing a path for faith (3:22–23).

The power of faith in Christ is wonderful. It frees us from subservience to the law because it makes us children of God in Christ (3:26). The sign of this sonship is the active presence in our hearts of the Spirit of the Son (4:6). Union with Christ through faith occurs at so deep a level that the distinction that existed between Jews and other nationalities in relationship to God completely disappears, as does every other distinction (3:28).

In salvation history two periods must be distinguished. The old period is one of guardianship under the dominion of the law of Moses, which is also the dominion of "the †elemental powers of the world" (4:3), since the law contains many material proscriptions such as dietary observances. The new period, introduced by the sending of God's Son and the Spirit, is that of freedom (4:5; 5:1) and adoption as sons and daughters (4:5–7). To illustrate this distinction Paul presents a †typological interpretation of Sarah and Hagar (4:21–31). For a Christian to seek justification by keeping the law (5:4) would be a lamentable step backward—indeed, a break with Christ. The only basis for justification is faith in Christ. The whole of Christian life is built on this foundation: it is "faith working through love" (5:6).

Part 3

Exhortation about How to Live as a Christian

Galatians 5:13–6:10

From here on Paul gives more-specific teaching about Christian living, a life of true freedom, and rejects some misconceptions of what this freedom means. To have an accurate understanding of Paul's theology in Galatians, it is necessary to hold together his doctrinal teaching (3:1–5:12) and his practical instruction (5:13–6:10).

By itself, the presence of an entire section devoted to exhortation indicates something important, since otherwise one could easily conclude that Paul's †gospel does not entail any teaching about conduct, but only a proclamation of the †faith that †justifies without works. Rather, Paul demonstrates that salvation by faith does not mean that people are saved merely through knowledge of the truth, which was the claim of certain pagan mystery religions and later of the heretical Gnostics. Nor is faith to be equated with mere assent to the truth or a powerful spiritual experience. Instead, faith involves the whole person and is intended to bring about a complete transformation. It requires a commitment not merely of the intellect but also of the will and the affections, and it expresses itself in action. Galatians 5:6 says that what "counts" is "faith working through love." This is why when Paul preaches faith he always includes a call to †*live* by faith.

185

Theologians sometimes distinguish two aspects of Paul's teaching by noting a change in his predominant usage from †indicative verbs, which present the *facts* of a situation (e.g., "As proof that you are children, God sent the spirit of his Son into our hearts," 4:6), to †imperative verbs, which summon readers to appropriate action in response (e.g., "Serve one another," "Bear one another's burdens," 5:13 and 6:2). Paul uses indicative verbs to tell about the gift of God, then follows with imperative verbs that instruct readers how to respond. What is stated in the indicative is always the foundation: it announces what God has done and what he has given to human beings, the radical transformation that Christ has accomplished. However, the indicative is not enough. God's gifts need to be received. Since these gifts convey life and activity, they cannot be received without human action that corresponds to the divine gift. God's gift of inner transformation always precedes and indeed makes possible our change in behavior.

In this respect the life of faith differs from life under the †law. It is true that under the law of Moses there was also an indicative that preceded the imperative. In the account of the Sinai †covenant, God's saving actions on behalf of Israel, his gifts (Exod 19:4; 20:2), are recalled before the commandments are imposed (20:3–17). However, there is an important difference. Under the first covenant, the gifts of God that preceded his commands were external interventions culminating in the exodus. There was no inner transformation of the people; the connection between the indicative and the imperative remained external. People needed to act according to the imperative, and if they did so they were considered righteous. In contrast, in the New Covenant, the indicative that comes first also includes interior transformation, a righteousness freely given by God in the Holy Spirit, and this interior gift is what makes it possible for his New Covenant people to do his will, to live out the imperatives of apostolic teaching.

Paul's writing in this section, as often in Galatians, seems rather spontaneous and improvised rather than carefully planned, requiring effort to understand the coherence of his thought. For example, Paul says that Christians are called to freedom (Gal 5:13) but in the same verse exhorts them to make themselves slaves of one another (the literal meaning of the Greek), which at first glance seems a contradiction. Then, having proclaimed freedom from the law, Paul presents fulfilling the law as an ideal (5:14), and then again says, "You are not under law" (5:18). In 6:2 the Apostle says, "Bear one another's burdens," but he affirms in 6:5 that "each will bear his own load." Paul does not seem concerned to express his ideas clearly enough to eliminate every possible confusion. Because of his manner of expressing himself, it is easy to draw false, incomplete,

---

Was the Old Covenant Only about Externals? BIBLICAL BACKGROUND

Several passages from both the Old and the New Testament con-trast the physical requirements of the Old Covenant with the in-terior transformation of the New.[a] Nevertheless, the Old Covenant was *not* only about externals. The exodus was an external divine intervention calling for a profound interpersonal response: "I bore you on eagles' wings and brought you to myself. Now, if you will really listen to my voice and keep my covenant, you will be my treasured possession among all nations" (Exod 19:4b–5a, author's translation). Moses clearly believed God's saving actions ought to evoke a heart response from the Israelites (Deut 10:16). This, indeed, is the central point of the book of Deuteronomy, with its emphasis on "Remember!" and "Love!"[b] The †law too is concerned with an internal response, as the com-mandments against coveting indicate (Exod 20:17; Deut 5:21). Examples of an interior response under the Mosaic †covenant can also be found in the prayers of the Psalter and the experiences of the prophets (Isa 6) and martyrs (2 Macc 7). Nevertheless, although God's acts of salvation in the Old Testa-ment deserved and sometimes evoked the love he sought from Israel (Deut 6:5), a greater interior †grace was necessary to overcome the power of sin in the human heart (Deut 30:6; Jer 31:33–34; Rom 7:7–25).

a. See, e.g., Jer 31:33; Ezek 36:26–27; Mark 7:18–23; 2 Cor 3:3; Gal 4:3, 9; Col 2:20–23; Heb 9:9–14.
b. For "remember," see, e.g., Deut 5:15; for "love," see especially Deut 6:5 and 10:12.

---

or one-sided conclusions from Paul's letters, as St. Peter observes in 2 Pet 3:16. Instead of seeking precision in his wording, Paul goes off first in one direction and then in the opposite direction. The result for the reader who succeeds at following the twists and turns of his logic is a certain equilibrium that is full of lively tensions, dynamic rather than static.

This third part of the letter (Gal 5:13–6:10), devoted to exhortation, begins with a contrast between the †flesh—that is, our self-centered tendencies—and love, which focuses on the good of others (5:13–15). Then Paul draws another forceful contrast between the Spirit and the flesh (5:16–25), followed by advice for community life (5:26–6:6). The Apostle concludes with a powerful exhorta-tion to the Galatians to do good, showing that Christian faith entails a serious commitment demonstrated by works (6:7–10). Paul's insistence on the need for works in a letter that has energetically proposed justification by faith could be confusing. Is Paul being unfaithful to his own doctrine? On the contrary, his vigorous exhortations to action contribute to a clearer understanding of his teaching. While Paul does not want works of the law to be regarded as the foundation of Christian life, a role reserved exclusively for faith, neither does he want faith to be sterile. He thus calls for works of charity that spring from faith (5:6), the fruit of a †grace to which believers must actively respond (1 Cor 15:10; 2 Cor 6:1).

Freedom, Love, and Life in the Spirit

Galatians 5:13–25

Now that Paul has demolished the idea that a Christian can be †justified by observing the †law of Moses and has instead proclaimed freedom from the law through †faith in Christ, the question naturally arises, how should a Christian conduct his or her life? If we are not called to observe the law of Moses, is there any rule of life? In this chapter Paul will speak of two guides to Christian conduct that are profoundly related: the law of love and the help of the indwelling Holy Spirit. Along the way Paul will describe the source of the resistance to God and to right conduct that is at work in fallen human beings, a tendency that he refers to as "the †flesh."

Freedom: Not License but Service in Love (5:13–15)

¹³For you were called for freedom, brothers. But do not use this freedom as an opportunity for the flesh; rather, serve one another through love. ¹⁴For the whole law is fulfilled in one statement, namely, "You shall love your neighbor as yourself." ¹⁵But if you go on biting and devouring one another, beware that you are not consumed by one another.

OT: Lev 19:18, 34
NT: Mark 10:43–44; 12:31–33; John 13:14; Rom 6:18–22; 13:8–10; 1 Pet 2:16
Catechism: love of neighbor, 2196; a law of love, grace, and freedom, 1972; the flesh is concupiscence, 2515

5:13 In the first sentence, which acts as a transition between the doctrinal and the exhortative sections of the letter, Paul shows he is aware of the danger that his teaching could be misunderstood and seized upon to justify dissolute conduct. He therefore feels the need to block the path to this erroneous conclusion, but without taking back anything that he has taught. Consequently, Paul begins this section by reaffirming his doctrine—**you were called for freedom**—before putting the Galatians on guard against a distorted interpretation of it.

By using the past tense, Paul refers to the time of the Galatians' conversion, when God established them in freedom. Paul has already urged them to keep themselves free (5:1). He does not repeat this exhortation, but as a realistic person he anticipates how it might be misunderstood and addresses the misunderstanding directly.[1] Does not proclaiming that Christians are no longer under the †law open the door to license and immorality? Not at all! Paul is firmly opposed to every temptation to **use this freedom as an opportunity for the flesh**. "†Flesh" here means the self-centered tendencies of human beings that lead to every kind of evil conduct; it is, therefore, roughly equivalent to what later Christian tradition refers to as concupiscence. Paul will give a concrete list of "the works of the flesh" in 5:19–21 so as to leave no doubt about the kind of conduct he is referring to.[2]

Paul contrasts this caricature of freedom to the Christian ideal: **rather, serve one another through love**. The Greek is more vivid: Paul presents this service paradoxically as slavery, using the Greek verb *douleuō*, "to serve as a slave," which he used earlier (4:8–9) to refer to the Galatians' servitude to the law and the †elemental powers. After saying that the Galatians should not turn back to slavery (5:1), here he counsels them to make themselves slaves! It seems contradictory, but actually it is not, as two phrases make clear. (1) The Galatians are invited to make themselves slaves to one another "through love." Whatever is done for love is done not by constraint but in freedom and joy. While, literally speaking, slavery is a form of oppression that crushes people and strips them of their dignity, serving as a Christian through love is a free commitment that lifts people up and confers great dignity upon them. We can add that if serving without love would be slavery, love without serving would be barren (see 1 John 3:17–18). Love and service go together. This teaching of Paul has Christ as its basis, the one who "did not come to be served but to serve and to give

---

1. In Romans, Paul mentions that he was accused of encouraging people to "do evil that good may come of it" (Rom 3:8).

2. Peter, in his first letter, also warns against the tendency to use freedom as a pretext for following evil inclinations (1 Pet 2:16). Whoever uses freedom to do evil quickly destroys that very freedom, since whoever commits sin "is a slave of sin" (John 8:34).

his life as a ransom for many" (Matt 20:28; Mark 10:45), and who "loved his own in the world . . . to the end" (John 13:1; see Gal 2:20). In addition, (2) true Christian service is service of "one another" in a mutual relationship that does not leave room for unilateral domination. In this love there are no masters on one side and slaves on the other, but each person is simultaneously master and slave, being served in certain matters and serving in others, according to the capacity and needs of each. Paul's wording points to a radical transformation of relationships among people based on a dynamic of love that comes from God—charity understood in all its dimensions.

At this point Paul makes an observation that might surprise some readers,   **5:14** since it could seem contrary to the perspective of the letter as a whole. Paul spoke of being "bound to observe the entire law" as something negative in 5:3. What he says here appears to reverse that: **the whole law is fulfilled in one statement, namely, "You shall love your neighbor as yourself"** (see Lev 19:18). But Paul is not contradicting himself. He is not saying that Christians should *keep* the †law of Moses, but rather that one who loves his or her neighbor *fulfills* the law—that is, achieves the purpose of the law. Paul says the same thing in Rom 13:8–10, where he provides additional details. His teaching corresponds to that of Jesus in the Gospels. In Matt 5:17, Jesus proclaims that he came not to abolish the law and the prophets but to *fulfill* them; in Matt 7:12, he summarizes the law as the golden rule; in Matt 22:37–40 he summarizes the law in the two precepts about loving God and loving one's neighbor.

If Paul had said that Christians are obligated to observe the system of the law and that this observance is the basis of their relationship to God, he would have

Figure 16. Torah manuscript (the law of Moses) on parchment, ca. 1270.

contradicted everything he said before. But Paul says nothing of the kind. His words about love fulfilling the law do not speak in favor of the whole Mosaic system of law, but rather speak against it. The single precept of love of neighbor is sufficient; a system of multiple precepts is unnecessary. Furthermore, Paul does not say that faithful observance of the commandment to love one's neighbor provides a sufficient foundation for a person's relationship to God. Rather, the foundation is †faith, through which a person receives the Spirit, and it is the Spirit who produces charity in the believer. Love of neighbor, an expression of charity, is thus not a human work through which a person can make himself or herself righteous before God but is rather a gift of divine life to which a human being responds (Gal 5:6, 22; Rom 5:5). The first and fundamental effort of a Christian is not, therefore, to practice charity, as though one could do so in one's own strength, but is rather to receive the divine †grace and action of the Holy Spirit that enable a person to love one's neighbor as oneself. Consequently, although believers have renounced any attempt to practice the law, they will discover that they have de facto fulfilled it and have done even more than the minute prescriptions of the law require (Rom 8:4).

5:15   Having said this, Paul puts the Galatians on guard against failures of charity in the community. He uses two powerful metaphors, **biting** and **devouring**, to describe animal-like ferocity in human relationships (see Ps 22:13–14, 21–22). Although it is always risky to speculate about the situation of a letter's recipients on the basis of such an exhortation, it appears that the Apostle is referring to rifts that were wounding the unity of the Galatian churches. When a crisis occurs, tensions almost inevitably provoke exchanges of words, harsh judgments, and personal attacks against the reputations of people on the other side of the issue. Paul warns against the real and present danger that they could be **consumed by one another**—that is, that mutual hostility could cause grave, permanent harm.

The Power of the Spirit over the Flesh (5:16–25)

[16]I say, then: live by the Spirit and you will certainly not gratify the desire of the flesh. [17]For the flesh has desires against the Spirit, and the Spirit against the flesh; these are opposed to each other, so that you may not do what you want. [18]But if you are guided by the Spirit, you are not under the law. [19]Now the works of the flesh are obvious: immorality, impurity, licentiousness, [20]idolatry, sorcery, hatreds, rivalry, jealousy, outbursts of fury, acts of selfishness, dissensions, factions, [21]occasions of envy, drinking bouts, orgies, and the like. I warn you, as I warned you before, that those

who do such things will not inherit the kingdom of God. ²²In contrast, the fruit of the Spirit is love, joy, peace, patience, kindness, generosity, faithfulness, ²³gentleness, self-control. Against such there is no law. ²⁴Now those who belong to Christ [Jesus] have crucified their flesh with its passions and desires. ²⁵If we live in the Spirit, let us also follow the Spirit.

OT: Isa 48:16–18; Jer 31:31–33; Ezek 36:27

NT: Rom 7:14–8:14; 13:13–14; 1 Cor 6:9–10; Eph 5:5–6; Col 3:5–10; 1 Tim 1:9; Jude 1:20–21

Catechism: the flesh is concupiscence, 2515; the Spirit is the new law, 1966, 1983; guidance and transformation by the Spirit, 736, 1695, 1832, 2744; penance and conversion, 1470; idolatry, 2113

Lectionary: 5:16–25: Pentecost Mass during the Day (Year B); Confirmation

---

While the commandment to love one's neighbor as oneself is indeed a sufficient objective guide to conduct that pleases God, we need more than a guide! The teaching about love of neighbor is a succinct statement of the moral law, summing up how a person should conduct himself or herself toward others. The problem, as Paul explains here (and more thoroughly in Rom 7), is that there is a self-centered inclination within each of us, which Paul calls "the [†]flesh" (Rom 7:25), that opposes God's will. The good news, however, is that the Spirit of God's Son that we received through [†]faith and baptism (Gal 3:27; 4:6) provides an interior power to overcome the [†]flesh and to [†]live in a manner that pleases God, to become people who in their character resemble Jesus Christ. However, this positive result is not automatic but requires active cooperation.

In this section (5:16–25) Paul describes the conflict between the Spirit and the flesh within a Christian, the difference between what the flesh produces and what the Spirit produces, and how Christians can cooperate with the Holy Spirit to become people who are Christlike.

How can people avoid falling into all the sinful patterns of conduct that we **5:16** human beings are so prone to? How can people resist **the desire of the flesh**, by which Paul means all human tendencies contrary to divine love, not only disordered bodily appetites like lust and gluttony? The Greek word translated "desire" refers to strong emotion, especially disordered desire; it is sometimes translated "passion," "lust," or "covetousness." The word translated "[†]flesh" has a wide variety of uses in the New Testament, even in Galatians[3] (see the glossary), but in the context of Gal 5 it refers to human nature's tendency to sin, ever since the fall of our first parents (Gen 3). Paul knows very well that human strength is not sufficient in this struggle. It is necessary to receive inner power from God the Holy Spirit, who is capable of overcoming the flesh. Paul then

---

3. E.g., 1:16; 2:16, 20; 4:13, 23; 6:13.

tells the Galatians to †live—literally, "walk"—**by** the light and power of **the Spirit**, with the assurance that in doing so, **you will certainly not gratify** the disordered inclinations of fallen human nature. The RSV translates this sentence as two parallel commands: "*Walk* by the spirit, and *do not gratify* the desires of the flesh" (similarly NRSV), but that misses the point. In the Greek, the first verb has the form of a command, while the second is a different verb form that indicates the inevitable result of keeping the command.

The Apostle is not merely pointing out that whoever chooses to follow the Spirit *does not* gratify the flesh because the two ways are incompatible. It is not a case of two opposing and equal principles, but rather that the Spirit is stronger than the flesh and brings victory over it. By contrast, the *Rule of the Community* of †Qumran explains that God has set before human beings two opposite dynamics: one is the "spirit of truth" and the other is the "spirit of perversion," two mutually opposed spirits.[4] Paul, however, talks not about two opposing spirits but about the antagonism between the Spirit and the flesh. Whoever welcomes the action of the Spirit is assured of overcoming the flesh. Therefore, a Christian's attitude can be positive. It is not a good strategy to be constantly preoccupied with avoiding sin—a gloomy outlook that only increases the likelihood of sinning. Rather, the wise path entails seeking to be attentive and obedient to the promptings of the Holy Spirit, trusting in his power, and availing oneself of the means that foster life in the Spirit. All of this is to live according to the Spirit, to set one's mind on the things of the Spirit (see Rom 8:5–6 NRSV).

5:17   Verses 17–25 explain the interior conflict between the tendencies of the †flesh and those of the Spirit. Paul is not preaching an easy, comfortable Christianity that involves no struggle. On the contrary, he places a choice before us between the **desires** of **the flesh** and those of **the Spirit**, since they **are opposed to each other**. The end of this verse, which expresses the consequences of this relentless opposition, is often misunderstood. Some commentators interpret it in light of Rom 7:19: "I do not do the good I want, but I do the evil I do not want." That leads them to think that the conclusion of Gal 5:17 means "so that you do not do what you want." But the Romans passage refers to the situation of human beings prior to or apart from a relationship with Christ, while the Galatians passage speaks of *believers united to Christ*. Verse 17 sums up the consequence of this opposition by saying, "so that you may not do whatever things you may desire" (literal translation). The conflict between the two dynamics in us makes

---

4. 1 QS 3:13–4:26.

it impossible to do everything that might attract us. A person might dream of satisfying all his or her desires: to live comfortably and yet be generous, to satisfy desires for sensual pleasure of every kind and yet experience spiritual joy and chastity, to dominate others and yet serve them humbly, and so on. Paul tells us that having it both ways is impossible; a choice is necessary. We must say no either to the desires of the flesh or to the godly desires that the Holy Spirit places within us.

In this section devoted to moral exhortation, Paul does not forget what he said   **5:18** earlier in the doctrinal section about Christian freedom from the †law. Rather, he boldly tells the Galatians, **If you are guided by the Spirit, you are not under the law.** People who are led by the †flesh find themselves under the law because they commit immoral acts that the law condemns and punishes.[5] In contrast, Christians who allow themselves to be led by the Spirit do nothing immoral and perform only good and generous acts that go above and beyond the realm of the law. Believers can fulfill the law without being "under" it, because there is a power in them enabling them to act righteously in a way that well exceeds the requirements of the law (Matt 5:20; Rom 8:4). To use an extreme analogy, a man who dearly loves his wife is not "under" the commandment against murder in regard to her; he does not need the law to keep him from murder because it is the furthest thing from his mind. In Christ the capacity to fulfill every part of the moral law superabundantly comes by the †grace of the indwelling Spirit.

The Apostle now paints contrasting portraits of what the †flesh produces   **5:19–21** (5:19–21) and what the Spirit produces (5:22–23). The way the two different results are designated is significant. In regard to the flesh, Paul speaks of "works," while in regard to the Spirit, he speaks of "fruit." In this way he contrasts a vital fruitfulness with merely external acts. The fruitfulness of which he speaks presupposes a union in love between the believer and Christ (2:20). In addition, "works" is in the plural while "fruit" is singular. This difference suggests that there is an organic unity among the various facets of the fruit of the Spirit, in contrast to the disjointed nature of **the works of the flesh**. Paul draws a similar contrast between works and fruit in Eph 5:11, where he speaks of "the fruitless works of darkness."

The list of "the works of the flesh" is obviously not meant to be exhaustive. It should be noted that these works are by no means limited to what we commonly call "sins of the flesh" but include attitudes and actions that have nothing to do with sex or gluttony—for example, hatreds, fury, and factions. The list clearly

---

5. Paul explains the continuing force of the law in regard to sinful conduct in 1 Tim 1:8–11.

Law in Catholic Tradition

LIVING
TRADITION

Paul's declaration that "you are not under the law" (Gal 5:18) might strike some people as a not very Catholic statement! What about natural law, moral law, civil law, and canon law, not to mention the Rule of St. Benedict and the statutes that govern other religious communities? The answer is that Catholic tradition embraces the Apostle Paul's nuanced teaching about †law (see the sidebar, pp. 146–47) but brings greater clarity to it by placing it within a broader context of reflection about law and the moral life (see Catechism 1950–86, especially 1963–66).

St. Thomas Aquinas teaches that the "new law" of the †gospel is the †grace of the Holy Spirit received through †faith. According to St. Thomas, this new law, unlike the old law of Moses, truly does make us just. "The new law is instilled into man by being added on to his nature by a gift of grace; it not only indicates to him what he should do, but also helps him to accomplish it."[a] Of course the gospel contains various commands and teachings. But according to St. Thomas, these elements, "the teachings of faith, and those commandments which direct human affections and human actions," while important to observe, are "secondary," in the sense that they do not †justify a person. Aquinas then quotes 2 Cor 3:6—"The letter brings death, but the Spirit gives life"—and says: "Augustine explains this [*On the Spirit and the Letter* 14, 17] by saying that the letter denotes any writing that is external to man, even that of the moral precepts that are contained in the gospel. It follows that the letter even of the gospel would kill, unless there were the inward presence of the healing grace of faith"—that is, the Holy Spirit.[b]

Another helpful insight of St. Thomas is his distinction between three kinds of precepts in the Old Testament: moral, ceremonial, and judicial.[c] The moral precepts of the law of Moses—for instance, the Ten Commandments—remain valid as standards of conduct to which human beings remain accountable.

shows what Paul means here by "the flesh"—namely, our fallen nature, the source of every sinful inclination. The first three works of the flesh are violations of chastity. The first, **immorality**, translates *porneia* in Greek, a term that refers to any improper use of sexuality, especially fornication or prostitution ("pornography" is related to this word). The second, **impurity**, is broader and can refer to a range of moral disorders that sully one's conscience (the same Greek word is translated "filth" at the end of Matt 23:27). When used together with *porneia*, it usually means sins against chastity (see Eph 5:3; Col 3:5). The same is true of the third word, translated **licentiousness** or "sensuality" (ESV, NJB). These three words are found together in a reproach to some Christians in Corinth

The ceremonial precepts—rules about sacrifices, †ritual purity, and festivals under the Old Covenant—function as †types that foreshadow the sacrifice of Christ and the worship of the New Covenant and thus in their literal sense are not binding on Christians. The judicial precepts governed Israel's life as a nation at a particular moment in history. While neither universal nor timeless as law, they contain many principles of enduring value—for instance, their insistence on impartiality and the need for two or three witnesses in judicial procedures (Lev 19:15; Deut 19:15) and their concern for the poor and vulnerable (Deut 15:7–11; 24:17–22).

Canon law arose from the decisions of Church councils early in the history of the Church in continuity with various apostolic rules found in Acts and in the letters of Paul.[d] The purpose of this kind of law is to preserve good order in the Church; its goal is "the salvation of souls, which is always the Supreme Law of the Church."[e] In addition there exist various communities within the Catholic Church that have their own constitutions and rules to express their spiritual ideals and to guide their common life. These rules are accepted voluntarily by members of these communities as aids to living a life of grace in the Holy Spirit.

a. Thomas Aquinas, *Summa theologica* I-II, 106. Translation slightly adapted from Fathers of the English Dominican Province (New York: Benziger Brothers, 1947), http://dhspriory.org/thomas/summa/FS/FS106.html#FSQ106OUTP1.

b. Thomas Aquinas, *Summa theologica* I-II, 106.

c. Thomas Aquinas, *Summa theologica* I-II, 99:4; 107:2.

d. E.g., Acts 15:28–29; 1 Cor 11:16; 2 Cor 13:1; 2 Thess 3:10–14; 1 Tim 5:19.

e. *Code of Canon Law*, Canon 752, the concluding words of the Code. In the document through which Pope John Paul II promulgated the current code of canon law, he wrote, "Although St. Paul, in expounding the Paschal Mystery, teaches that justification is not obtained by the works of the Law, but by means of faith (cf. Rom. 3:28; Gal. 2:16), he does not thereby exclude the binding force of the Decalogue (cf. Rom. 13:8–10; Gal. 5:13–25; 6:2), nor does he deny the importance of discipline in the Church of God (cf. 1 Cor. 5–6). . . . This being so, it appears sufficiently clear that the Code is in no way intended as a substitute for faith, grace, and the charisms in the life of the Church and of the faithful. On the contrary, its purpose is rather to create . . . order in the ecclesial society" (*Sacrae Disciplinae Leges* [*Laws of Sacred Discipline*], January 25, 1983).

(2 Cor 12:21). Sexual disorder was common in Greco-Roman society, as it is today in Western culture, so Paul uses a variety of terms to fortify his †Gentile Christian communities against the patterns of sin common to their culture.[6]

We can wonder why the Apostle lists **idolatry** after sexual immorality. There is a connection, however, and it is rooted in biblical tradition that considers idolatry on the part of the chosen people, married to the †Lord by †covenant, to be immorality (see Ezek 16:15, 25; Hosea 1:2). In addition, in the pagan world the worship of idols sometimes involved sexual relations with temple

6. See 1 Cor 5:1–13; 6:13–18; 1 Thess 4:3–8.

prostitutes. The book of Wisdom says that "the source of wantonness [*porneia*] is the devising of idols" (Wis 14:12). Paul saw a relationship of cause and effect between idolatry and sexual disorders. When a personal relationship with the true God is missing, human relationships become disordered, and the most serious sexual depravities can follow (see Rom 1:23–27).

After idolatry comes **sorcery**, or magic, a practice that is mentioned only here, in Acts, and in Revelation in the New Testament but is severely condemned in the Old Testament.[7] Magic refers not to the illusionist tricks of entertainers but to the use of drugs, potions, and spells in witchcraft.

What follows next is a long series of disorders in personal relationships between individuals (**hatreds, rivalry, jealousy, outbursts of fury** . . . **occasions of envy**) and groups (**dissensions**, **factions**). The meaning of the Greek word translated **acts of selfishness** is unclear; it could mean disputes. The list ends with **drinking bouts** and **orgies** or "carousing" (NRSV), words that suggest excess in food, drink, and sex. Viewed as a whole, the works of the flesh that Paul depicts are repulsive. He underscores the negative aspect of these behaviors again by a warning about their final consequence: exclusion from the promised †inheritance, the kingdom of God. A horrific prospect indeed!

5:22–23   In contrast to the works of the †flesh, the description of **the fruit of the Spirit** does not focus on specific kinds of acts but describes the character of people whose lives are led by the Holy Spirit. The list does not begin by emphasizing chastity and purity to counterbalance fornication and impurity, but begins with "love, joy, peace," which sets a very different tone. The Holy Spirit does not follow the path of the flesh to counter it, but rather pursues his own independent course. His fruit is above all generous **love** (Greek *agapē*), divine charity: "The love of God has been poured out into our hearts through the holy Spirit that has been given to us" (Rom 5:5). Whereas the works of the flesh are all manifestations of self-centeredness, the fruit of the Spirit is always a manifestation of love, but in diverse forms. Love brings with it **joy** because love satisfies the heart's deepest desire and most ardent aspiration, since human beings were created to love and to be loved. Alongside joy, there is **peace**. The Spirit establishes peace in people's hearts as he leads them to be in harmony with God's fatherly will and gives them victory over all their disordered tendencies, which would otherwise entangle them in endless interior conflict. In addition, the Spirit brings peace among people because he directs them to benevolence and harmony.

7. See Acts 8:9, 11; 19:19; Rev 9:21; 18:23; 21:8; 22:15; in the Old Testament, see Deut 18:10; Wis 12:4; 18:13; Isa 47:9, 12.

Christian Conduct Surpasses the Law

In the *Epistle to Diognetus*, an anonymous Christian in the second century sought to help pagan readers in the Roman Empire understand his fellow believers. Among other things, the author describes how Christians measure up to the laws of society:

> Christians are differentiated from the rest of humanity neither by land, nor by language, nor by clothing. . . . Rather, dwelling in both Greek and non-Greek cities . . . and following the local customs in clothing, food, and the rest of life, they demonstrate the amazing and undeniably remarkable character of their citizenship. . . . They marry as all do, they have children, but they do not expose their offspring. They set a common table, but not a common bed. They find themselves to be in the flesh, but they do not live according to the flesh. They remain upon earth, but they have their citizenship in heaven. They obey the set laws, and in their own lives they surpass the laws.[a]

a. *The Epistle to Diognetus* 5.1, 4, 6–10, in *A Patristic Greek Reader*, by Rodney A. Whitacre (Peabody, MA: Hendrickson, 2007), 211.

After these three foundational aspects of the fruit of the Spirit, Paul lists a few particular qualities: **patience** or forbearance, which knows how to wait; **kindness**, which is ready to serve; **generosity** or goodness, which is not afraid to give; **faithfulness**, which can be relied upon; **gentleness** or meekness, which refrains from using force or violence. The last word in this series, translated **self-control**, often refers to continence in sexual matters.[8] It should come as no surprise that the Spirit of the Son, whom the Father sent into the hearts of his sons and daughters (Gal 4:6), should transform their character and conduct to be like that of his Son (Rom 8:29).

At the end of his description of what the Holy Spirit produces, Paul adds an observation that underscores his doctrine of Christian freedom (as in Gal 5:18): **Against such there is no law**. A person who †lives a life guided by the Holy Spirit bears the fruit of the Spirit, a way of conducting oneself that is far from violating the †law of Moses—or any reasonable human law, for that matter. First Timothy 1:9 makes a similar point: "Law is meant not for a righteous person but for the lawless and unruly, the godless and sinful." The person who is led by the Spirit lives well above the minimum that the law requires.

8. The Clementine Vulgate of 1592 and some Greek manuscripts confirm this interpretation, adding the word "chastity" to this list.

5:24   Paul's next two sentences, verses 24–25, conclude the contrast between †flesh and Spirit. The first sentence speaks about the struggle against the flesh and recalls Jesus' crucifixion. The situation of Christians follows from their union with Christ: in baptism they "clothed" themselves with Christ (3:27) and now belong to him. Consequently, since Christ was crucified, **those who belong to Christ [Jesus] have crucified their flesh with its passions and desires**. This forceful sentence defines the situation of Christians in a manner that might seem incompatible with freedom. How can someone nailed to a cross be free? The reason Christian freedom is in perfect harmony with Christian crucifixion is that what is crucified is the obstacle to freedom, the "flesh," with "its passions and desires"—fallen nature with its disordered inclinations and appetites. This crucifixion means union with Christ in love, which brings freedom (see 2:19–20).[9] This severe statement is very valuable for spiritual life. It protects against illusions and shows the path of true freedom. Christian life is founded not only on freedom from the †law but also on freedom from one's own ego. In fact, freedom from the law cannot be complete without victory over self-centered tendencies.

5:25   In order for Christians to really be free from the domination of the †flesh, and therefore to be free from the †law by surpassing its requirements, they must learn to be docile to the Holy Spirit. The Apostle employs a simple metaphor to invite readers to this attentive obedience, urging them to "follow"—more literally, "keep in step with" (NIV)—the Spirit. Much like the †indicative-†imperative logic noted earlier (see the introduction to part 3, pp. 185–88), the *fact* that **we live** by the †grace of **the Spirit** makes possible the conduct that the Apostle urges: **let us also follow the Spirit**. Again we may note that the gift that is given, the Holy Spirit, requires active cooperation. The Apostle states his invitation in the first-person plural, "Let us follow," indicating that the exhortation is addressed not only to the Galatians but also to himself.

Reflection and Application (5:16–25)

Paul's use of the past tense in verse 24 challenges the reader. "Those who belong to Christ [Jesus] *have crucified* their flesh with its passions and desires" (italics added). Have I really crucified my †flesh? Paul is probably referring to baptism as the moment when Christians definitively die to the old self and put on

---

9. Paul's teaching corresponds to the requirement of carrying the cross to follow Jesus, expressed in the Gospels (Mark 8:34–35 and parallels). Paul's words are even more paradoxical, since he speaks not merely about carrying the cross but of having been crucified on it.

Christ (Rom 6:6; Col 3:9). However, other statements by Paul indicate that this is an ongoing process. He acknowledges an enduring interior conflict between the Holy Spirit and the "crucified" flesh in Gal 5:17; elsewhere he indicates that Christians still have need to "put to death the deeds of the body" by the power of the Spirit (Rom 8:13; see Col 3:5); in another text he exhorts his readers to "put away the old self . . . , be renewed in the spirit of your minds, and put on the new self" (Eph 4:22–24). While Christian identity is founded on what God has done for us in Christ, it nevertheless requires a firm decision, enabled by †grace, which must be renewed daily, to say yes to Christ and no to sin and self (Matt 16:24; 2 Cor 5:15).

True education leads learners to freedom; it is an education of the heart. Teachers, parents, and others engaged in spiritual formation, however, are often tempted to focus on external aspects of formation and to neglect the interior. But doing so only forms slaves, not free men and women. The learner's perfection in exterior things nourishes pride in both the learner and the educator, while the more difficult task of freeing the heart keeps both humble.

There is an immense difference between the dynamics of the flesh and the Holy Spirit. The flesh is the natural self corrupted by original sin, incapable of attaining true holiness by observing laws. The †law has nothing to offer against these sinful inclinations other than commands and prohibitions: "You shall . . . You shall not . . . ," indicating the minimum standard of conduct necessary so as not to displease God. The Spirit, on the other hand, motivates and empowers loving conduct that is not content with minimums but presses forward to the freedom of giving our whole selves. By making this total self-gift possible, the Spirit enriches us in a marvelous way.

The gift of the Spirit that brings love, joy, and peace comes to us through the sacrifice of Jesus, a total self-offering; through his sacrifice and his Spirit, the complete freedom of the risen †Lord is born in us. The next time we participate in the Eucharist, let us ask for the grace to †live more consistently in the freedom of those who have been raised with Christ.[10]

---

10. Adapted from Cardinal Albert Vanhoye, *Il pane quotidiano della Parola: Commento alle letture feriali della Messa ciclo I e II* (Casale Monferrato: Piemme, 1994), 733–34.

Advice for Christian Community Life

Galatians 5:26–6:10

In this section Paul passes from exhortations that set forth general principles for Christian conduct—loving one's neighbor, following the Spirit, and crucifying the †flesh—to specific instructions. What is interesting is that when Paul gets specific, his exhortations pertain mostly to life in Christian community. Christian life is not primarily about individual holiness and salvation, but about the progress of our spiritual family, the Christian community to which we belong, toward holiness and salvation. Of course, the welfare of the community absolutely depends on the conduct of each of its members.

Not Conceit but Solidarity (5:26–6:6)

²⁶Let us not be conceited, provoking one another, envious of one another. ^{6:1}Brothers, even if a person is caught in some transgression, you who are spiritual should correct that one in a gentle spirit, looking to yourself, so that you also may not be tempted. ²Bear one another's burdens, and so you will fulfill the law of Christ. ³For if anyone thinks he is something when he is nothing, he is deluding himself. ⁴Each one must examine his own work, and then he will have reason to boast with regard to himself alone, and not with regard to someone else; ⁵for each will bear his own load.

⁶One who is being instructed in the word should share all good things with his instructor.

OT: Prov 9:8; 25:12; Sir 11:7
NT: Matt 18:15; Rom 15:1–3; 1 Cor 9:11; 2 Cor 5:10; 1 Thess 5:14; 2 Tim 2:24–26
Catechism: fraternal correction, 1829

Verse 26 is a hinge verse. It may be taken either with the previous verse as   **5:26**
reinforcing the call to "follow the Spirit" by exhorting against contrary †fleshly
conduct or as introducing the practical advice about relationship problems
in the Christian community (alluded to earlier, 5:15). The first problem Paul
addresses is bearing oneself in a prideful manner, becoming **conceited**, which
inevitably provokes other people, arouses envy, and poisons the atmosphere.

Nevertheless, there is a solution. One could suppose that when a member of   **6:1**
the community is **caught in some transgression**, Paul would recommend forceful
correction. Instead he proposes that those **who are spiritual**, those whose lives
manifest the fruit of the Spirit (5:22–23), should **correct** the guilty party **in a
gentle spirit**—literally, "a spirit of meekness." "Gentleness" or meekness, in fact,
is named among the fruit of the Spirit (5:23).[1] Paul offers a very useful thought in
favor of this attitude, that is, the reminder of one's own moral fragility—**looking
to yourself**—and also regarding the risk of being **tempted**. Who can be sure of
always resisting temptation? How would I want to be corrected?

Paul applies the advice given in verse 1 more generally: Christians should   **6:2**
always **bear one another's burdens**. The Spirit nudges us not only to gentleness but also to solidarity with one another. The word "burdens" refers to all
the hardships that arise in life: exhausting work, sickness and physical pain,
psychological suffering, loneliness, strife, failure, and so on. In light of the
preceding verse, this includes bearing with the sins, defects, and weaknesses
of brothers and sisters (Rom 15:1; 2 Cor 11:29). In so doing, Christians **will
fulfill the law of Christ**. This law obviously does not consist of a long series
of precepts and prohibitions. It consists of only one commandment: love and
serve as Christ did, by the †grace of Christ. Here Paul's teaching overlaps with
the Gospel of John. Paul's invitation to "bear one another's burdens" parallels
Jesus' words in John 13:14: "You ought to wash one another's feet." Paul's "law
of Christ" corresponds to Jesus' "new commandment" (John 13:34), which is
to "love one another as I love you" (15:12).

At first glance, the flow of Paul's thought in verses 3–5 is perplexing. To un-   **6:3**
derstand it we need to note that the first sentence of the paragraph (v. 1) brings

---

1. In Titus 3:2–3 Paul uses the same word for how Christians should conduct themselves toward
outsiders and offers a similar reason. He urges "graciousness" or courtesy (the same Greek word as
"gentleness" here) toward all because "we ourselves were once foolish, disobedient, deluded, slaves
to various desires and pleasures, living in malice and envy, hateful ourselves and hating one another."

together two different topics: brotherly assistance and self-examination. Verse 2, which speaks of bearing one another's burdens, describes brotherly assistance. Verses 3–5 take up the second topic—self-examination. Paul admonishes those who, in examining themselves, think too highly of themselves: **if anyone thinks he is something when he is nothing, he is deluding himself**. Perhaps the underlying idea is the same as Paul wrote the Corinthians: "What do you possess that you have not received? But if you have received it, why are you boasting?" (1 Cor 4:7).

6:4–5   Then Paul narrows in on a particularly defective way of examining oneself that involves comparing oneself to others in a way that leads to being proud or critical of others. Paul disapproves of this approach and invites his readers to examine their own conduct without comparisons by a reminder: **each will bear his own load**. The point is similar to something Paul says in Rom 14:10–12: "Why then do you judge your brother? Or you, why do you look down on your brother? For we shall all stand before the judgment seat of God. . . . So [then] each of us shall give an account of himself [to God]." The contradiction between "bear one another's burdens" and "each will bear his own load" (Gal 6:2, 5) is thus only apparent, because the contexts are different. The first is said about brotherly assistance (v. 2), while the second is about how a person should evaluate himself or herself (v. 5). If it is a question of helping, mutual relationships are encouraged: we must "bear one another's burdens" (v. 2); if it is a question of judging, what other people do is irrelevant, because "each will bear his own load" (v. 5). The point, it would seem, is that we should not be complacent about our apparent superiority to another person in some respect, because we will be judged by God not on relative superiority to others but on the value of our own actions in God's eyes.

6:6   Paul returns to the topic of brotherly assistance, focusing on the particular case of teachers. The Greek verb translated **instructed** here is the root from which we get the words "catechumen" and "catechesis." Catechesis was of the greatest importance to the young communities of the early Church, and it has become a high priority again as society has become less Christian. Paul is very concerned to ensure that those who are teaching receive the material support they need to fulfill their ministry. He is not satisfied with half measures: the person who is taught **the word should share all good things with his instructor**. Although Paul did not ask support for himself but was able to live by his own labors (sometimes supplemented by donations for his mission from some churches),[2] here and elsewhere he teaches plainly that Christian teachers ought

---

2. See Acts 18:3; 20:34; 1 Cor 9:11–12, 15; Phil 4:14–18; 1 Thess 2:9; 2 Thess 3:8.

to be compensated (1 Cor 9:9–14; 1 Tim 5:18; see Matt 10:10). It remains a high priority for Catholics to generously support the priests, deacons, and laypeople who preach and teach the word of God.

Doing Good to All (6:7–10)

> ⁷Make no mistake: God is not mocked, for a person will reap only what he sows, ⁸because the one who sows for his flesh will reap corruption from the flesh, but the one who sows for the spirit will reap eternal life from the spirit. ⁹Let us not grow tired of doing good, for in due time we shall reap our harvest, if we do not give up. ¹⁰So then, while we have the opportunity, let us do good to all, but especially to those who belong to the family of the faith.

OT: Job 4:8; Prov 20:4; Sir 6:19
NT: Rom 8:13; 13:14; 1 Cor 9:11–14; 2 Cor 9:6–11; Heb 12:3; 13:16

Speaking about financial generosity leads Paul to think about the analogy of planting and harvesting (see 1 Cor 9:11; 2 Cor 9:6, 9–10), but in this case Paul applies the metaphor more broadly, not just to the support of ministers of the word but as a principle that informs all of Christian life.

The agricultural metaphor of seed and harvest underscores the close link **6:7** between the quality of an activity and its final result. It is another way of speaking about the judgment of God, "who will repay everyone according to his works" (Rom 2:6; see Prov 24:12). However, instead of presenting a negative outcome as a deliberate divine punishment, the metaphor suggests that the outcome of a person's life will be a natural consequence of his or her conduct. Whoever sows barley will harvest barley, not wheat. Similarly, whoever **sows** evil will **reap** evil.

Now the Apostle shifts the metaphor. Instead of focusing on what kind of seed **6:8** is sown, he focuses on the field in which it is being sown, the field of the †flesh ("for his flesh") or the field of the Spirit ("for the spirit"). The NABRE, unlike other translations, presents "spirit" (lowercase) twice in this verse, interpreting Paul to mean the human spirit (as in 6:1, 18). However, the fact that we "will reap eternal life from the spirit" (v. 8) clearly indicates that Paul is referring to the divine Spirit. This reintroduces the contrast between flesh and Spirit that marked the beginning of the previous section (5:16–25). The two clauses of verse 8 are parallel but point to opposite results: **the one who sows for his**

flesh will reap corruption from the flesh, but the one who sows for the spirit will reap eternal life from the spirit. The flesh is contrasted to the Spirit, and corruption to eternal life. Paul highlights the connection between the activity and its result. Those who follow their disordered, self-centered tendencies will find themselves subject to moral and spiritual death. In contrast, those who follow the Spirit are assured of entering into eternal life because the Spirit is the giver of life. Although the baptized receive the life of Christ into themselves here and now (see 2:20), at the moment of judgment they will receive it in its fullness in a definitive manner (see Rom 8:11).

6:9   Verses 9 and 10 round out Paul's exhortation, addressing both his readers and himself: **Let us not grow tired of doing good**. Building on the harvest metaphor of the preceding verses, he adds: **for in due time we shall reap**. The hope of an abundant **harvest** spurs us on. The conclusion of the verse adds a condition, **if we do not give up**, using a verb that means to "collapse" or "lose heart" (Matt 15:32; Heb 12:3–5). Perseverance is necessary.

6:10   **So then** indicates that what follows is both the logical conclusion and the practical application. **Let us do good to all**, Paul urges us, either **while we have the opportunity** or "whenever we have an opportunity" (NRSV). A saying by John Wesley, the founder of Methodism, expresses the desired attitude: "Do all the good you can, in every way you can, as long as you can." "To all" indicates the suitable recipients of Christian kindness—no one is excluded. The fruit of the Spirit implies an active love "to all" because Christ "died for all" (2 Cor 5:15). However, a certain priority is appropriate: **especially to those who belong to the family of the faith**, or "household of faith" (RSV), since members of our spiritual family, the Church, are the neighbors who are nearest and whose claim on us is greatest (Matt 12:48–50; 1 Tim 5:8).

Summary of Paul's Concluding Exhortation (5:13–6:10)

Galatians 5:13–6:10 concludes the third and last major section of the letter. Even though it is quite different from the preceding sections, it is profoundly linked to them. It continues the theme of Christian freedom in contrast to life under the †law (5:18, 23) and shows the relationship of freedom to the gift of the Spirit. What distinguishes this section is Paul's persistent exhortation to be on guard against the desires of the "†flesh," understood in a negative sense as the source of the evil tendencies in human beings.

This final section adds a necessary completion to Paul's message in Galatians. It clearly shows that the †gospel of freedom preached by the Apostle does not at all mean license, the freedom to do whatever a person feels like doing, but radically opposes it. Indeed, Christian freedom entails a resolute struggle against all self-centered tendencies, and even presupposes the crucifixion of passions and disordered desires (5:24). In addition, this section prevents misinterpreting Paul's teaching on †justification by †faith to mean that a person's works do not matter. Paul certainly excludes works as the basis for initial justification, since faith alone is its foundation. This does not mean, however, that after initial justification a person made righteous by God can disregard his or her conduct and count on a faith without works for final justification. Paul combats this illusion and insists that Christians "not grow tired of doing good" (6:9) and "do good to all" (6:10). Paul is not contradicting his earlier rejection of "works of the law" (2:16), because the works Paul now commends are not works of the law but works of faith, carried out in vital union with Christ (2:20) through the interior action of the Holy Spirit (5:16, 22–23). Consequently, these works are not a human accomplishment that a person could boast about. They are a gift of God actively received by the believer, a gift that leads to humble and joyful thanksgiving.

Paul's Final Words and Signature

Galatians 6:11–18

Up to this point Paul has been dictating his letter to a secretary. For the final lines of his letter he picks up the reed pen himself to authenticate what has been written. Not content to merely write a closing greeting, he adds a few lines of final argument against the †Judaizers and in defense of himself (vv. 12–14, 17). He ends as he usually does, wishing his readers "the grace of our Lord Jesus Christ," but adds the word "brothers," an affectionate final touch that is unique to Galatians.

Paul's Postscript (6:11–18)

[11]See with what large letters I am writing to you in my own hand! [12]It is those who want to make a good appearance in the flesh who are trying to compel you to have yourselves circumcised, only that they may not be persecuted for the cross of Christ. [13]Not even those having themselves circumcised observe the law themselves; they only want you to be circumcised so that they may boast of your flesh. [14]But may I never boast except in the cross of our Lord Jesus Christ, through which the world has been crucified to me, and I to the world. [15]For neither does circumcision mean anything, nor does uncircumcision, but only a new creation. [16]Peace and mercy be to all who follow this rule and to the Israel of God.

[17]From now on, let no one make troubles for me; for I bear the marks of Jesus on my body.

[18]The grace of our Lord Jesus Christ be with your spirit, brothers.
Amen.

OT: Pss 125:5; 128:6
NT: Rom 6:4; 2 Cor 5:17; 10:12; 11:22–31; Gal 5:6, 11; Phil 3:3–8
Lectionary: 6:14–18: St. Francis of Assisi; Common of Saints

Instead of writing, "This greeting is in my own hand," as he says in other letters,[1]　**6:11**
Paul draws attention to the difference between his handwriting and his secretary's. His **writing** is in **large letters**, matching Paul's self-affirming character
(unless, as some think, it was due to eye problems; see 4:15).

In a final effort to counter the propaganda of the †Judaizers, who promoted　**6:12**
circumcision, the Apostle takes aim at their motives, which deserve criticism.
He points out their desire to enhance their own reputations and to avoid persecution. Ambrosiaster, a fourth-century commentator on Paul, remarks on
his boldness: "Paul was never intimidated by his opponents. He consistently
refused to keep silent about the truth."[2] Paul asserts that the Judaizers want **to
make a good appearance in the flesh**. What does this odd-sounding phrase
mean? It is obvious that the word "†flesh" here does not have the same meaning
it had earlier when it referred to human sinful tendencies (5:16–24; 6:8). Here
it refers to the physical body and, in particular, to circumcision, an operation
on "the flesh" (Eph 2:11). The fact that Paul goes from one meaning to another
without drawing attention to the difference is deliberate. In Paul's eyes there is
a real connection between seeking glory through what is external and physical
("flesh" in one sense) and the self-centered tendencies of a sinner ("flesh" in
the other sense).

Of course, the Jewish nation of Paul's day did not see it that way. Whoever
was circumcised was regarded positively, because circumcision was the sign of
belonging to the chosen people, the descendants of Abraham (see Gen 17:9–14).
For Jews, retaining the foreskin evoked repugnance and disdain because it was
a sign of belonging to the pagan world. In Philippians, Paul explains that if he
had wanted to, he could have been "confident in flesh" like the Judaizers, above
all because he was "circumcised on the eighth day" (Phil 3:4–5).

In addition to their desire to make a good impression, Paul discerns a lack
of Christian courage in the motives of the Judaizers. They want to avoid being
persecuted for the cross of Christ. †Faith in the crucified Christ did arouse
persecution from Jews who could not bring themselves to believe in a †Messiah

---

1. Col 4:18; 2 Thess 3:17; see 1 Cor 16:21.
2. Ambrosiaster, *Epistle to the Galatians* 6:12, in ACCS VIII:101.

who, by crucifixion, had become "a curse" (Gal 3:13). Before his conversion Paul had actively persecuted the followers of Jesus.[3] After his conversion he became a victim of persecution himself (see 5:11; 2 Cor 11:24). The Judaizers could reduce the hostility of their fellow Jews by preaching circumcision to converts from paganism, thereby showing that faith in Christ was contributing to the expansion of ethnic Israel.

6:13   Paul elaborates on his point, telling the Galatians that the †Judaizers want to have reason to **boast of your flesh**—again, †flesh in the physical sense, through the circumcision of the Galatians. Persuading converts from paganism to accept circumcision was a feather in the cap of the Judaizers since it demonstrated to other Jews that they had won a victory for Judaism over paganism, using the Christian faith as the means of that victory. Paul denounces this quest for human boasting as a lack of uprightness in their intentions and as a kind of hypocrisy. The Judaizers claimed to seek the good of the Galatians; in reality they were seeking their own advantage and did not deserve to be listened to.

A third reason for mistrusting the Judaizers was their inconsistency. They were urging †Gentile Christians to be circumcised and observe the †law of Moses but did not **observe the law themselves**. Paul does not explain what part of the law the Judaizers were not observing. In 5:3 Paul stated emphatically that circumcision made people "bound to observe the entire law." Being circumcised and then transgressing the law is inconsistent and contradictory behavior that deserves to be condemned. On the one hand, through circumcision they enter into the exclusiveness of Judaism; on the other hand, by not observing the law, they remain outside it. Such inconsistency demonstrated that their conduct was inspired not by any genuine conviction but by other considerations—namely, to "make a good appearance" (6:12), to "boast" (v. 13), and to avoid being "persecuted for the cross of Christ" (v. 12).

6:14   Paul instead is perfectly consistent. He excludes any boasting that is not related to the cross of Christ. He preaches "Jesus Christ . . . crucified" (3:1; 1 Cor 2:2) and has renounced boasting for any human reason. He boasts instead **in the cross of our Lord Jesus Christ**. It is paradoxical to speak of boasting in the cross, since crucifixion was regarded as the most shameful of all punishments. Besides inflicting incredible pain, crucifixion was intended precisely to expose the condemned person to public humiliation. The crucified Jesus was mocked and insulted.[4] How is it even conceivable to boast in the cross of Jesus? Only by going beyond appearances to recognize the profound meaning of that event can

---

3. Gal 1:13; Acts 8:3; 1 Cor 15:9; Phil 3:6.
4. Matt 27:39–44; Mark 15:29–32; Luke 23:35–39.

a person perceive an action of God whose results are positive beyond imagining. Contemplating Jesus' cross, Paul recognizes a sublime demonstration of love: the Son of God "has loved me and given himself up for me" (Gal 2:20; see Eph 5:2, 25). Jesus surrendered himself to his enemies to be nailed to the cross and die on it. Already glorious in itself, such a feat of love became even more glorious because of its wonderful fruitfulness: "by becoming a curse for us" Christ "ransomed us from the curse of the law" (Gal 3:13), because his death on the cross procured for him—and for us—new life that is no longer subject to the †law (2:19). God truly "raised him from the dead" (1:1) and made him "†Lord" of all (1:3; Phil 2:8–11) and, more personally, "our Lord" (Gal 6:14, 18). All believers can now exclaim, "I live, no longer I, but Christ lives in me" (2:20), and this leads them to boast in the cross of Christ.

Since it is the cross *of the Lord*, it is glorious. Nevertheless, it remains a cross and thus marks a radical break with the world for Christ and for believers. Paul is keenly aware of this and expresses it with a twofold declaration: **through which the world has been crucified to me, and I to the world**. This statement is puzzling for various reasons. First, because it speaks of the world in relation to the cross of Christ, but mostly because it declares that the world was crucified by means of the cross. Why would Paul say the world is crucified? Certainly, the one who was crucified was Jesus! How is it possible for the world to be crucified? The answer is that Paul understands the event at Calvary as bringing a kind of destruction on the harmful entities that exist in the world. "World" here is intended negatively to refer to the totality of the powers of evil that wreak havoc on earth. These forces raged against and attacked Jesus' mortal body and were, in a certain sense, destroyed along with it. Jesus' crucifixion has deprived them of the power they previously possessed (John 12:31–33; 16:33; Col 2:15). A passage in the Letter to the Romans offers an analogous interpretation. "We know," says the Apostle, "that our old self was crucified with him, so that our sinful body might be done away with" (Rom 6:6; see 8:3). In a certain sense, the world was nailed to Jesus' cross to be conquered by it. Paul's words express a mutual repudiation: Paul has broken with the world, and the world has broken with Paul because he has been "crucified with Christ" (Gal 2:19).

Now Paul unexpectedly returns to the issue of circumcision. The connection to the foregoing lies in the fact that **circumcision** and **uncircumcision** are earthly realities. In contrast, the Apostle's life—and that of every believer—is found at another level of existence that Paul calls **a new creation**. In Isaiah, God announced that he would create "new heavens / and a new earth" (Isa 65:17; see 66:22). This prophecy found its fulfillment in Christ's resurrection,

6:15

Fathers of the Church on Glorying in the Cross

LIVING
TRADITION

Like us, the Fathers of the Church found Paul's words in these verses both moving and thought-provoking. Here are a few of their insights:

> But what is this boasting in the cross? That on my behalf Christ took the form of a slave and suffered what he suffered on account of me the slave, the enemy, the ingrate. . . . By *world* he means not heaven nor earth but the affairs of life, human praise, distinguished positions, reputation, wealth and all things that have a show of splendor. All such things are dead to me. Such should be the case for all Christians. (John Chrysostom, *Homily on Galatians* 6.14)

> When in that mystery his body hung from the cross and in it crushed the power of this world, the whole world was crucified through him. In the cross he identified with every person in the world. In doing so he made everything that he suffered universal, that is, he caused all flesh to be crucified in his death. Therefore I too am fixed to the cross. (Marius Victorinus, *Epistle to the Galatians* 2.6.14)[a]

a. ACCS VIII:102–3.

---

so that "whoever is in Christ is a new creation" (2 Cor 5:17) and has "put on the new self, created in God's way in righteousness and holiness of truth" (Eph 4:24). For the believer, in a profound way earthly conditions have now been surpassed. Circumcision has lost its religious importance, while uncircumcision had none. At the end of his Letter to the Romans, Paul acknowledges a difference between God's relation to Jews and his relation to the †Gentiles because of God's special history with Israel,[5] but the Apostle does not mention this distinction in this letter. Instead, the particular crisis in Galatia led him to emphasize the complete absence of distinctions at the deepest level, where "there is neither Jew nor Greek" and all are "one in Christ Jesus" (Gal 3:28). This is the essential message of the letter. †Judaizers considered circumcision fundamentally important because it was a means by which people could enter into Abraham's line of descent. But Paul denies its importance and demonstrates that †faith in Christ makes a person enter Abraham's line of descent in a far more valid manner. Circumcision and the legal system of the Jews were in the

---

5. "I tell you that Christ became a servant to the circumcised to show God's truthfulness, in order to confirm the promises given to the patriarchs, and in order that the Gentiles might glorify God for his mercy" (Rom 15:8–9 RSV; see Luke 2:32).

process of being reduced to expressions of Jewish national identity, legitimate as such, but which absolutely must not be imposed on Gentile converts from paganism.

Paul considers his declaration in verse 15 as a **rule** that the Galatian Chris- **6:16** tians need to **follow** (the same verb used in 5:25). The Apostle pronounces **peace** (see 1:3) and **mercy** from God (see Rom 15:9) to those who keep in step with this rule. He adds **and to the Israel of God**, a phrase that does not occur elsewhere in the New Testament. There are two psalms that end with the wish, "Peace upon Israel!" (Pss 125:5; 128:6). By specifying that he is referring to the Israel *of God*, Paul is making a distinction. Some people suggest that he is distinguishing between the Church as "the Israel of God" and the Jewish people as "Israel according to the †flesh" (1 Cor 10:18). However, Paul's wording does not favor this interpretation. After invoking peace and mercy on "all who follow this rule," referring to Galatian Christians who reject the †Judaizers' teaching about the necessity of circumcision, he adds, "*and* to the Israel of God," apparently a distinct category of Christians. Consequently, "the Israel of God" probably designates not the Church but rather a part of it, Jews who believe in Christ and are therefore authentic children of Abraham, as opposed to those who are children only according to the †flesh (Gal 3:7; 4:22–23; Rom 9:6–9).[6]

Before writing his final greeting, the Apostle lets slip a moving request in **6:17** which he reveals his weariness after the battle he has fought in this letter. He asks now to be spared any more trouble and gives as a reason **the marks of Jesus** that he bears on his body. Although the Greek term for "marks" is *stigmata*, Paul is not saying that he bears the five wounds that marked Christ's body (St. Francis of Assisi was the first to experience that †grace), but rather he refers to the scars he bore from his apostolic sufferings. Paul lists some of these sufferings in 2 Cor 11:24–25, which include receiving thirty-nine lashes five times, three beatings with rods, once being stoned (Acts 14:19), besides other hardships. Paul calls them the "marks of Jesus" because his scars are the direct consequence of his service to Jesus. They constitute a participation in Jesus' passion[7] and therefore deserve deep respect. Paul invites the Galatians to consider them.

As is true in Paul's other letters, the last sentence is a prayer-wish of †grace **6:18** for his readers. Instead of saying, "Grace . . . be with you" (as in Rom 16:20 and 1 Cor 16:23), he says, "**Grace . . . be with your spirit.**" The spirit of a person is

---

6. Some scholars, nevertheless, interpret Paul as referring to only one group, the Church, and base their argument on the context of Galatians as a whole, since Paul has argued that those who have faith are "children of Abraham" (3:7) and has forcefully stated that there is "neither Jew nor Greek" in Christ (3:28).

7. 2 Cor 4:10–11; Phil 3:10; Col 1:24.

his or her inmost self, capable of receiving divine grace, so that he or she may be raised up to a vital union with Christ.

At the end of this letter, Paul's prayer for **the grace of our Lord Jesus Christ** takes on an intense significance, since all the Apostle's effort in this very passionate letter has aimed at keeping the Galatians from a temptation that would have led them to be "fallen from grace" (Gal 5:4) and to "nullify the grace of God" (2:21) by putting conformity to the †law at the foundation of their Christian lives instead of the free gift of God.

In contrast to the reprimand that called the Galatians "stupid" (Gal 3:1), the last word, **brothers**, expresses the Apostle's affection for the Christians of Galatia and gently invites them to remain united to him.

Suggested Resources

Commentaries from the Christian Tradition

Aquinas, St. Thomas. *Commentary on Saint Paul's Epistle to the Galatians*. Translated by F. R. Larcher, OP. Aquinas Scripture Series. Albany, NY: Magi, 1966. Careful exposition in light of the whole of Scripture and the questions of classical theology. Available online at https://dhspriory.org/thomas/SSGalatians.htm.

Chrysostom, St. John. *Homilies on Galatians*. Six homilies that treat the entire letter verse by verse. Each sermon includes exposition followed by exhortation. Available online at http://www.newadvent.org/fathers/2310.htm.

Edwards, Mark J., ed. *Galatians, Ephesians, Philippians*. Ancient Christian Commentary on Scripture: New Testament VIII. Downers Grove, IL: InterVarsity, 1999. This series offers selections from patristic writings on every passage of the biblical text.

Scholarly Commentaries

Matera, Frank J. *Galatians*. Sacra Pagina. Collegeville, MN: Liturgical Press, 1992. An excellent study by a respected Catholic scholar.

Moo, Douglas J. *Galatians*. Baker Exegetical Commentary on the New Testament. Grand Rapids: Baker Academic, 2013. An excellent recent study by a respected evangelical scholar.

Midlevel and Popular Works

Byrne, Brendan. *Galatians and Romans*. Collegeville, MN: Liturgical Press, 2010. A balanced, accessible study by a former member of the Pontifical Biblical Commission.

Hahn, Scott, and Curtis Mitch. *The Ignatius Catholic Study Bible: The New Testament*. San Francisco: Ignatius, 2010. The thirteen pages of text and notes on Galatians in this study Bible provide a helpful explanation of the main issues from a Catholic perspective.

Perrotta, Kevin. *Galatians: Free in Christ*. Six Weeks with the Bible. Chicago: Loyola, 2006. An excellent resource for small-group Bible study.

Witherup, Ronald D. *Galatians: Life in the New Creation*. New York/Mahwah, NJ: Paulist Press, 2019. A new pastoral-spiritual commentary by a highly respected Catholic scholar.

Paul and Pauline Theology

Gorman, Michael J. *Apostle of the Crucified Lord: A Theological Introduction to Paul and His Letters*. 2nd ed. Grand Rapids: Eerdmans, 2017. This volume, by a Protestant scholar who teaches at a Catholic seminary, provides rich information about the world in which the Apostle preached, an overview of his life and message, and an examination of each of the letters.

Matera, Frank J. *God's Saving Grace: A Pauline Theology*. Grand Rapids: Eerdmans, 2012. The author sets forth what Paul says about the principal theological topics he treats. He understands Paul's theology as arising from the Apostle's personal experience of God's saving grace.

———. *New Testament Theology: Exploring Unity and Diversity*. Louisville: Westminster John Knox, 2007. This volume presents the theology of each letter in the Pauline tradition and relates that tradition to the other theological streams in the New Testament.

Glossary

anagogical sense: the spiritual sense of Scripture that has to do with the life to come.

carnal: see **flesh, fleshly**.

covenant: a solemn agreement between two parties that establishes a special relationship. In the Old Testament, God makes a covenant with Abraham (Gen 15; 17) and later with Israel as a whole on Mount Sinai (Exod 20; 24). In the New Testament, Jesus establishes a new and eternal covenant through his passion, death, and resurrection (Luke 22:14–20). The Greek word for covenant in the †Septuagint is *diathēkē*, which also means "will" or "testament," a meaning that Paul employs in Gal 3:15.

doxology, doxological: prayer that ascribes glory or praise to God.

ecclesial: something that pertains to the Church (Greek *ekklēsia*); for example, ecclesial discipline refers to church discipline.

elemental powers (Greek *stoicheia*, "elements"): Paul uses this term in Gal 4:3, 9 to refer to what held both Gentiles and Jews in subjection prior to the coming of Christ. Although interpreters debate what exactly Paul means, this commentary takes the term as having its usual meaning in Greek literature of the period—that is, it refers to the four elements (earth, water, air, and fire) that Greek thinkers regarded as composing the physical world. It is Paul's way of expressing what humanity was subject to—that is, what is merely physical, earthly, and of this age, in contrast to the new possibility in Christ of living as children of God who are led by the Holy Spirit.

eschatological (from Greek *eschata*, "last things"): all that belongs to the end of human history and the fulfillment of the new age in Christ. The New Testament teaches that the new age began with Jesus' passion, death, and resurrection and the gift of the Spirit and will reach its fullness when Christ returns (1 Cor 10:11; Eph 1:13–14; Heb 9:26; see commentary on Gal 1:1–4).

faith (Greek *pistis*): (1) belief, such as belief in Christ, in God, or in the gospel proclamation that justifies a person (Gal 2:16; 3:2; see the sidebar, "What Does Paul Mean by 'Faith'?," p. 100); (2) faithfulness in a relationship (see the sidebar, "'Faith in Christ' or 'the Faithfulness of Christ'?," p. 86); (3) the content of the gospel (Gal 1:23).

flesh, fleshly (Greek *sarx*): (1) the body (Gal 2:20; 4:13); (2) what is merely human (3:3; 4:23); (3) fallen human nature characterized by sinful inclinations and disordered desires (5:13, 16–21). Elsewhere in the New Testament "flesh" has the anatomical meaning of muscle or soft tissue (Luke 24:39); in John 6:51–56, "my flesh" refers to Christ's eucharistic body.

Gentile, Gentiles (Greek *ethnē*, also translated as "nations" in 3:8): people of non-Jewish nationality. In other books of the New Testament, "Gentiles" is sometimes used to refer only to unbelieving Gentiles, who lack relationship with God and who live immorally and unjustly (e.g., Eph 4:17; 1 Pet 2:12; 4:3).

gospel: the message (literally, "good news") about salvation through the death and resurrection of Jesus Christ, which calls for a response of faith and repentance. Although there is only one gospel (Gal 1:6–9), Paul acknowledges a difference in how it is presented to Jews and Gentiles (2:2, 7), a difference that is evident in the apostolic preaching in Acts (e.g., 13:14–41; 17:22–31). "Gospel" (capitalized) later came to refer to each of the four canonical narratives of the life of Jesus.

grace (Greek *charis*): (1) an attitude of favor, generosity, or magnanimity (Gal 1:6, 15); (2) a gift, benefit, or other effect (e.g., blessing, justification) that results from this attitude (1:3; 2:21); (3) the gift of the Spirit acting in or through a person for their benefit or for that of the Church (2:9). The distinguishing character of "grace" is that it is freely given, not earned.

imperative mood: a grammatical term referring to verbs that convey a command or instruction—for example, "Do not get drunk on wine . . . but be filled with the Spirit" (Eph 5:18). Verbs in the imperative mood instruct readers about how they are to live their new identity in Christ (Gal 5:13b, 16b; 6:1–2).

indicative mood: a grammatical term referring to verbs that describe matters of fact—what was, is, or will be. Verbs in the indicative mood often recount what God has done in Christ and the change that it has brought about for believers (Gal 2:16, 20; 3:11).

inheritance: a term in Scripture that often refers to a share in the land that God promised to Abraham and his descendants (see the sidebar, "What Is

Abraham's Inheritance?," p. 107). As the story of salvation has progressed, the understanding of this inheritance has deepened, so that in the New Testament it often refers to eternal life with God.

Judaizers, Judaizing: people who taught that it was necessary for Gentile Christians to be circumcised and keep the law of Moses.

justify, justification: according to its most basic sense, "to justify" means to judge that a person's conduct meets God's standards, which for a Jew meant the law of Moses. Paul, however, on the basis of many Old Testament texts and his encounter with the risen Lord, came to see that no human being will be found truly righteous before God on the basis of conduct (Gal 2:16; Ps 143:2; see Rom 3:9–19). He discovers instead that human beings need to be justified in a more radical sense—namely, to be *made righteous* by a divine act that not only grants forgiveness of sins but also transforms a person from within by the Holy Spirit. The basis of this justification is Christ's death on the cross for our sins (Gal 2:20), and the way to receive this gift is through faith in Christ (see the sidebar, "What Does It Mean to Be Justified?," pp. 82–83).

law (Greek *nomos*; Hebrew *torah*): refers to the first five books of the Bible— that is, the Pentateuch or the law of Moses—and, occasionally, the entire Old Testament (e.g., Rom 3:19). Paul usually uses "law" to refer to God's commandments but sometimes focuses on the law as divine revelation (both senses are found in Rom 3:21b and Gal 4:21). For more, see the sidebars, "What Are 'Works of the Law'?," p. 84, and "Paul's Nuanced View of the Law," pp. 146–47.

live (Greek *peripateō*, "walk"): to conduct oneself in a particular manner. In Galatians, Paul uses this word to refer to the Christian way of life (5:16).

Lord (Greek *kyrios*): (1) in common usage, a term of respectful address (like "Sir") or the title used for a slave master or for the Roman emperor; (2) in the †Septuagint, a word that translates the divine name YHWH and refers to God; (3) in the New Testament, a title of Jesus that refers to his divinity and royal authority (Phil 2:11). Catholics use this title in the liturgy when they pray, "*Kyrie, eleison*," "Lord, have mercy."

LXX: see **Septuagint**.

Messiah (from Hebrew *mashiah*, "anointed one"; in Greek *Christos*): the descendant of King David promised by God, who Jews of Jesus' day hoped would come to restore the kingdom to Israel. The early Christians recognized Jesus as the Messiah promised in the Jewish Scriptures, the Christ, whose eternal kingdom includes people of every nation.

nations: see **Gentile, Gentiles**.

Qumran: an archaeological site northwest of the Dead Sea, thought to be an Essene settlement, near which the Dead Sea Scrolls, a treasure trove of Jewish religious writings, were discovered. The Essenes were a Jewish sect at the time of Jesus and are known from the writings of Philo and Josephus.

rhetoric, rhetorical: (1) the science and art of persuasive oratory developed by Aristotle and his successors (see "Genre" in the introduction, pp. 18–19); (2) persuasive ability in speech or writing. Rhetorical questions do not expect an answer but are intended to make a point.

ritual: (1) as a noun, a (religious) rite or ceremony; (2) as an adjective, referring to regulations of purity or procedure that govern daily life and especially acts of worship. Thomas Aquinas referred to this type of legislation in the law of Moses as the ceremonial law (see the sidebar, "Law in Catholic Tradition," pp. 196–97).

Septuagint: Greek translation of the Hebrew Bible dating from the third and second centuries BC, commonly abbreviated LXX because of the tradition that it was the work of seventy scholars. As the Bible used by Greek-speaking Jews and Christians, it is often quoted in the New Testament.

Torah (Hebrew for "law" or "instruction"): the first five books of the Bible, attributed to Moses and thus also called the law of Moses, the books of Moses, or the Pentateuch. "Torah" is also used more broadly to refer to all God's teachings in the Old Testament on how to live an upright life in covenant relationship with him.

tropological sense: the spiritual meaning of Scripture that has to do with Christian conduct; also called the moral sense.

type, typological: describes a person, place, institution, or event in an earlier stage of God's plan that foreshadows God's action at a later stage in Christ, the Church, the sacraments, or the future kingdom.

Index of Pastoral Topics

This index indicates where Galatians mentions various topics that may be useful for evangelization, catechesis, apologetics, or other forms of pastoral ministry.

anathema, 1:8–9

baptism, 2:19–20; 3:27–28; 6:14

Cephas. *See* Peter and Paul

children of God, 3:26–27; 4:4–7

Christology, 1:1, 3, 15–16; 3:13–14, 16, 26; 4:4–6

Council of Jerusalem, 2:1–10

cross of Christ, 1:4; 2:19–21; 3:1, 13; 5:11, 24; 6:12, 14, 17

crucifying the flesh, 5:24; 6:14

death of Christ. *See* cross of Christ

ecclesiology, 2:7–10; 3:7, 14, 28–30

faith of Abraham, 3:7–14

faith working through love, 5:6

financial support of teachers, 6:6

flesh, works of, 5:17, 19–21

fraternal correction, 6:1

freedom in Christ, 4:8–10, 26–31; 5:1, 13

Galatians' relationship with Paul. *See* Paul, relationship with the Galatians

generosity, 6:6–9

good works, 6:9–10

gospel, no other, 1:6–9, 11–12

gospel to circumcised and uncircumcised, 2:7

grace, 1:3, 6, 15; 2:9, 21; 5:4; 6:18

heir. *See* inheritance

Holy Spirit. *See* Spirit

hope, 5:5

humility, 6:3–5

inheritance, 3:14, 18, 29; 4:7

Jews and Gentiles in Christ, 2:7–9; 3:28–29; 5:6; 6:15

justification by faith, 2:15–16, 19–21; 3:11, 22, 24

kingdom, conduct that is incompatible with, 5:19–21

law, dying to, 2:19

law, purpose of, 3:19–24; 4:1–5

law, works of, 2:16; 3:2–5, 10; 5:3

love of Christ, 1:4; 2:19–20

love toward others, 5:13–14; 6:2, 10

marks (*stigmata*) of Jesus, 6:17

miracles, 3:5

mutual care among Christians, 5:13–14; 6:9–10

new creation, 6:15

Paul, call and conversion, 1:13–23

Paul, physical weakness of, 4:13–14

Paul, relationship with the Galatians, 1:2, 6–7; 3:1; 4:11–20; 5:10; 6:18

people-pleasing, 1:10

perseverance, 6:9

Peter and Paul, 1:18; 2:7–14

reward, 6:7–9

sexual immorality, 5:19–21

slavery and freedom, 1:10; 3:28; 4:7–10;
5:1, 13
speech, 5:15
Spirit, baptism in, 3:2–3
Spirit, fruit of, 5:22–23
Spirit, living (walking) in, 5:16–18, 25

Spirit, received by hearing in faith, 3:2–5,
14
Trinity, 4:6
truth, 2:5, 14; 4:16; 5:7
vices to avoid, 5:15, 19–21, 26
world, the present age, 1:4; 4:3; 6:14

Index of Sidebars

Abraham's Inheritance, What Is?   107

Anathema, The Origin of, in the Christian Tradition   38

Antioch, The Church of   74

Child of God, Is Everyone a?   142

"Children of God," Understanding   128

Deep Magic in Narnia   182

"Faith in Christ" or "the Faithfulness of Christ"?   86

"Faith," What Does Paul Mean by?   100

Fathers of the Church on Glorying in the Cross   212

"Gospel," The Meaning of, in the New Testament   36

Jerusalem Council, Paul's Visit and the   61

Jerusalem, Mother of All Nations   164

Jerusalem, The Fourfold Meaning of   161

Justified, What Does It Mean to Be?   82

Law, Christian Conduct Surpasses the   199

Law in Catholic Tradition   196

Law of Moses, Did Paul Keep the?   174

Law of Moses, Diverse Biblical Perspectives on the   120

Law, Paul's Nuanced View of the   146

Paul's Confrontation with Peter in the History of Interpretation   78

Paul's Gospel   62

Peter, Cephas Is   54

"Son of God" in the Bible   50

St. Augustine on the Purpose of the Letter to the Galatians   65

St. John Chrysostom on Paul's Pastoral Skill   154

Tone, Diverse Insights into Paul's Change of   157

Was the Old Covenant Only about Externals?   187

"Works of the Law," What Are?   84

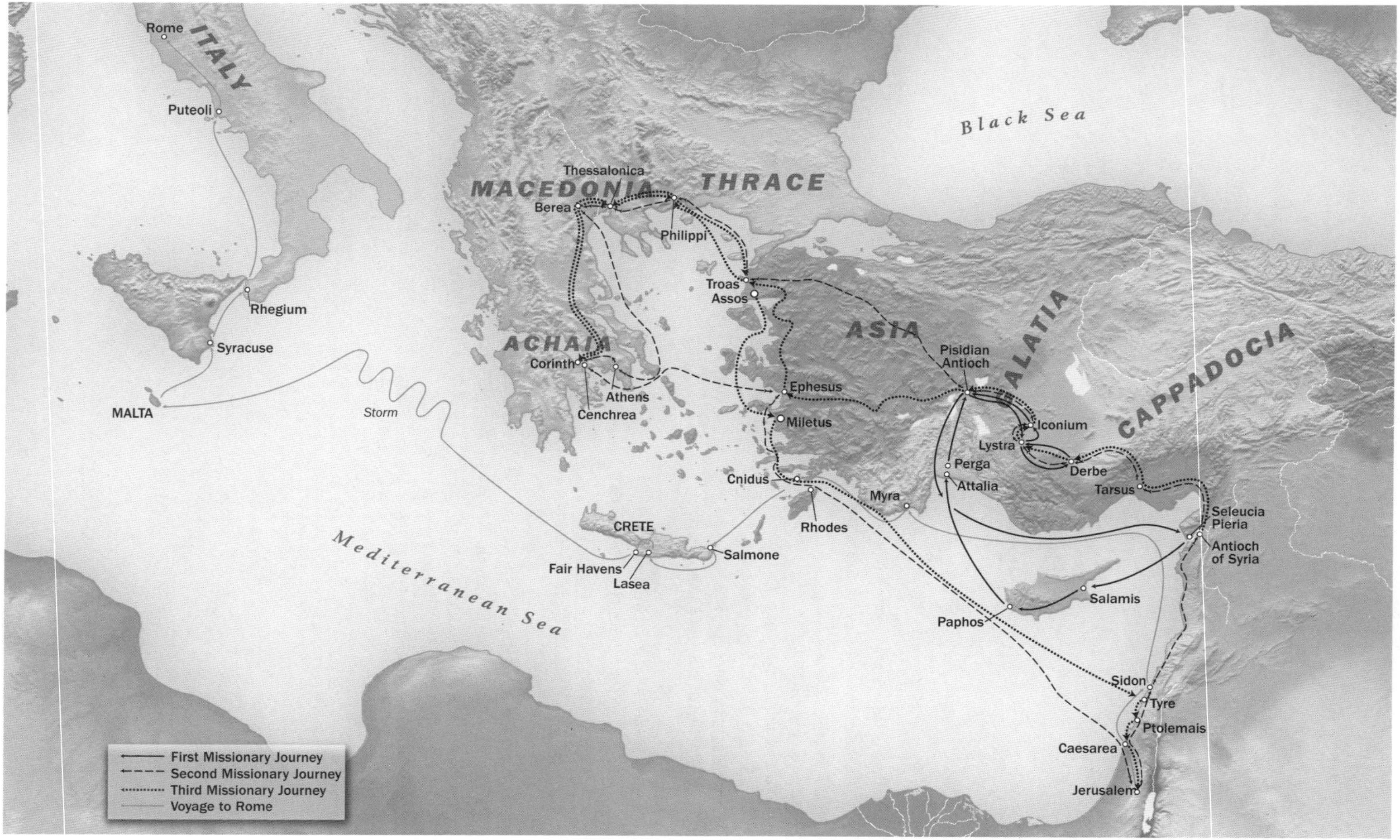

Figure 17. The journeys of St. Paul according to the information supplied in Acts of the Apostles.